Adcreep

Adcreep

The Case Against Modern Marketing

Mark Bartholomew

Stanford Law Books
An Imprint of Stanford University Press
Stanford, California

Stanford University Press
Stanford, California

Printed in the United States of America on acid-free, archival-quality paper

Library of Congress Cataloging-in-Publication Data

Names: Bartholomew, Mark, 1971– author.
Title: Adcreep : the case against modern marketing / Mark Bartholomew.
Description: Stanford, California : Stanford Law Books, an imprint of
  Stanford University Press, 2017. | Includes bibliographical references and
  index.
Identifiers: LCCN 2016040091 (print) | LCCN 2016040663 (ebook) |
  ISBN 9780804795814 (cloth : alk. paper) | ISBN 9781503602182 (ebook)
Subjects: LCSH: Advertising laws—United States. | Marketing—Law and
  legislation—United States. | Advertising—Social aspects—United States. |
  Marketing—Social aspects—United States.
Classification: LCC KF1614 .B37 2017 (print) | LCC KF1614 (ebook) |
  DDC 343.7308/2—dc23
LC record available at https://lccn.loc.gov/2016040091

Typeset by Bruce Lundquist in 10/15 Minion Pro

For Hank and Clara

Contents

Adcreep

Introduction

IN 1999, Steven Spielberg was working on a new movie, an adaptation of Philip K. Dick's short story "The Minority Report." Although the story was science fiction, set in an undated time in the future, Spielberg wanted the film's details to be realistic. The director did not want an over-the-top dystopian fantasy but a plausible vision of what might come to pass in fifty years. To help him build this vision, Spielberg convened a group of technology experts and asked for their prognostications. Front and center in their discussion was advertising. They predicted a world where advertising had become more personalized, more insistent, and more effective. The experts envisioned omnipresent and, thanks to facial recognition technology, individually targeted ads. Spielberg used their insights in the film, describing a future where advertising doubles as a surveillance tool, helping to keep citizens under the thumb of shadowy bureaucratic overlords.[1]

That future is now. New advertising techniques, some of them forecast in *Minority Report*, follow every step of our lives. Surveillance technologies (including facial recognition software) compile digital dossiers on potential consumers, the data shuttled along an impenetrable web of veiled third parties and used to craft individualized ads. Marketing messages adorn once ad-free zones like schools and state parks. Through a barrage of carefully choreographed blasts of online information, celebrities engineer a calculated familiarity, entreating us to "follow" and "like" them so they can further quantify and monetize their personal brands. Neuroscientists perform the ultimate market research, using brain scans to reach into consumers' heads and calibrate advertising campaigns for maximum appeal. As in Spielberg's film, these techniques are becoming embedded into the fabric of daily life. This is adcreep—modern marketing's march to create a world where advertising can be expected anywhere and at any time. Whether we realize it or not, adcreep has come, transforming not just our purchasing decisions but our relationships, our sense of self, and the way we navigate all spaces, public and private.

The marketing techniques detailed in the following pages are not the stuff of science fiction. They are currently being implemented by the most powerful companies and people in our society. A skeptic might argue that we have nothing to fear from adcreep. Consumers adjusted to past marketing innovations, like radio and television, and they will do so again. But the selling strategies of today—what I describe as the "new advertising"—are revolutionizing the relationship between advertiser and consumer. By deploying a variety of new marketing devices, businesses can expand the areas where their messages can be heard, develop rich and portable records of consumer preference, deliver advertising customized for the idiosyncratic thought processes of individual commercial targets, and obscure their own role by mobilizing others to convey their advertising messages for them. These techniques let advertisers know us on a deeper, more intimate level than ever before, dramatically tilting the historical balance of power between advertiser and audience. The algorithms that advertisers use to analyze our Facebook likes do a better job of identifying our personalities than our friends, lovers, or families do. Automated systems decode our facial expressions, revealing emotions we would otherwise be able to hide. Brain scans and biometric measurements tell marketers what we are feeling even when we cannot verbalize those feelings ourselves. Meanwhile, in a world of omnipresent advertising, corporate America can hide in plain sight. When no space is off-limits to commercial appeals, we become numb to the ideology of advertising, lowering our defenses, accepting Madison Avenue's suggestions for self-definition, and no longer considering alternative, non-market-based perspectives.[2]

Like the air we breathe, modern marketing inescapably infuses our environment. By some estimates, the average American is exposed to over three thousand advertisements each day.[3] But this marketing torrent does not need to flow unrestricted. Legal authorities have the capacity to channel it in ways that advance marketplace efficiency and consumer welfare. A complex system of legal regulations already exists to serve these ends. Yet when it comes to the latest round of marketing innovation, this system remains dormant, oblivious to the changes around us. In my teaching and writing on the latest developments in intellectual property and privacy law, I came to the realization that the most important cases I read often centered on new advertising technologies. They might be described by most legal scholars as intellectual property cases or privacy cases, but they were really *advertising* cases. And, for the most part, the advertisers have been winning these cases.

Legal Failure

This is not the first time that marketing technologies have threatened to upend the consumer-advertiser relationship. We live in a commercial world. Whether it was the machinery of mass production or the creation of the Internet, technological upheaval is inevitable and so is its immediate appropriation by marketers. Sometimes innovative advertising can prove socially beneficial. Mass marketing spread the word about new kinds of products, like refrigerators and dishwashers, that gave people more opportunities for leisure. Amazon's predictive analytics can reduce the time we spend searching for consumer goods. But advertising's innovations need to be interrogated before new patterns are established and it becomes too late to evaluate their costs against a historical benchmark. As the philosopher Helen Nissenbaum notes, different social arenas have different norms that should be investigated to determine the potential toll from a loss of privacy. Similarly, in wrestling with the consequences of the new advertising, different environments need to be studied so we get a sense of their contextual integrity and what might be lost by allowing today's marketing strategies to proceed unabated. And when the consequences appear too grave, law needs to be used to restrain opportunistic and invasive practices.[4]

Law is the necessary referent to compare what is possible with what is not possible when it comes to modern marketing. It forms a backdrop for what advertisers can and cannot do, setting the line between swindling and selling, fraud and commercial honesty. Sometimes citizens can protest overzealous selling tactics by voting with their pocketbooks. Markets are not a cure-all, however. History shows that at different moments, as advertisers leveraged new technologies for their persuasive projects, legislators and judges set boundaries on commercial behavior. Highway billboards, subliminal sales techniques, and the digital resurrection of deceased celebrities all provoked legal responses. Understanding these historical episodes is important not because they provide perfect analogies for today's advertising tactics, but because they reveal the need for thoughtful analysis of the potential economic, social, and cultural disruptions generated by new forms of commercial persuasion.

Unfortunately, there has been scant discussion of the potential harms of commercial surveillance, advertising in public spaces, the celebrification of online identity, or the marriage of neuroscience with marketing, particularly by legal officials and academics. Even rarer are comprehensive accounts of advertising's simultaneous spread on a variety of fronts. Instead, with little public debate, many of these marketing initiatives were introduced in the middle of an economic downturn, amid a willingness by private and public entities to realize new revenues by opening up spaces to advertisers. Even when these entities have tried to restrict advertiser access, they have come up against legal roadblocks. Advertising is a global industry, but this is a particularly American story. A variety of novel legal interpretations in the U.S. legal system provide an environment hospitable to the new advertising and hostile to its regulation. By enshrining commercial speech with vigorous First Amendment protection, the Supreme Court handcuffs those who would limit advertising's entry into traditionally civic spaces. Contract law gives advertisers a free hand to induce consumers to bargain away their privacy interests with the click of a button. Expanding intellectual property rights let companies and celebrities censor unauthorized communications that conflict with their desired messaging. These trends in legal doctrine allow advertising and its concomitant free market philosophy to spread and become naturalized. As a result, the insistent creep of invasive advertising is taken as a given in most quarters, a tax that has to be paid for life in the modern world. Adcreep has consequences, however, and these consequences should be recognized and considered before deciding to allow the new advertising to continue unimpeded.

The New Advertising

We might not always notice advertising given its near ubiquity, but that is part of the point. The new techniques of commercial persuasion leverage advertising's prosaic nature to lull us into acceptance, dismantle our skepticism, and bypass review by the authorities charged with safeguarding consumer well-being. This book is an exploration of these techniques and their ramifications. It relies on advertisers' own words—from marketing texts to industry magazines to published research studies—to reveal how the successors to *Mad Men*'s Don Draper are plying their trade in a new era of technological advancement and scientific understanding. It also uses a variety of interdisciplinary tools to offer a holistic portrait of the consequences of the new advertising.

To understand these consequences, it helps to have a historical referent in mind. Over the course of the twentieth century, the legal system responded on multiple occasions to the challenges posed by new marketing strategies. These legal reforms put in place a carefully negotiated system of trade-offs in our advertising regulatory scheme meant to arm consumers with a variety of protections against advertising's worst abuses. Chapter 1 examines the law's historical relationship with advertising. Not every advertising innovation triggered a legal response; consumers bore some responsibility for navigating the commercial world on their own. Unresolved debates over consumer rationalism, government paternalism, and the professional status of advertisers all played a part and continue to play a part in assessing the need for regulatory intervention. Exploring this backdrop also helps explain some of the current legal paralysis when it comes to the new advertising.

One technique of the new advertising involves increasing advertiser infiltration of once ad-free spaces. As described in Chapter 2, advertising is no longer limited to traditional media like print, radio, and television. It now enters any social arena, including public institutions like government and schools, and traditionally private spaces like the home and human body. Life in a wired world makes almost any object a potential carrier for commercial come-ons. Ads can now be delivered via smart refrigerators and home thermostats, beamed back at us through wired wearables. These new intrusions are not a mere annoyance. Recent research on the formation of human identities shows the importance of spaces where we can be free to examine and participate in different social groupings so as to develop an independent sense of self. When advertisers infiltrate these spaces, they also influence who we are and what it means to be a part of a particular social enclave. Adcreep also erodes the ability of civic spaces to communicate noncommercial values. As areas traditionally cordoned off from advertiser control, like schools, state parks, and editorial pages, are auctioned off to marketers, commercial values become dominant and noncommercial alternatives harder to find.

Modern advertisers are not only entering once commercial-free spaces; they are using that entry to gather more information on consumer behavior than ever before. Chapter 3 discusses the importance of data collection to modern advertising. The ability to compile and aggregate large quantities of consumer data gives advertisers a new ability to influence purchaser behavior. The apps we use, the electronic books we read, and the digital coupons we shop with may be convenient, but they also provide marketers with an increasingly fine-grained map of our daily activities. Advertisers can leverage this information in all sorts of ways and not necessarily for the good. Digital surveillance resembles a one-sided mirror that businesses can use to manipulate consumers without their knowledge. Evading advertising's digital dragnet is difficult, if not impossible. As consumers become aware that they are under continuous observation, their lives will resemble a commercialized panopticon. They will need to assume that they are never free from the advertiser's gaze, a recipe for distrust and psychological dysfunction.

As modern advertisers compile massive digital dossiers on individual consumers, they are also developing increasingly in-depth psychological profiles of how consumers make decisions. Chapter 4 investigates the emerging field of neuromarketing, which combines insights from neuroscience with the study of consumer behavior. It allows purchasing behaviors and motivations to be probed, false memories to be planted, and emotional susceptibilities to be targeted, all without the consumer's conscious participation. Even if some of its practitioners have a tendency to overclaim, neuromarketing suggests an unprecedented ability to enter consumers' minds, one that fundamentally alters the dynamic between consumer and advertiser. Market research once required a dialogue, providing consumers an opportunity to consciously shape the ads they watched and the products they bought. Advertising guided by neuroscience threatens to replace that dialogue with interventions that impinge on free will and stifle consumer voices.

One out of every four ads features a celebrity.[5] Chapter 5 explores the way in which celebrities sell products and themselves in the age of social media. Society's definition of celebrity has changed, shifting from a focus on unapproachable glamour to accessible artifice. The change has facilitated more celebrity advertising as stardom no longer seems inconsistent with hawking merchandise. It also encourages consumers to adopt their own techniques of "micro-celebrity," gaming their disclosures to others in efforts to build a personal brand and accumulate followers. Of course, life has always involved a certain amount of presentation and exposition. But by commandeering large swaths of the Internet, celebrities (along with their marketing managers and publicists) encourage all of us to frame ourselves as commodities. Aping the techniques of reality stars and professional athletes, everyday actors now carefully curate their online personas in an effort to build followings and keep their localized fan bases stimulated. These techniques of micro-celebrity necessitate personal disclosures, which, conveniently for social media interests and their associated advertisers, can be quantified in the form of "likes," "shares," "retweets," and "followers." When you are constantly selling yourself, it becomes less disconcerting to sell for others. As a result, from the planting of bogus user reviews on social media sites to the increasingly cozy relationship between advertisers and journalists, it becomes more and more difficult to determine who is being genuine, who is trying to sell to us, and where the difference lies.

It doesn't have to be this way. Legal intervention is meant to keep the relationship between consumer and advertiser in balance. Advertisers have a right to inform consumers of their wares and to make a fair case for their purchase. But consumers should also be able to resist and have an accurate understanding of the product being sold and the entity that is attempting to sell to them. In the past, law has been the tool for this consumer empowerment, but it has stood still during the latest wave of advertising innovation. Chapter 6 proposes reforms to restore some of the balance of power back to consumers. A new consumer movement needs to alert somnolent public servants to the dangers of adcreep. Reform is still possible, but change will need to come quickly while we can still recognize the difference between cinematic predictions of the future and the world we really live in.

Advertising on Trial

IN THE 1930s, Americans were confronted with startling evidence of the mendacious nature of early twentieth-century advertising. The U.S. Senate held hearings on a potential new law regulating food and drug advertising, the first major legislation in this area since the pioneering Pure Food and Drug Act of 1906. To illustrate the deficiencies of the current regulatory regime, Food and Drug Administration (FDA) inspectors supplied Congress with an exhibit showcasing the harmful and fraudulent products being freely sold in the marketplace. One example was Lash Lure, an eyelash dye that its manufacturer promised would benignly help its purchasers "radiate personality." It turned out that the product was made from coal tar, a now well-known allergen. Use of the product caused infection in many women's eyes, one case resulting in permanent blindness. In their exhibit, the inspectors included graphic photographs of one Lash Lure user's now ravaged eyes. When First Lady Eleanor Roosevelt toured the exhibit, according to *Time* magazine, she came upon the Lash Lure display, pressed the grisly photos to her breast, and cried out, "I cannot bear to look at them!"[1]

Dubbed the "Chamber of Horrors," the exhibit created by the FDA inspectors became a sensation. It traveled from the Senate to the White House to the 1933 Chicago World's Fair, and then on to various women's clubs and other civic organizations across the country.[2] As the exhibit graphically demonstrated, advertising blatantly misled Americans as to the actual ingredients and effects of the products they purchased. Consumers in the 1930s faced a gauntlet of misleading labels, packages with false bottoms, and newspaper and magazine advertising chock full of fraudulent claims. Although a furious counteroffensive by the affected industries slowed the legislative push produced by the Chamber of Horrors, eventually new federal legislation was secured. Congress granted the Federal Trade Commission (FTC) new powers to issue cease-and-desist orders for false advertising. The 1938 Food, Drug, and Cosmetic Act allowed the FDA to set new standards for food and cosmetics labeling and impound offending products. Lash Lure was the first product forcibly removed from store shelves after the act's passage.[3]

This chapter describes the evolution of U.S. advertising law. The legislative response to the Chamber of Horrors is just one example of a long-standing pattern involving advertising and legal reform in this country. Advertisers seize on opportunities provided by technological or social developments; lawmakers respond with laws and regulations designed to rein in what they deem to be predatory behavior. Early twentieth-century advances in transportation and industrial production allowed foods, health remedies, and cosmetics to be sold across the country to buyers who had little to no information about their sellers. The Chamber of Horrors starkly illustrated the dangers of leaving this system unregulated, and Congress reacted. Other episodes in the history of advertising regulation have left their mark as well, producing a host of rules and mechanisms that remain in place for restraining different objectionable marketing technologies and behaviors. After describing the various entities that populate the advertising law ecosystem, the chapter lays out three thematic fault lines that guided past regulatory responses and continue to influence this policy domain today.

The Advertising Law Ecosystem

The call and response of advertising and government regulation has occurred many times, not just in the 1930s. Before the Industrial Revolution, legal rules for advertising through trademarks were slow to develop. The law offered little protection for consumers who might be deceived by misleading uses of brand names. But as national brands emerged in the American marketplace in the late nineteenth century, courts pivoted, expanding trademark law to protect purchasers from mistaken purchases (as well as to shield the advertising in-

vestment of mark holders).[4] In the early 1900s, mass marketers used photo-
graphic technology to suddenly thrust the faces of unaware individuals into
national advertising campaigns. State courts responded by birthing a new
"right to privacy" to prevent such activities. In the 1910s and 1920s, companies rushed in to take advantage of a new advertising space, public roadways,
subjecting drivers to a scenery obscuring billboard barrage. Municipalities
fought back, adopting zoning laws that restricted roadside ads. In the 1950s,
advertisers were accused of abusing the relatively new medium of television
by broadcasting split-second commercials designed to stimulate subconscious
sales. Public outrage triggered bans on the practice. After a period of federal
legal desuetude coinciding with the Reagan presidency, state attorneys general began filing an increasing number of cases aimed at consumer protection,
particularly with regard to harmful products targeted at the young. The most
notable among these was the multistate litigation strategy that produced the
Tobacco Master Settlement Agreement of 1998, which ended many established
cigarette advertising strategies.

Not every new advertising move has been checked by a legislative or judicial counter. Sometimes new marketing strategies failed to inflame public sentiment. On many other occasions, political calculations defeated the objections
of consumer groups or effectively neutered new advertising regulations. Nevertheless, the history of select legal interventions in the world of advertising is
instructive. Each of the controversies mentioned above, like the uproar over
the Chamber of Horrors, generated a new legal response. The sum total of these
responses produced a constellation of interweaving regulatory provisions designed to calibrate the consumer-advertiser relationship and set the boundaries
of acceptable advertising.

A number of different governmental and private actors make up this constellation. Foremost among government regulators is the FTC. It files suit to
prevent egregious or particularly high-profile deceptive advertising practices.
It also provides nonbinding guidance for advertisers, like its disclosure rules
for bloggers endorsing products on social media.[5] Other government agencies
have enforcement powers against advertisers in specific fields. For example, the
FDA (thanks to the Chamber of Horrors) regulates labels on food and beverage products while the Federal Communications Commission promulgates advertising guidelines for broadcasters.[6] State attorneys general sometimes issue

rules for specialized marketing strategies within their jurisdictions. Through private lawsuits, holders of intellectual property rights stop certain advertising behaviors by contending that advertising campaigns infringe their copyrights or rights to control use of their name or likeness.

For the most part, however, competitors, that is, other advertisers, are meant to be the main vindicators of American advertising law. Competitors can sue under trademark law, which prevents confusing and dilutive uses of a business's trademark, and false advertising law, which is designed to prevent false and misleading advertising claims. Aggrieved businesses can also turn to the National Advertising Division, a private, voluntary self-regulation system administered by the Better Business Bureau.

Consumers themselves take little part in this regulatory apparatus. Rigorous standing requirements prevent consumers from taking on advertisers under either false advertising or trademark law. Individual state consumer protection laws and common law actions for fraud and breach of warranty provide a vehicle for consumers to sue advertisers directly. But the injuries contemplated by such laws are often minimal, often rendering individual litigation infeasible, and recent judicial interpretation of the procedural rules for aggregate litigation makes it increasingly difficult for large groups of aggrieved purchasers to successfully prosecute class actions against mendacious marketers.[7] Instead, consumers have their battles fought through proxies, chiefly businesses concerned with neutralizing the competitive advantages their rivals attempt to secure through marketing. Regardless, the advertising law ecosystem is undeniably complex. Multiple actors exist to police what is fair and foul when it comes to the commercial blandishments we experience.[8] Undergirding the decisions of these actors is a set of normative frames further complicating the question of advertising's proper role.

Assessing the Consumer-Advertiser Relationship

There are three main stakeholders when it comes to advertising regulation: consumers, regulators, and the advertisers themselves. Assessments of these interest groups and their proper relationship to each other determine the scope of advertising regulation. These assessments are not stable; they vary depending on the theoretical currents of the time. Historical examples reveal changing

visions of consumer rationalism, regulatory competence, and advertiser professionalism, visions that shaped the advertising law framework and continue to
affect the kinds of ads we are exposed to today.

Consumer Rationalism

In 1931, a former bootlegger from Enid, Oklahoma, opened what was to be
come the most famous nightclub in the world. Sherman Billingsley's Stork
Club, just off Fifth Avenue in Manhattan, became the place to see and be seen
as a who's who of the rich, famous, and royal vied to pass through its doors.
On the right night, one could rub elbows with Kennedys, Roosevelts, the duke
and duchess of Windsor, Judy Garland, Ernest Hemingway, Ethel Merman, or
Marilyn Monroe. Billingsley ran his establishment with a firm hand, buying
out the New York mobsters who had initially financed the club, banning Hum-
phrey Bogart and Jackie Gleason for what he deemed overly rowdy behavior,
and fighting efforts to unionize the club's employees. He also advertised heavily,
spending hundreds of thousands of dollars to promote the club in newspapers,
magazines, direct mail, books, national radio programs, and an early television series, as well as through the award of lavish gifts and Stork Club–branded
merchandise. Billingsley's marketing blitz worked. As one society writer of the
1940s described it, "To millions and millions of people all over the world the
Stork . . . means fame; it means wealth; it means an elegant way of life among
celebrated folk."[9]

In 1945, Billingsley learned that a small tavern was operating in San Francisco's notorious Tenderloin district under the name "Stork Club." One didn't
patronize the San Francisco bar for its elegance or glamour. The tavern had a
total of ten bar stools and served only the bare minimum of food to "conform
with the law regulating the operation of bars." Nevertheless, perceiving a threat,
Billingsley pounced, hiring a pair of high-powered attorneys to sue for unfair
competition and trademark infringement. At heart, their argument was that
consumers were being misled, somehow associating the San Francisco dive bar
with the glitzy New York City nightclub. The tavern's proprietor argued that a
reasonable onlooker would quickly realize that his modest establishment had
nothing to do with the other. But a federal court in San Francisco disagreed,
finding for Billingsley and interposing its own assessment of consumer thought:
"One would not have to be uncommonly naïve to assume that even a 'humble'

café at Turk and Hyde Streets, San Francisco, might be an unpretentious branch of a glittering New York night spot."[10]

The Stork Club case illustrates a court attempting to answer a question at the heart of advertising regulation: How do consumers perceive advertising? In large part, the law of advertising is governed by legal hypotheses about the cognitive abilities and habits of consumers. Most of the advertising law ecosystem is built on the principle that advertising's value lies in the informational signals it broadcasts to consumers. Because advertisers supply consumers with the facts needed to make informed purchasing decisions (price, location, product specifications), they are providing a social good, helping consumers choose the best resources available to them and, relatedly, fueling the development of more competitive markets.[11]

But these facts need to be accurate. False information, instead of making the market run more effectively, throws sand in its gears, causing consumers to make purchases for the wrong reasons. Falsehoods can also destroy the incentives for investments in product quality and increase cognitive burdens on consumers. Because the San Francisco tavern was perceived to be falsely telling potential patrons that it was affiliated with the New York nightclub, it was enjoined from further use of the "Stork" name. One of advertising law's main purposes is to screen the information provided to consumers, preventing misleading information from infecting the marketplace. The desired rigorousness of this screening process depends on one's view of consumer psychology. The Stork Club case characterized consumers as spending little time evaluating brand names and contextual cues. Rather than bemoaning this view of the consumer as "a moron in a hurry,"[12] trademark doctrine has come to celebrate it, maintaining that the law in this area is meant to reduce consumer "search costs."[13] In line with this thinking, one court described the average consumer as follows: "He acts quickly. He is governed by a general glance. The law does not require more of him."[14] Similarly, the Stork Club court explained: "It may well be true that a prudent and worldly-wise passerby would not be so deceived. The law, however, protects not only the intelligent, the experienced, and the astute. It safeguards from deception also the ignorant, the inexperienced, and the gullible."[15]

By envisioning a harried, unthoughtful consumer, judges reduce search costs by preventing conflicting trademark uses that might demand more care and attention on the part of shoppers. At other times, courts give consumers more credit for using their deliberative faculties. Like trademark law, false advertising law is meant to filter out bogus information that jeopardizes marketplace efficiency. It takes as its subject not the presentation of a brand name, but advertising involving factual claims. The provisions governing false advertising and trademark infringement appear side by side in the U.S. Code and are worded almost identically. But thanks to judicial interpretation, false advertising law operates under a different view of consumer decision making. It assumes greater consumer engagement, taking as a given that thoughtful consumers will not be swayed by outrageous boasts or patently unverifiable statements. Similarly, vague claims of superiority over another product or hyperbolic assertions are not actionable. In general, false advertising law posits a more discerning consumer, one who marshals her rational faculties to separate truthful from false advertising to the best of her abilities.[16]

Despite these differing approaches, a consistent theme emerges in the law of advertising of a rational consumer who looks to ads for information, not emotional sustenance. For judges evaluating false advertising claims, consumers are like Joe Friday, examining "just the facts" and ignoring noninformational content. Even in the trademark context, consumers may be harried, but only because they have other things on their minds and expect the brand names they see to be consistent sources of information as to source and product quality. The problem, however, is that the overwhelming majority of advertising contains little in the way of factual information. Marketers use atmospherics to tug at the heartstrings and stir up anxieties. Famous trademarks signal not just a product's source of manufacture but status, prestige, and conspicuous displays of difference. Most advertising is designed not to inform but to persuade.

How should the law evaluate advertising that entices, insists, shouts, and flatters? Two views have emerged, radically different, and each dependent on a particular view of consumer rationalism. On one side is the argument that persuasive advertising directly influences consumers, causing them to consume in ways that are inimical to their own self-interest. For those holding this position, persuasive advertising is a threat to consumer autonomy. For example, in his work *The Affluent Society*, John Kenneth Galbraith accused advertisers of erecting a false idol before an expanding middle class. Postwar Americans were working harder and harder to obtain an array of modern conveniences that did nothing to increase citizen satisfaction. Instead, advertising spurred a "craving for more elegant automobiles, more exotic food, more erotic clothing, more elaborate entertainment—indeed for the entire modern range of sensuous, edifying, and lethal desires."[17] For Galbraith and others, this was more than economic waste—it was manipulation. Rather than merely relying on consumers' internal preferences, marketers were shaping those preferences from the outside and eroding consumer sovereignty. Cultural critics since Galbraith have railed against advertising's ability to persuade us to buy things we do not really want, to crave things that won't make us any happier. Instead of believing in a strictly rational consumer who deeply discounts advertising's unverifiable, abstract promises, these critics contend that persuasive advertising works all too well on an average consumer who processes commercial messaging irrationally, just as advertisers intend.[18]

The other side contends that rather than accepting persuasive advertising at face value, consumers use such advertising for their own purposes, thereby enhancing their autonomy. Those partial to this argument make two key analytical moves. First, they treat persuasive advertising, in effect, as informational advertising by positing a rational consumer who ignores the nonfactual atmospherics of commercial speech. Current false advertising law follows this mold, holding that arguably unverifiable advertising claims like "fits more naturally" for diapers and "America's best loved coffee" are mere "puffery," a legal term signifying that no sensible consumer would give such vague claims credence.[19] Some proponents of persuasive advertising go further, arguing that not only do rational consumers disregard the specific meaning of these claims, but they astutely reinterpret them for evidence of corporate stability. Even advertising devoid of any factual content, it is maintained, still signals to consumers that the advertiser has sufficient resources to stand behind its product. This hyper-rational consumer disregards marketing promises not susceptible to objective measurement, instead peering behind the advertiser's actual message for what the ad's presence can truly tell her about corporate finances. Others contend that even when advertising's emotional appeals work, their effects are short-lived, giving other businesses the ability to compete by presenting new, compelling information to consumers.[20]

The second analytical move is to view consumers as accurately assessing the potential costs of exposure to persuasive advertising and making choices in a way that maximizes individual preference and overall utility. For this "venture consumer," persuasive advertising is not a threat to individual autonomy but an opportunity to make a mutually beneficial trade-off with a corporate part- ner. As we will see, technology can render advertising's influence more opaque, thereby making efforts to exercise rationality more difficult. Particularly in a world of online tracking and messaging, advertisers are able to influence con- sumers through clandestine means, using digital data to target consumers in ways that are often calculated to appear organic and serendipitous. But others celebrate technology for enabling a consumer "who knows what she wants out of her media, knows where to get it, and is aware of the risks and costs in- volved."[21] This tech-savvy shopper chooses to accept advertising as the price to be paid for consuming particular content yet also consciously fashions this consumptive experience on her own terms. She embraces product placement as a favorable alternative to interspersed commercials that can interrupt one's immersion in entertainment. She elects to watch programming online and via DVR recording to have more control over the timing and playback of content, as well as the ads attached to that content. Under this theory of consumer be- havior, persuasive advertising, rather being an external force that manipulates preferences, is a neutral commodity that the consumer can take or leave as she sees fit, fully aware of the risks and rewards of continued advertising exposure. This view of consumer psychology fits well with online architectures that allow consumers to consent to various advertiser requests, sacrificing privacy to mar- ket researchers in return for other calculated gains.

There is a considerable difference between viewing consumers as ratio- nal decision makers and viewing them as susceptible to irrational influences. Under the first approach, the consumer successfully navigates the marketplace, extracting accurate signals from advertising and consciously choosing to act on those signals in a way that optimizes individual welfare. The other approach finds consumers outgunned by a relentless persuasive marketing machine that instills exogenous preferences. Each view has vied for dominance when policy- makers consider regulation of new advertising technologies. Both sides would agree on one thing, however. If it could be demonstrated that advertising of a particular stripe actually manipulates consumers, making it impossible for them to apply their own rational faculties to the marketer's message, then that advertising poses a threat.

In 1957, Vance Packard alerted Americans to just this kind of threat in his book *The Hidden Persuaders*. Packard's best-seller listed a variety of techniques— Freudian psychoanalysis, hypnosis, subliminal advertising—that he maintained were manipulating postwar consumers without their awareness. In Packard's view, psychologists in league with Madison Avenue knew too much about how the mind worked, using their expertise to stimulate consuming preferences subconsciously. Packard ultimately gave advertisers of the day too much credit, accepting their claims instead of truly investigating the real-world effects of the new marriage between psychology and marketing. But his book attracted a lot of attention, causing some (including the Kennedy administration) to question the relatively blank check that advertisers had been given so long as they did not lie in their ads. Packard tapped into a concern that remains implicated in the regulation of advertising today. In large part, limits on advertising regulation stem from the idea that consumers can successfully navigate the shoals of the marketplace on their own. The legally constructed rational consumer can handle persuasive advertising and truthful informational advertising without the need for government intervention. But techniques that have the potential to take free will out of the equation are another matter. Once it becomes evident that advertisers are guiding behavior and shaping preferences without awareness, consumer autonomy is jeopardized, and the argument for legal intervention becomes stronger. In general, the advertising regulatory system has been reluctant to countenance this vision of the marketplace, adopting a view of consumers as rational and resistant to commercial persuasion, let alone manipulation. But legal actors have kept one wary eye open for advertising that threatens to subvert our rational faculties without our knowledge.[22]

Private/Public Competence

Print ads for patent medicine represented the lion's share of advertising expenditures in the early 1900s. These advertisements routinely made outlandish claims. For example, B. & M. External Remedy promised to kill "all tested disease-producing bacteria," thereby curing "tuberculosis, pneumonia, laryngitis, bronchitis, pleurisy, influenza, la grippe, asthma, coughs, colds, catarrh, rheumatism, lumbago, neuritis, neuralgia, locomotor ataxia, blood poisoning [and] bites of poisonous insects."[23] Under a strictly rational view of consumer behavior, one might assume that these kinds of claims would be ignored and are therefore harmless. Nevertheless, patent medicine advertising attracted public outrage and the concomitant attention of lawmakers. The progenitors of *Consumer Reports* blamed the free presence of such deceptive content on "the extraordinary safeguards thrown about business operations by our legal system to prevent interference with 'private initiative' and 'freedom of contract.'"[24] The law changed. New regulatory authorities were created, tasked with verifying product claims and safeguarding the health and safety of consumers. This was a situation where faith in consumer rationalism was trumped by a belief in the need for government authorities to scrutinize advertising that threatened public health. Hence, a second theme in the law of advertising is one of institutional competence. When should government authority be invoked to screen commercial messaging, and when should it stay on the sidelines and allow free market forces to flourish?

The answer to this question depends on assessments of the competence of both the government and private markets. In the late nineteenth century, the American marketplace was viewed as the place where character was formed. Rather than supporting government efforts to shape that marketplace, the prevailing view was that citizens needed to be exposed to an unbridled commercial sphere filled with both bad and good information as well as temptations in order to shape their character. Teddy Roosevelt spoke for many when he proclaimed that private markets taught self-reliance and initiative to both merchants and consumers. Even members of the nascent consumer movement agreed with the general premise that the marketplace favorably shaped the moral development of its participants and was not overly influenced by corporate interests. This all counseled in favor of a relatively unregulated marketplace where it was up to the individual to exercise self-restraint, not the government or advertisers themselves. To be sure, some anticapitalist critics at this time were calling for more regulation, but in general, people saw business as a neutral field for personal striving and heroic endeavor that should not be altered through government interference.[25]

This view began to shift as policymakers noted the consequences of an unregulated marketplace. It was hard to justify the outright falsehoods attached to B. & M.'s External Remedy as valuable tools for character formation. Industrialization produced national supply chains impossible for even the savviest consumer to interrogate on her own. It no longer seemed like a good idea to

build character in a place where no amount of proactive conduct could separate the truth from lies. In the Progressive era, a belief in expertise, wielded
by government, counterbalanced faith in the marketplace. The Progressives reacted against the prior century's efforts to translate laissez-faire attitudes into
legal doctrine, instead urging the adoption of scientific methods in government
and law. The Pure Food and Drug Act of 1906 was a direct response to unsafe
food products and patent medicines like B. & M. External. Under the law, the
U.S. Bureau of Chemistry, the precursor to the Food and Drug Administration,
examined drugs for false representations and made sure that they did not fall
below federally mandated purity levels.[26] Government experts had a clear role
to play in regulating the behavior of producers and marketers.

Other attempts to install legal experts to review advertising have foundered
over fears of government incompetence. Judges have been accused of being too
sure of their abilities in determining the truth of advertising claims and the
likelihood of consumer confusion under trademark law. The result has been judicial reliance on "objective" proxies (such as survey evidence and the amount
spent by a trademark holder on advertising) to decide trademark cases and
judicial unwillingness to expand false advertising law to consider noninformational claims. When the FTC tried to ban television advertising targeting
children in the late 1970s, a proposal pejoratively labeled the "kid-vid rule,"
Congress cut off funding to the agency, forcing a temporary shutdown. The
congressional response channeled a larger public outcry against government
intervention in an area that could be adequately addressed by parents and the
private market. Many objected that the FTC could not separate commercial
messaging designed for children from that meant for adults, thereby censoring
information meant for rational consumers. Another concern was that through
such restrictions, the FTC would harm an already faltering economy.[27] A subsequent director of the FTC described the kid-vid controversy as "a lesson in
the proper role of government."[28]

Others object to government involvement in advertising regulation not so
much because of incompetence but because of an objection to government
paternalism. In the kid-vid controversy, commentators accused the FTC of
overstepping its bounds and becoming a "national nanny."[29] A *Washington Post*
editorial implied that even a more limited proposal banning ads for sugary ce-
reals during Saturday morning cartoons did not give parents enough credit for

being able to ignore "the wailing insistence of their children." Resisting children's unreasonable requests, it chided, "is one of the roles of a governess . . . not a proper role of government."[30] Similarly, in 1975, Ronald Reagan criticized calls for a federal consumer protection agency. In a series of radio addresses and op-eds, he took dead aim at the agency's proponents for their paternalistic view of consumers, castigating would-be advertising regulators for "promoting the notion that people are too dumb to buy a box of corn flakes without being cheated."[31] For Reagan, the reformers' failure to trust the invisible hand of the marketplace reflected not just misplaced faith in government but an assault on the autonomy of individual shoppers. "Professional consumerists are, in reality, elitists who think they know better than you do what's good for you," he wrote.[32]

Taken to its extreme, the paternalism argument considers potential manipulation of consumers by private actors preferable to the structuring of consumer preferences by government. Depending on one's perspective, government regulation of advertising, by censoring commercial expression, is just a different form of manipulation, but a form that is less efficient and one that narrows the range of choices available to us. Today the chief legal frame for this argument is the First Amendment. Government regulation of advertising represents a threat to free speech. And once one accepts the general premise that commercial speech is preferable to government speech, manipulation at the hands of advertisers doesn't seem so bad. At the very least, concerns with government paternalism trigger a great deal of skepticism when considering the evidence brought forth by regulators of the harmful effects of certain advertising. It also causes legal authorities to look at government efforts to use its own messaging to shape public attitudes with a jaundiced eye. If the government is inept when compared to the private market, then it has little business in restraining private advertising or in attaching its own messages to those private communications. Along with assessing consumer capabilities, an examination of the government's ability to screen helpful from harmful commercial information forms a central theme in the history of advertising regulation.

Status and Property

Fred Astaire died of pneumonia in 1987. Pursuant to California law, after Astaire's death, the rights to commercially use his celebrity persona passed on to his wife, Robyn. Over the objections of Astaire's daughter from a previous marriage (and many fans), Robyn licensed the use of Astaire's digitized image in a 1997 Super Bowl commercial that showed the famed song and dance man hoofing it with a Dirt Devil vacuum cleaner. Robyn also tried to use her rights to prevent a company from selling dance instructional videotapes containing two clips of Astaire dancing on film. When alive, Astaire authorized the company's use of his name and photograph. But Robyn contended that the film footage was not covered by the agreement and its use represented an unauthorized appropriation of her rights in her deceased husband's image. A federal court sided with the company, interpreting California law to permit such uses after a celebrity's death. Undeterred, Robyn asked the California legislature to change the law, teaming up with eighty celebrities and the Screen Actors Guild to sponsor legislation lifting restrictions on postmortem publicity rights. "Fred left me in charge of his legacy, and I promised to oversee his creative property as he would have," she told the California Assembly Judiciary Committee.[33] Her lobbying worked. The legislature enacted a new law, dubbed the Astaire Image Protection Act, expanding the rights of successors in interest to block use of deceased celebrity likenesses and extending the duration of these rights to seventy years after the celebrity's death.

The legal battle over postmortem rights in Fred Astaire's image illustrates a third theme running through the history of advertising regulation. Long before it was possible to digitize the images of deceased celebrities, political economist Max Weber observed a process by which particular social groups win legal privileges. When groups achieve higher social status and that status exhibits a period of stability, the legal perks start to flow.[34] Weber's observation holds true in advertising law. As celebrities like Astaire gained greater social legitimacy among legal elites, judges and legislators expanded the ability of celebrities to control use of their images for advertising, even after death. Similarly, efforts by advertisers to professionalize their craft enhanced their social standing and led to a set of judicially constructed doctrines that bolstered their ability to control the emotional valences they instilled in their brands. In both situations, lawmakers became more willing to designate such control as a "property" right, implying a legal privilege of some durability and resistant to the imposition of outside limitations.

The more that advertisers have succeeded in demonstrating possession of an exclusive skill, putting them in the same realm as professional elites like doctors, lawyers, and academics, the more receptive legal authorities have become to granting them property rights in their creations. Ironically, advertisers have often suffered from deep public relations problems. Unlike others who had successfully professionalized their craft, early advertisers had trouble demonstrating that they possessed special qualifications. It didn't help those advertisers seeking to rehabilitate their image that they were viewed as part of the same club as purveyors of patent medicines and get-rich-quick schemes.

But over time, advertisers could lay claim to some of the requirements of professional status. They convinced legal officials that their work did require specialized expertise. They also acted to exclude the more undesirable elements of their profession—the snake oil salesmen who gave advertising a bad name. Exclusion is a critical component of any group's efforts to achieve professional respectability. By pushing for professional codes and local truth-in-advertising laws designed to kill off patent medicine sellers, early twentieth century advertisers successfully burnished their image, and they began to be held in higher regard by legal elites. Judicial opinion shifted, describing advertising as an "art," a skill that required "mastery" and expertise in the arrangement of "delicate factors."[35] Simultaneously, judges began to award broader rights to trademark holders (i.e., the advertisers' clients), making it easier to demonstrate trademark infringement in a variety of ways. And legal scholars, noting the value in the advertisers' craft, championed robust intellectual property protection for their labors.[36]

A similar phenomenon occurred in the 1980s and 1990s with celebrities and their publicists. Once criticized as "professional poisoners of the public mind," the work of publicists and their celebrity clients came to be accepted as having social value.[37] The legal system rewarded celebrities with a broad new right to block unauthorized commercial use of their personas, even a century after death. Over time, courts grew more comfortable describing this right as a "property" right, abandoning earlier contentions that whatever legal ability celebrities had to prevent use of their personas, it did not rise to the level of "property." This rhetorical move had real-world consequences, as the property label implied that the value in celebrity visibility deserved robust protection and could be transferred to others and extend beyond the celebrity's lifetime.[38]

At other times, skepticism over the advertisers' craft has produced a reluctance to legally privilege their creations. Perceptions of the advertiser itself have been central. Sometimes negative perceptions of particular industries led to marketing restrictions. Criticism of patent medicine advertisers spurred critical responses from legislators, judges, and even fellow advertisers. Revelations about the cigarette industry translated into legal limits on its ability to market on billboards, radio, and television. Anxiety over the undemocratic and unpredictable nature of celebrity held back earlier efforts to expand the ability of celebrities to control use of their personas in the 1960s and 1970s. It was a changing view of fame, as more rationalized and democratic, that made more recent expansions in legal protection for celebrity advertisers, like the Astaire Image Protection Act, possible.

More generally, concerns with inauthenticity have dogged the advertising profession, sometimes causing lawmakers to decide against its interests. In contrast to other persuasive communications, the advertiser's motivation to trigger purchase can be viewed as tainting her message. This view was summed up by F. Scott Fitzgerald who, for a time, turned to writing advertising copy to support himself. "Advertising is a racket, like the movies and the brokerage business," he wrote his daughter. "You cannot be honest without admitting that its constructive contribution to humanity is exactly minus zero."[39] Following Fitzgerald, sometimes regulators draw a line between art (which is highly valued legally) and advertising. For example, copyright law contains provisions specifically precluding stronger protections when a particular work is deemed an "advertisement."[40] More broadly, the law treats commercial expression differently than it treats noncommercial expression, precisely out of skepticism over the authenticity of the speaker's message. For decades, "purely commercial advertising" was viewed as a low-value type of communication not subject to the protections of the First Amendment.[41] The Supreme Court later revised this position, recognizing that advertising could both communicate valuable information to consumers and represent an important personal avowal for the advertiser-speaker. At the same time, however, the Court determined that advertising enjoys a "subordinate position" in First Amendment jurisprudence because commercial motivations render its claims to serving the autonomy interests of its creators suspect.[42]

Tensions between advertiser professionalism and inauthenticity, consumer protection and self-reliance, and government paternalism and expertise have shaped the law of advertising for over a century. The legal framework designed to navigate these tensions was meant to optimally balance commercial freedom with consumer protection. The framework has been adjusted over time to accommodate different views of marketer and consumer power, but the need for a balance has been accepted as part of the law of advertising for decades. That balance is now threatened by the array of modern marketing techniques that make up the new advertising.

As detailed in the following chapters, advertisers increasingly insert themselves into our lives, colonizing once-commercial-free territories, surveilling our every keystroke and mouse click, studying and scripting our emotional responses, and encouraging us to mimic the same techniques of self-presentation as celebrity pitchmen. The advertising regulatory system needs to evolve in response. So far, it is standing still.

2

Colonizing New Advertising Spaces

IN NOVEMBER 2013, the U.S. Postal Service announced that it was going to release a set of twenty postage stamps celebrating that great American . . . Harry Potter. Although a citizens' advisory committee exists to vet postage stamp choices, the Postal Service intentionally bypassed the committee to ensure the boy wizard's selection. According to Postmaster General Patrick R. Donahoe, the Harry Potter decision reflected a need for the Postal Service "to change its focus to stamps that are more commercial."[1] Before the Harry Potter decision, the Postal Service hired a former Coca-Cola executive as its director of marketing, and the citizens' committee bowed to pressure to change its charter to allow corporate advertising on stamps. Stamps commemorating Mattel's Barbie doll, Kentucky Fried Chicken's Colonel Sanders, and cartoon characters Snoopy and Dora the Explorer have been discussed or approved. Members of the stamp collecting community express great discomfort at turning stamps into mini-billboards for companies and celebrities. "The stamp program should celebrate the things that are great about the United States," says former Postmaster General and stamp collector Benjamin Bailar. "To prostitute that goal in the pursuit of possibly illusory profits does not make sense to me."[2]

The shift to more commercial subjects for postage stamps is emblematic of advertising's growing infiltration of formerly commercial-free (or at least commercially resistant) spaces. New technologies and marketing strategies now inject advertising into almost every physical or virtual space, markedly changing the environments in which we live. The simple act of mailing a letter now becomes a choice to affiliate one's self with a particular corporate symbol. Cognizant of an audience that tries to tune out traditional commercials, advertisers are turning to new, untapped areas for their appeals. They have muscled their way into government-run spaces that have been traditionally cordoned off from marketing, like national forests and public schools. Modern product placement technologies give advertisers the ability to add updated sales pitches to movies, television, and video games after their release. Social media marketing campaigns count on users themselves to generate and share brand-friendly content. No longer limited to print media, radio, and television, advertisers rely on new communications devices to confront their subjects at every moment of their online lives.

This chapter describes advertising's colonization of new and once historically ad-free spaces and how this has made advertising a nonstop presence in our lives. This ubiquitous persuasion, the constant voice in our ear, comes at a cost. Ultimately, advertising's shift to new territories is a project of governance, meant to monitor, inform, and persuade. When advertising never stops, it becomes normalized, invisibly influencing the consumer. A world where advertising can be expected anywhere and anytime is a world where our abilities to recognize and defend ourselves against advertising become less effective. Advertising's infiltration of civic spaces changes their character, narrowing their capacity to instill nonmarket-based values. By limiting the ability to escape to ad-free zones, advertisers can more directly influence our efforts at self-definition. With nowhere to hide, we lose alternative, noncommercial means of telling our own stories.

Advertising's annexation of new territories is not inevitable. In the early 1900s, complaints over billboards erected on the private lands alongside newly built roadways were taken seriously enough by courts and legislators to halt the growth of this particular type of commercial speech. Today, however, lawmakers have shifted their view of the appropriate boundary between the public interest and the rights of private entities to advertise. Under current judicial interpretation, the First Amendment assists advertisers seeking new territories for their marketing messages while simultaneously hobbling efforts to preserve the noncommercial character of civic spaces.

Invasion of the Ads

Today's advertising industry is obsessed with "guerrilla marketing." There are many descriptions of guerrilla marketing out there, but perhaps the best simply refers to advertising in previously "commercially dormant zones."[3] Television commercials, magazine spreads, radio jingles, and banner ads are not guerrilla marketing. We expect these media to be filled with persuasive entreaties and have already installed defenses against them, ready to deploy the moment we see or hear an advertisement in a familiar space. Even preschoolers can condition themselves to delineate these traditional sorts of commercials from regular programming (although their ability to differentiate the motivations behind these communications lags until about age eight).[4] Consumers rely on mental (tuning out while a commercial plays on the radio) and physical strategies (getting up to use the bathroom while commercials play during a television show) to blunt advertiser efforts. Technological defenses are used as well. Digital video recorders allow commercial targets to skip past the commercials interlaced with their favorite television shows. Pop-up blockers and spam filters help screen out undesirable and distracting online ads.

These mental, physical, and technological techniques of self-defense are a big reason why guerrilla marketing exists. The goal of any guerrilla ad is to sneak past the defenses audiences have built up against more traditional marketing techniques. The placement of an ad in an unusual or unexpected space can be disruptive and attention grabbing. But, somewhat paradoxically, advertising in these unexpected spaces is also meant to casualize the exercise of market power. These campaigns are not one offs but carefully calculated marketing blitzes conducted by sophisticated advertising firms on behalf of some of the world's biggest corporations. The more spaces occupied by advertisers, the more consumers come to accept advertising's presence. The territory of guerrilla marketing can be divided into two particular kinds of spaces: spaces originally created by commercial actors and civic spaces controlled by government authorities.

Reinforcing Commercial Space

A familiar marketing strategy in recent years is to layer additional advertising onto preexisting commercial spaces. The examples are numerous. Advertisers now claim space on the handles of shopping carts, seatback tray tables in airplanes, and the surface of supermarket eggs. Talking urinal cakes confront bar patrons. To avoid technologies that permit the skipping of stand-alone commercials, advertisers are increasingly turning to product placement, integrating their advertising message into programming voluntarily selected by consumers. New technologies allow updated advertisements to be inserted into television shows, motion pictures, and video games years after their first viewing. Technology also permits commercial videos to be shown in captive spaces like elevators, automated teller stations, doctors' offices, and gas station fueling areas where targeted audiences have little choice but to experience the advertiser's message. In another captive space, the workplace, employers are turning to internal branding programs that use in-house marketing to cultivate employees as consumers while they work.[5]

There are also wholly new spaces for advertising, ones that did not exist in any form years ago, as advertisers and their business partners erect new platforms for their messages. Advances in processing power facilitate real-time marketing messages on home thermostats, car dashboards, and refrigerators.[6] Search engine advertising allows commercial missives targeted to an individual Internet user's daily interests and discoveries. Social media facilitates another sort of guerrilla marketing as consumers generate branded content hand in glove with advertisers. Social media platforms allow advertisers to design websites festooned with corporate logos and advertiser-generated content, as well as promotions that prompt consumers to upload their own brand-friendly material. For example, Disney used the video-sharing website Vine to invite users to submit videos "showing their Disney side." The winning entry won a vacation to a Disney park along with $10,000 in funding to create further videos designed to promote Disney to other Vine users.[7] There are analog examples as well: marketers sponsor parades, festivals, historical commemorations, and other gatherings in physical space to showcase their products.

This is by no means an exhaustive list of the different ways in which marketers have asserted a presence in new commercial territories, but it reveals the spread of advertising into the geography of daily life. One might ask why there has not been more resistance to these tactics, a boycott of businesses using their control of commercial space to force more and more advertising into the consumer's field of vision. The answer is twofold. First, guerrilla marketers often take pains to portray their work as an organic cultural outpouring rather than an obvious attempt to construct an advertising platform. For example, communications scholar Michael Serazio relates how Pabst Blue Ribbon organized bike messenger races to promote its beer, but opted to keep signage to a minimum so that participants could seemingly "choose PBR rather than having the brand chosen for them."[8] Such so-called stealth marketing is harder to detect and less likely to trigger consumer protest.

Second, consumers do resist some advertising invasions, but this resistance typically fades unless it is translated into some sort of legal prohibition. Cinematic commercials are a good example of this phenomenon. Prefilm advertising is a relatively new feature in the moviegoing experience. In this country, it dates back only to the early 1990s. Before then, a viewer might have seen promotions for other films or for the theater's snack stand before a film's opening credits, but those commercials still fit within the fantasy milieu of the theater. Now, advertisers view moviegoers as a captive audience and, with few inhibitions, force them to witness ads for a wide range of products before the film begins, and then, only slightly more subtly, they embed advertisements within the film itself. Theaters make over half a billion dollars each year on prefilm advertising, showcasing ads that usually have little to nothing to do with the film being viewed or the moviegoing experience.[9]

How did this happen? For nearly a century, films were shown without these kinds of advertisements. Movies were considered separate from the more commercialized media of radio and television that had a history of relying on brand sponsorship. Injecting obviously unrelated advertising into this forum threatened the escapism that many viewed as the sine qua non of the moviegoing experience. At first, citizens and even some elected officials reacted harshly to the introduction of non-cinema-related commercials before the screening of the feature film itself. Frustrated audience members audibly howled at the prefilm commercials. Surveys, perhaps unsurprisingly, showed widespread objection to their presence.[10] Class action lawsuits for breach of contract and deceptive business practices were filed by angry consumers against the theater chains. Various state legislators proposed legislation banning the new advertising practice. According to a Maryland assemblyman who introduced legislation outlawing cinematic ads on Maryland theater screens in 1991, "You pay enough money to go to the movies. I'm not sure you have to cheapen the moviegoing experience by sitting through these horrid commercials."[11]

This initial outburst of legal protest quickly subsided, however. The lawsuits stalled and the legislation never passed. Consumers did not retaliate by leaving the theater; ticket sales have remained steady since the introduction of cinematic ads in the early 1990s, and art house theaters now show prefilm commercials as well.[12] Instead, public attitudes changed. Years of advertising at the movies inured audiences to the experience. Surveys now suggest that audiences have become ambivalent to the presence of prefilm commercials.[13] Sitting through minutes of commercials has come to be expected, a levy on our desire to escape into film that consumers have resigned themselves to paying.

Infiltrating Civic Space

As marketers have filled more commercial spaces with advertising, they have also moved to open up governmental spaces historically antagonistic to the entry of commercial forces. The government has long engaged in marketing to its citizens (often with the help of private industry), so it would be inaccurate to describe these spaces as commercial free until the present. Yet we are now witnessing a time when the government no longer limits the marketing conducted under its auspices to its own products (e.g., bonds, political candidates). Instead, private enterprise increasingly employs government property for its own commercial purposes.

Advertisers now use government infrastructure as a commercial canvas. In 2012, Chicago mayor Rahm Emanuel announced a new initiative to put ads on city property, including trash cans, parking pay boxes, and the pillars of a historic bridge. A few years before, Kentucky Fried Chicken topped fire hydrants in Indianapolis with plastic "wing buckets" advertising their new fiery chicken wings. The transportation authorities in New York City and Philadelphia have sold off naming rights to their subway stations for millions. Municipalities sell sponsorship rights in public safety, agreeing to prominently display corporate brands as part of the bargain. In Los Angeles County, lifeguards not only must wear Izod-branded swimsuits, but their towers, beach towels, and boats also have to bear the Izod name. In Florida, Georgia, Indiana, Louisiana, Maryland, and New York, state vehicles that assist stranded travelers are emblazoned with the State Farm logo. In 2011, the Erie County Holding Center in Buffalo, New York, began to sell ads (typically purchased by defense lawyers and bail bondsmen) on television screens viewed by arrestees. The company that arranged this new public-private partnership described the viewers of the ads as "the ultimate captive audience."[14]

Perhaps even more glaring is the introduction of corporate advertising to public lands. The visual costs of advertising on fire hydrants and parking meters may not be readily apparent, but scenic landscapes are a different matter. Recent years, however, have witnessed a new willingness to integrate corporate advertising with public conservatorship of natural wonders. In 2012, Florida governor Rick Scott signed a bill allowing advertising on Florida's "greenways" and trails. New Hampshire has a state park sponsorship agreement in place with sporting goods retailer Eastern Mountain Sports. Maryland and Virginia have similar deals with outdoor clothier North Face. As part of the sponsorship deals, North Face can post its logo and scannable discount codes on trailhead signs. California and New York have brokered similar bargains with companies like Nestlé, Coca-Cola, and Odwalla. Although the National Park Service continues to ban most advertising in its parks (despite efforts by the Bush administration to relax the ban in 2006), in 2015, it reversed a long-standing policy barring the display of corporate donors' logos. In national forests, companies can now put up advertisements along roads and trails, inside concession buildings, and other areas.[15]

Like government infrastructure and public lands, public schools now regularly showcase commercial appeals. History shows a long list of marketers seeking to infiltrate the classroom. But only recently has in-school commercialism become the norm rather than an outlier. Today's students, rather than viewing the isolated in-school advertisement, now face an unremitting gauntlet of commercial messages from the moment they walk through schoolhouse doors. More than 80 percent of American public school students witness some form of overt non-school-related advertising every school day.[16]

Modern marketing infiltrates the schoolhouse in a variety of ways. Sometimes cash-strapped schools simply provide advertising space in return for financial payment. Schools receive cash payouts or supplies in exchange for renting out their hallways and bus space to advertisers and featuring corporate logos on curricular materials, scoreboards, and student athlete jerseys. Contracts with beverage companies mandate copious brand promotion, including signage; book covers; ads on vending machine panels; and logos on sports equipment, cups, and even report cards. Borrowing a page from municipalities and professional sports franchises, schools are increasingly selling naming rights to school facilities.[17]

Schools have also turned to corporate America to supply new educational materials. Many schools have incentive programs for scholastic achievement that come with corporate backing and attendant corporate advertising. Although not as big a presence as it once was, Channel One produces twelve-minute "news broadcasts" that are transmitted to thousands of middle and high schools throughout the country. Schools with Channel One contracts receive TVs, DVRs, and satellite dishes but are required to show Channel One's entire daily broadcast, including two minutes of commercials (unless they pay for a subscription). Schools are increasingly turning to corporate supply of Web-based services for out-of-class reinforcement of scholastic concepts, as well as communication hubs for students, teachers, and parents. These social sharing sites are also used to coordinate school athletic leagues. Such online resources do not come for free. In addition to requiring students and parents to divulge personal information that can be tracked for marketing purposes, the sites also often show third-party advertisements to after-school users.[18]

Advertisers also influence the drafting of actual lesson plans. There are numerous examples. The oil company BP helped write a new environmental curriculum for California schools, resulting in the adoption of a high school textbook lauding BP's donations to universities for environmental studies. Thanks to the provision of materials from Nabisco, thousands of teachers integrate Oreo cookies into elementary school math lessons. Salad dressing company Hidden Valley joined forces with Weekly Reader Custom Publishing to provide math, language arts, and science lessons for thousands of elementary school students. The lessons emphasized the importance of eating vegetables, although that topic was unrelated to the academic material covered.[19]

A skeptic might contend that consumers have reached their saturation point and that these advertising incursions simply wash over their targets, unnoticed and ineffective. Advertisers themselves fret over "ad blindness." In 2006, former advertising executive Maurice Saatchi complained of "the strange death of modern advertising," contending that today's relentless commercial bombardment allowed only brutally simple ideas to break through the advertising clutter.[20] Since there has been advertising, there have been complaints about its expansionist tendencies. In 1759, Samuel Johnson noted that "advertisements are now so numerous that they are very negligently perused."[21] As soon as the first advertising industry was formed in the early twentieth century, admen warned of a future of unreachable consumers inundated by an overabundance of ads.

Yet the advertisers' prophesies have not come to pass. Saatchi's comment notwithstanding, commercial bombardment does not necessarily reduce advertising's effectiveness. In some ways, it strengthens it. Even when ads become part of the scenery and are processed at a low level of attention, they still have an influence. The expansion of advertising and consequent normalization of its messages makes it easier for advertisers to get past our defenses and convince us to purchase. In this crowded environment, it may sometimes be more difficult for an individual marketing campaign to resonate. Yet there is a cumulative toll from advertising's geographic advances, one that makes it more difficult to recognize the source of commercial appeals. Decades ago, maybe it was clear that the didactic voices on the radio or television had a plan for us to buy that was not necessarily in our self-interest. But when advertising is everywhere, who to trust and who not to trust is not so obvious.

I Shop, Therefore I Am

Some already bristle at advertising's intrusion into these new territories. Political scientist Michael Sandel maintains that advertising corrupts these spaces. According to Sandel, there are certain places where "market values and commercial sensibilities" are not appropriate because these places stand for something else, a preserve of personal contemplation or an environment meant to communicate civic values.[22] In a similar vein, David Marquand writes of the need to "carve out from the encircling market and private domains a distinct, self-conscious and vigorous public domain governed by non-market and non-private norms."[23] Others have zeroed in on particular territories, like schools or public lands, arguing that commercial influences betray their unique character.[24]

But to really explore the normative consequences of this process of geographic colonization, we need to understand how this process works. One of the fundamental questions about advertising is its relationship to consumer agency. If advertising simply offers consumers opportunities that they are completely free to accept or reject, then its presence, even in new spaces, becomes less objectionable. But if it exercises significant influence over audiences, particularly if these audiences are unaware of this influence, then one might feel less sanguine about its expansion. In other words, policymakers investigating adcreep need to grapple with the question of power. In particular, one might ask how advertising's colonization of new territories structures the relationship between advertiser and consumer.

What kind of power is exercised when advertisers claim new spaces, and how does that power operate? The French philosopher Michel Foucault distinguished disciplinary power from the direct punishment once exercised by the sovereign. According to Foucault, in a historical shift, "the marks that once indicated status, privilege and affiliation were increasingly replaced . . . by a whole range of degrees of normality indicating membership of a homogeneous social body but also playing a part in classification, hierarchization and the distribution of rank."[25] Throughout modern history, authorities have used disciplinary techniques to govern their subjects without their awareness, articulating what was "normal" and policing human behavior accordingly. Foucault engaged in profuse use of spatial metaphors to describe the operation of these disciplinary techniques. By mapping the regions where disciplinary power is exercised, he argued that one could better understand different forms of this power and their social effects.[26]

In Foucault's terms, guerrilla marketing is a disciplinary project meant to train bodies to do something they would not otherwise have done. By monitoring and shaping the expressive content found in particular territories, guerrilla marketers project norms for others to follow, identify "abnormal" behavior that does not match those norms, efface their own role in articulating normal and abnormal behavior, and circumscribe the discourse surrounding their products in ways that reinforce the desired norms. These techniques, described in more detail in the following sections, reveal the exercise of a normalizing discipline on consumers. Advertising's advance into new spaces shapes our sense of self while masking its own ability to do so.[27]

Projecting Norms

Advertisers are in the business of articulating what should be considered "normal." Like other cultural authorities, they hail individuals with their own made-up definition of the self, "generat[ing] a script that identity bearers must heed."[28] By interpellating a particular vision of the relevant consumer, the advertiser offers a norm to be followed and encourages consumers to imitate and internalize that norm. One might contest this account, maintaining that consumers are free to ignore or reshape the identity templates that advertisers proffer. But even acknowledging that consumers resist and reconfigure some commercial entreaties, there is little doubt that advertising shapes identity formation.[29] Individuals acquire self-definition by conjuring images of themselves engaged with external objects. If humans naturally build their identities from the cultural materials surrounding them, the growing omnipresence of advertising must be influencing the formation of modern identities.

The tactics of guerrilla marketing suggest a norm of self-promotion for all individuals. Recipients of these marketing messages are meant to use the particular brands and logos that the advertiser presents to perform their own identities. They are encouraged to reenact a particular vision of personhood that relies on competition, persuasion, and the erasure of any boundary between commercial and noncommercial behavior. Targeted consumers are meant to become brands themselves, constructing their own marketable self-presentations and accepting their role in a society organized by battles for individual attention.

Evidence of this normalizing process can be seen in both the guerrilla marketing tactics that occur online and the resulting displays of identity occurring in that discursive space. As more and more of our lives are lived in digital territories, social media and other online platforms have become increasingly important locations for representing the self. Teenagers and young adults now spend their online time uploading "haul videos": home movies showcasing the filmmaker's particular brand shopping choices and articulating the reasons why these brands fit his or her own sense of style. Guerrilla marketing encourages this process by paying the makers of such videos, in effect, refashioning the video into a marketing display designed to attract others engaging in their own journeys into identity formation. Popular haul video makers compete for lucrative endorsement contracts. Marketers create contests for the "best" haul video, turning a mode of personal expression into a competition for who can best shill for a particular product.[30]

The haul video is one example of a larger social phenomenon where everyone, not just marketing professionals, is encouraged to "build their own brand." Advertising's infiltration of new spaces facilitates this process by making anywhere an appropriate site for self-promotion. In business, academia, and even social settings apart from the workplace, individuals are now advised to employ strategic marketing processes to make themselves stand out as a recognizable and attractive commodity to others. In contrast to an earlier time of more playful, shifting online identities, today's technologies encourage consistent self-branding as those using social media and contributing user-generated content compete for status in the quantifiable forms of online "friends," "likes," "followers," and "retweets." Part and parcel of the new norm of self-marketing is a blurring of the boundary between commercial and noncommercial spaces. Once the term sellout was a widely recognized shorthand for someone who had transgressed this boundary by allowing commercial forces to enter a space where norms suggested they should be disallowed. But people coming of age in a world of adcreep no longer know what being a "sellout" means. In an environment of ubiquitous advertising, where commercialization and self-branding are hardwired into the technologies made for personal expression, failure to separate market-based from non-market-based motivations is not recognized as a failure at all.[31]

Advertisers communicate not just one norm but a variety of them. The disciplinary potential of interpellation increases the more the hailed individual sees the advertiser's call as individually tailored. Research in psychology reveals that we are naturally attracted to definitions of self that involve our membership in a particular group. Niche marketing allows advertisers to call out to consumers with these potential group identities in mind. Consider, for example, recent marketing efforts directed at gays and Hispanics. These communities are perfect examples of demographic groups that marketers aggressively and specifically target.[32] Advertising, even as it identifies a social category, also has the power to define it. Advertisers have chosen a vision of gay sexuality that is predominantly monogamous. Worried about the stereotype of the promiscuous gay male, advertisers have done their best to "straighten up" their advertisements by placing cultural totems that suggest monogamy (e.g., pets, homes, or children) next to their gay referents. These representations fail to recognize those who choose to adopt less conventional manners of outward appearance and more transgressive representations of their individual sexuality. By precluding other equally accurate representations of homosexuality, these advertisements push viewers toward a more limited understanding of gay identity, disciplining those who do not follow the same monogamous course.

A similar phenomenon can be seen in marketers' attempts to categorize Hispanic consumers. According to one scholarly treatment, the very term Hispanic was popularized by advertisers and "as if it were a brand, became the symbolic handle by which everyone could refer to a population that had been seen as disparate before."[33] Advertisers have chosen to define Hispanics in a particular way. Hispanics are portrayed as rooted in traditional gender roles, leaving out Hispanic consumers who chafe at conservative male/female distinctions. In contrast to appeals to other social groups that emphasize individuality, marketing to Hispanic women reproduces stereotypes of conformity and lack of individual ambition. For example, Avon advertised to the general public with individual images of independent professional women but also ran a separate advertisement targeting the Hispanic market that featured a group of women surrounded by family and friends and a voice-over touting their feminine characteristics.[34]

Any depiction of a particular social group in a commercial will, to some degree, exclude other potential depictions of that group. But this does not mean that the advertisers' choice to depict social identity in a particular way should avoid scrutiny. By hailing and at the same time proposing definitions of its audience, marketers discipline their targets. They articulate a particular vision of what the recipient's identity should be. When this vision does not match a prospective group member's actual characteristics, that prospective member may feel left out and unvalidated, causing that person to change his or her behavior accordingly.

Group members are even more likely to internalize the advertisers' vision in an environment where there are few opportunities for social identity formation outside the advertiser's gaze. Marketing experts call for ad campaigns that use sites of community development like parades and holidays to make the advertised brands relevant to group self-representation. By planting advertisements in group meeting places, whether in the form of a traditional advertisement or through a group member mobilized by a word-of-mouth marketing campaign, advertisers embed themselves in some of the chief milieus where social identities are made. Spaces for group politics and coalition building are increasingly under the influence of corporate advertisers. Gay publications, for example, have become centered on consumerism, not civil rights, while gay bookstores are dying out as the technology that propels Amazon allows for individualized servicing of the need for gay-themed communications. To overcome Hispanic consumers wary of commercial appeals, marketers emphasize the need to mobilize political and religious leaders and infiltrate spaces like church halls and community centers.[35]

Identifying Abnormality

Normalization depends on more than the articulation of a model for a human subject to follow, whether it be marketers' conception of gay or Hispanic identity or their broader vision of all consumers engaged in social competition and self-promotion through brands. The normalizing process also relies on displays of abnormality to give content to norms and rationalize further disciplinary techniques. "The abnormal is the 'other' that defines the 'normal.'"[36] Advertisers showcase the abnormal by encouraging comparison, hailing consumers with a label meant to apply to them but also presenting alternative visions meant to define an "other" that the consumer can react against. In an earlier era, advertisers relied on broad-based entreaties meant to appeal to an undifferentiated mass of consumers. By contrast, the Internet architecture and sophisticated data collection of today allow for customized encounters with audiences. The sheer number of new spaces available for broadcasting advertising messages further enables more localized interactions with consumers. These new ways to narrowcast advertising permit advertisers to posit lines of difference with other social groups without risk of offending other segments of their customer base.

Again, advertising campaigns to the Hispanic and gay communities are instructive, this time in revealing how marketers convey what they do not want us to be. Anthropologist Arlene Davila has chronicled how niche market advertising to Hispanics is constructed in comparison to an Anglo other.[37] Here is the advice given to marketing professionals in one text on Hispanic advertising:

> Hispanics are more likely than Anglos to believe that nature and the supernatural control their lives. This is very much in contrast with the Protestant belief that humans can control the world around them. Although the majority of Hispanics would endorse the notion that destiny controls or influences their lives, generally Anglos would state that they believe they can shape their future and that destiny does not hold sway.[38]

These markers of difference promoted by advertisers are meant to realign subjects to a desired model—in this case, a norm presenting Hispanics as fatalistic, religious, and family dependent rather than self-reliant or secular.

By the same token, media studies professor Katherine Sender contends that gay magazines articulate the notion of the tasteful gay consumer to interpellate a subsegment of the gay community particularly desirable to advertisers.[39] As part of this project, gay marketers contrasted the high-status, high-class tastes of the aspirational gay consumer with low-status, low-class tastes of those deemed outside the community. Advertising to the gay community depicted male homosexuals as somehow having a sixth sense for which products and styles should be consumed, contrasting them with heterosexual consumers completely lacking this ability. Such appeals to taste naturally fit with the process of comparing social groups and reinforcing cultural differences. At the same time, these appeals discipline gay consumers, forcing self-categorized gay individuals who do not fit the ordained model of conservative, tasteful gay sexuality to choose between giving up any claim to "good taste" or abandoning a type of sexual identity that advertisers do not recognize.[40]

Masking Authority

Another essential component of the normalization process is the masking of authority. Guerrilla advertising often relies on an effacing of the advertiser's role. According to Foucault, disciplinary power reflects a more pervasive yet at the same time decentralized form of control than the brute punishment once inflicted by the sovereign. Subjects are influenced not by direct prohibitions but through disciplinary techniques that transform people's experiences of themselves. These disciplinary techniques work by being internalized, not by being explicitly forced on individuals, and this requires camouflaging the articulation of a norm.

Consider, for example, product placement. This kind of advertising embedded within films and television represents a softer form of coercion as compared to the didactic approach of a typical thirty-second television ad. In such an ad, representative of most advertising for a number of years, the advertiser actively entreats the consumer to buy a particular item. In contrast to this hard sell, the actors in sponsored content merely show their audience what they are doing with a particular brand name item, then leave it to the audience's discretion whether to engage in similar consumptive practices. By effacing the advertiser's role in this way, branded entertainment subverts consumer defenses. Product placement steers consumers into mimetic attempts to recreate the experience of the character using the planted product. It also, by portraying use of the product in one setting, helps create acceptance for advertising in other settings. Product placement does not directly ask anyone to make a purchase, leaving the advertiser's role in interpellating the consumer somewhat hidden.[41]

Another example comes from online advertising campaigns that rely on user-generated content. Brand advertising distributed by fellow consumers appears more authentic to onlookers, manifesting as grassroots, personal expression rather than a pedantic missive from the advertiser itself. Like product placement, this sort of advertising helps obfuscate the advertiser's role by using a third-party intermediary instead of the advertiser to deliver the advertising message. Voted one of the most successful advertising campaigns ever, Apple's famous Get a Mac campaign presented an "abnormal," bumbling, untrendy PC user in counterpoint to a "normal," hip, unflappable Mac user. Although initially introduced through traditional television spots, part of the value of the Get a Mac campaign came from its re-creation in thousands of imitative unauthorized videos. Some of these videos reinforced the desired dichotomy between the fuddy-duddy PC user and the savvy Mac user. But even when the Get a Mac campaign was used to create videos with an alternative message, the unauthorized content suggested authentic engagement with the original and subtly reinforced and strengthened interest in Apple's campaign.[42]

The use of civic spaces for advertising represents yet another attempt to efface the advertiser's role, this time by drawing on the authority of the chosen space. Marketers and their clients are attracted to advertising in civic locations in part because of their noncommercial histories. We expect artificiality from television commercials and, in fact, inherently suspect anything that comes in that format. By contrast, civic territories with long histories of noncommercialism give advertisements placed there a feeling of authenticity they otherwise would not enjoy. Advertisements in schools and city infrastructure rely on their surroundings to suggest tacit endorsement by a governmental or educational authority. As their experience with advertising in these contexts deepens, consumers eventually may adopt the same skeptical posture that they have learned to adopt in more traditional, commercialized spaces. But even this may end up working to the advertisers' advantage. By establishing a beachhead in the public sphere, advertisers accelerate the normalization of advertising across geographies, making these long-standing marketing holdouts appear no different from other spaces with longer commercial histories.

Controlling Discourse

Finally, guerrilla advertising works by controlling discourse, exercising power over its subjects not only by articulating visions of normal and abnormal behavior, but by channeling communications in ways designed to reinforce its project of governance. This discourse-shaping function of guerrilla advertising works in two chief ways. First, by flooding physical spaces with advertising, marketers make their chosen signifiers a primary source for expression. According to one industry analysis, more than 50 percent of people's everyday conversations revolve around brands.[43] In contrast to the more information-driven advertising of an earlier time, brands are now associated not with product specifics but rather with emotional valences. People drive Toyota Priuses and buy Seventh Generation cleaning products to be part of an environmentally conscious lifestyle, wear Brooks Brothers suits to signal personal conservatism and aspirations to high managerial positions, and drive Harleys to display an inner value structure that favors machismo and freedom from workplace restrictions and social conformity. The Apple name and logo communicate personal creativity. Skinny Girl food and beverage products are meant to be irreverent and social. As advertisers are allowed to enter more and more expressive arenas, their advertisements take on greater importance as raw materials for modern communication.[44]

Second, in cultivating new expressive spaces for advertising, marketers are careful to delimit the boundaries of that expression. Campaigns relying on user-generated content appeal to the individual creativity of users. Contests encouraging the development of such content dangle the ability to win money or consumer goods over would-be auteurs. This incentivizes the kind of content creation that best meshes with the advertiser's brand image and goal of persuading others to purchase its product. By mandating use of the particular brand, limiting the time and technologies that can be employed in the creative process, and requiring the creator to sign over legal control of her creation, advertisers restrict expression that potentially conflicts with their desired norms.[45]

Advertisers also police the boundaries of brand discussion by clandestinely inserting their representatives into the conversation. While trying to foster seemingly organic tableaus for commercial discussion, advertisers are simultaneously using individuals and businesses to steer that discussion in particular directions. Advertisers are advised to "simulate informal networks" in order to appeal to particular demographics on the basis of social identity.[46] Sometimes advertisers hire individual infiltrators to plant their message within a social organization. Word-of-mouth marketing strategies recruit individuals to observe and articulate markers of community difference when making sales pitches to consumers of an identified subgroup. Consider the Girls Intelligence Agency, which claims to have forty thousand teen and preteen girls that it can leverage for product seeding and market research. Described as "secret agents" in the agency's own promotional materials, these girls are paid to organize slumber parties and surreptitiously determine their friends' reactions to particular products and brands.[47] As described in more detail in Chapter 5, our online activities reveal a web of interconnected personal relationships that can be monetized by marketers. Advertising agencies use these social graphs to find and recruit individuals to sing product praises to their friends on social media. By using third parties in this fashion for surveillance and brand proselytizing, advertisers can imbue themselves with an outsider's authenticity while obscuring their own authority and commercial intent.[48]

Admittedly, these grassroots marketing campaigns represent a much more dynamic relationship between advertiser and consumer when compared to the favored advertising formats of the past like the thirty-second television spot. In Foucauldian terms, these campaigns rely not on threats or coercion, but on interpellating a vision of the consumer that the consumer herself wants to become. This relationship is not unidirectional but rather reflects "the multiplicity of force relations" at play in the dialogue between consumer and advertiser.[49] Sometimes efforts to generate brand-friendly content can backfire, producing messages antithetical to the advertisers' desired message.[50] In the main, however, communicating in these new spaces permits advertisers to relinquish some control over their message while still exercising power over their consumer subjects.

Normalization of advertising expansion causes us to no longer see advertising's corrupting influence, to no longer recognize those areas that we do not want to become commercialized. The problem is not that advertisers offer potential choices for identity development; it is that they structure those choices largely without our awareness. Many guerrilla marketing techniques rely on clandestine behavior. Even techniques that are more transparent, like the advertising now found in movie theaters, schools, and public lands, have the effect of desensitizing consumers to the advertisers' presence. As a result, consumers become more and more likely to use this advertising to form identities and adopt the same persuasive strategies and modes of presentation as the advertisers themselves. Healthy identity formation requires the ability to pick and choose from a wide array of contrasting messages. In an environment where every space represents an opportunity for advertisers to call out to their chosen subjects, advertisers define what it means to be part of a social group, leaving out alternative perspectives like Hispanics that are not family oriented or gays not equipped with "good taste."

I want to make clear the limitations of this argument. I am not saying that all advertising produces negative social effects, that it should never be used to fashion identities, or that its messages are impossible to resist. Advertising is not an omnipotent force. Targeted consumers can search out different norms being articulated by noncommercial interests and select the personal vision they like best. But the normalization process that occurs when advertising is free to enter new territories makes those alternative norms less salient and co-opts resistance to the norms articulated by advertisers. Advertising does not merely tap into preexisting lines of self-identification and difference. It articulates a particular vision of the consumer that has discursive power, actively constructing identities and narrowing the ability of individuals to seek self-definition outside of an ever-expanding commercial sphere.

I am also not claiming that the only spaces for identity development are those currently occupied by advertisers. Commercial space is only part of a collection of spaces that people claim and use for identity construction. Our sense of self is produced by many factors. Family, friends, childhood traumas, and workplace triumphs all shape our development. Instead, my normative claim is that the expansion of advertising into new spaces crowds out and devalues competing perspectives. Allowing advertisers to infiltrate schools, government infrastructure, and public lands makes it harder to recognize the alternative perspectives those environments once conveyed. When any space is a potential site for commercial persuasion, individuals become more likely to adopt market-based strategies in their personal lives and the definitions of self proffered by marketers. If no spaces are cordoned off from advertising, the advertiser perspective threatens to become the dominant perspective that audiences internalize.

Law, Advertising, and the Public/Private Divide

One potential response would be to put laws in place to restore a balance and create safe zones where citizens can retreat, knowing that they will not be subject to the commercial gaze. For example, legal authorities in western European nations heavily regulate product placement, sometimes enforcing outright bans on such practices in films and television.[51] In the United States, past legislative commitments sometimes restricted advertising's entry into particular territories. More and more, however, advertisers are allowed to infiltrate new spaces with the blessing of political and legal authorities. In this section, I describe how legal doctrine has changed from blocking to facilitating advertising's colonization of new spaces.

Setting up legal fences is a critical and recurring judicial project. As the political theorist Michael Walzer noted, "Justice is alert to differences, sensitive to boundaries."[52] Institutions occupy spaces, and then those spaces can become contested because they provide areas where opposed discourses may occur. In American legal thought, what has been particularly important in these contests over space is the boundary between public and private. These two categories are used to help to determine the appropriate borders for government regulation. Once a space is deemed private, government regulation of that space becomes constitutionally suspect. Yet when the regulation governs a public space, judges are more likely to defer to the regulatory initiative. Defending this distinction, legal philosopher Martha Minow explains that even though the public/private distinction is inherently contestable, it is a necessary "stand in for liberal democratic commitments to extend the norms of inclusion and equality as common guarantees while also protecting freedom for individuals and groups to express and define themselves safe from government control."[53]

The public/private distinction is a doctrinal tool for assessing the limits of government power, not an all-consuming legal binary. Courts recognize that even areas deemed private still may require some government regulation. For example, in the context of advertising, judges enforce trademark and unfair competition laws to police misleading statements in the private marketplace. Meanwhile, in the right situation, courts willingly limit government authority in public areas. So rather than being outcome determinative, the public/private distinction merely suggests when government regulations should be presumed legitimate. Its salience varies according to the kinds of practices being scrutinized. Nevertheless, the distinction plays an important role in determining the ability of government to restrict advertising's geographic expansion. The public/private boundary is now set in a way that facilitates advertiser entry into historically ad-free zones while effectively blocking the government from participating in zones traditionally controlled by advertisers. The particular legal mechanism used to accomplish this spatial rearrangement is the First Amendment.

Keeping Government Out of Private Space

As described in the first part of this chapter, advertisers have moved to colonize two different kinds of spaces: commercial space and civic space. In each category of space, the public/private boundary has been operationalized in a different way. With regard to government regulation of commercial spaces, judicial treatment of the boundary can be divided into three distinct eras. In the early twentieth century, the public/private distinction was construed broadly as courts gave legislatures wide latitude to restrict advertising on private property. This was exemplified through the legal battle over outdoor advertising in which the courts quickly came to view the scope of the public "police power" as far greater, in this particular regard, than the rights of private property owners. In 1980s and 1990s, the First Amendment's commercial speech doctrine became a new focal point for the public/private distinction. Judges attached a "reasonableness" requirement to government restraints on advertising in private spaces. In the most recent era, courts have come to view commercial space as a preserve that should be governed primarily by private market forces and not by paternalist public actors.

Banning Billboards

Only a decade or so after the introduction of the Model T, a legal battle raged between outdoor advertisers and those seeking to preserve the aesthetic integrity of the roadside environment. In the early twentieth century, billboards were a much more insistent presence than they are today. Early billboards often were clustered in end-to-end rows and stacked on top of each other. In both the cities and the countryside, citizens chafed at their ubiquity. The president of the American Civic Association complained in 1908, "Along the roads . . . all are alike begirt with whiskey, phonographs, fly screens, corsets, tobacco, beer and razors, often to the second and third tiers of shouting signs, between which one can but seldom see the landscape, because of the prevailing signscape—from which there is no escape!"[54]

In response, cities passed zoning restrictions to reduce billboards' effects on the landscape. When advertisers challenged the restrictions, judges initially agreed that the local governments' reach had exceeded their grasp. The local governments' efforts to act in the public interest were trumped by the interests of private property holders wishing to install outdoor advertising on their land. In finding against the cities, courts held that restrictions on commercial sign-age could not be justified by mere aesthetic discomfort at its presence. For example, the Illinois Supreme Court rejected a law restricting billboard signs and locations because the law's "purpose . . . seems to be mainly sentimental, and to prevent sights which may be offensive to the aesthetic sensibilities of certain individuals."[55] Unsightliness, mused the Pennsylvania Supreme Court, was in the eye of the beholder and could not justify a government ban.[56] Zoning re-strictions inspired by a mere desire to avoid commercial eyesores were judged an unfair taking of private property and an illegal government intrusion on a private space. These early decisions protected the private sphere from public beautification attempts. As one court explained, "Aesthetic considerations are a matter of luxury and indulgence rather than of necessity, and it is necessity alone which justifies the exercise of the police power to take private property without compensation."[57]

Shortly thereafter, however, judges adjusted their decisions, holding that civic beautification efforts should overcome private property interests. In other words, when it came to advertising, the judges affirmed a strong governmental role in the private, commercial sphere. Justification for advertising restrictions was found in the local government's police power, even though the traditional concerns of the power—regulation necessary for the health and safety of the citizenry—did not really apply to the aesthetic concerns at the heart of bill-board bans. The cases demonstrate a great deal of judicial maneuvering to justify these advertising bans on the basis of public safety. For example, a New York Supreme Court decision in 1898 upheld a Rochester billboard law that limited billboard height and required outdoor advertisers to register with the city. The court deemed this a suitable use of local authorities' police power, explaining that tall billboards could potentially blow over during strong winds, presenting "a constant menace to the lives and limbs of those who are obliged to pass along in front of them."[58] Other billboard bans were upheld on the public safety rationales of fire risk, sanitation, and potential driver distraction, despite little corresponding evidence.[59]

As time went on, the courts became more comfortable with the bans, going so far as to justify them simply on the basis of aesthetics. Upholding a Los Angeles restriction on the size of outdoor advertising structures, a California judge maintained that "the views in and about a city, if beautiful and unobstructed, constitute one of its chief attractions, and in that way add to the comfort and well-being of its people."[60] A Florida court announced the importance of "so called aesthetic, but really very practical" legislative considerations.[61] New York's highest court endorsed local government's ability to shield drivers from "obnoxious sights of public nuisances."[62] The U.S. Supreme Court weighed in supportively on billboard restrictions, noting not potential public safety hazards but the particularly intrusive nature of this sort of advertising:

> The young people as well as the adults have the message of the billboard thrust upon them by all the arts and devices that skill can produce.... The radio can be turned off, but not so the billboard or street car placard.... The Legislature may recognize degrees of evil and adapt its legislation accordingly.[63]

In just a couple of decades, aesthetic concerns became a sufficient rationale for billboard restrictions, their rapid embrace representing a decision to expand the sphere of government authority at the expense of private interests.[64]

One might have expected advertisers and private landowners to challenge the billboard laws not only as surpassing the boundaries of the police power but also as restrictions on their right to free expression. But in a unanimous 1942 decision, the Supreme Court concluded that advertising was not protected by the First Amendment. Although the government may not unduly burden freedom of communication, the Court explained, the Constitution imposes no such restraint on government as respects "purely commercial advertising."[65] Well into the second half of the twentieth century, states and municipalities had broad discretion to quarantine the spread of advertising, even in "private" domains.

Balancing Commercial Expression with Public Welfare

This dynamic changed in the mid-1970s as the First Amendment was used to more rigorously police the boundary between public authority over advertising and private space. In a 1976 case, the Supreme Court abruptly reversed its prior course, announcing that commercial speech enjoyed constitutional protection. The case, *Virginia State Pharmacy Board v. Virginia Citizens Consumer Council*, involved a Virginia law preventing pharmacies from advertising prescription drug prices. Writing for the majority, Justice Harry Blackmun justified new constitutional safeguards for commercial speech by noting the autonomy interests of advertising's targets. He explained that "if there is a right to advertise, there is a reciprocal right to receive the advertising." Commercial speech, Blackmun maintained, provides material through which human beings may express themselves. It also offers information vital for citizens to make decisions in a market economy. Hence, according to Blackmun, restrictions on such speech strike at listener autonomy and should be deemed inherently suspect.[66]

Blackmun's opinion reflected a new antipaternalist impulse in advertising law fused to a different calibration of the public/private boundary. It set off a wave of decisions shielding advertisers from government regulation based on the right of listeners to be exposed to commercial expression. Of course, almost by its very nature, government acts paternalistically by taking steps to restructure people's choices on their behalf. In a wide range of areas, from motorcycle helmet requirements to antiprostitution laws to food sanitation rules, this sort of government behavior triggers no serious constitutional complaint. But Blackmun contended that there is something more damaging to human autonomy in the regulation of commercial speech than there is in the regulation of commercial conduct. For Blackmun, government should not be in the business of restricting the free flow of expression, particularly when operating out of fear that people will use truthful information to make bad choices. Instead, a market—"the marketplace of ideas"—will sort out good ideas from bad.[67]

At the same time, however, there was a recognition that the new line between public authority and expression in private, commercial space was not meant to be watertight. The commercial speech doctrine tolerated a certain amount of restriction on advertising, pragmatically balancing the autonomy interests of listeners with the policy goals of legislators. The commercial speech cases of the 1980s and 1990s held that some deference is due to legislative judgments, even when those judgments involve restrictions on commercial expression. Shortly after the *Virginia Pharmacy* decision, the Court articulated a three-part test for determining when a government restriction on nonmisleading commercial speech could survive a First Amendment challenge. Under what is called the *Central Hudson* test, to be constitutional, a commercial speech regulation must (1) address a "substantial government interest," (2) "directly advance" that interest, and (3) not be "more extensive than necessary to serve that interest."[68] Two things are notable about this test. First, it treats commercial speech differently from other types of expression, giving the government more latitude to restrict it. As the Court explained, commercial speech enjoys "a limited measure of protection, commensurate with its subordinate position in the scale of First Amendment values, while allowing modes of regulation that might be impermissible in the realm of noncommercial expression."[69] Hence, at the same time that the Court recognized the First Amendment rights of advertisers, it designated commercial speech as inferior to other kinds of communication like political and artistic expression.

Second, the criteria in the three-part test are fairly vague. Over the next two decades, the Court filled in its gaps in ways that permitted a certain amount of government freedom to regulate commercial spaces. The Court specified that the *Central Hudson* requirement that the regulation not be more extensive than necessary does not require proof that the government regulation is the least restrictive means possible of achieving the government's interest. Rather, the judgment of the government merely has to be "reasonable."[70] When the government can tie its speech regulation to a sufficiently weighty interest and show that its regulation can work without too much collateral damage, it has arguably satisfied the test and is not acting in an overly paternalistic fashion. At least until recently, if the government met this burden, it could restrict advertising to help consumers avoid making bad decisions. In 1993, the Court upheld a federal law banning broadcast advertisements for state lotteries outside of states that actually conduct lotteries, accepting the government's argument that the law directly advanced Congress's interest in balancing the interests of both lottery and nonlottery states.[71] It did not matter to the Court that some border residents of lottery states might be denied the ability to hear lottery advertisements when they listened to a radio station located in a nonlottery state. In another case, even as it struck down a state law banning advertisements of retail liquor prices, the Court suggested that another price advertising ban could be constitutional if it was shown that it would "*significantly* reduce alcohol consumption."[72] Under the early commercial speech jurisprudence, efforts to restrict commercial expression for consumers' own good were naturally suspect but that suspicion could be overcome if the government made a compelling case for the need and efficacy of its restriction.

One more feature of this earlier era of commercial speech jurisprudence deserves mention. The Court gave even greater leeway to legislative intervention in the private marketplace that forced commercial actors to carry certain messages on behalf of the government. In general, the First Amendment treats government requirements to speak as inherently suspect. Yet such mandates were not viewed with suspicion when it came to commercial speech. Even in the *Virginia Pharmacy* case, the Court carefully noted that the First Amendment does not prevent the government from mandating "that a commercial message appear in such a form, or include such additional information, warnings, and disclaimers, as are necessary to prevent its being deceptive."[73] In the 1985 case of *Zauderer v. Office of Disciplinary Counsel*, the Court specifically held that commercial speech mandates raise only weak constitutional concerns. When it came to compelled speech, the government had wide latitude to influence advertising's content in private commercial spaces.[74]

Antipaternalism Ascendant

In recent years, legal attitudes toward governmental efforts to restrict advertising in commercial spaces have changed markedly. If the early 1900s construction of the police power gave governmental authorities full discretion in this regard and the commercial speech doctrine of the 1980s and 1990s attempted to balance listener autonomy with regulatory objectives, the current approach treats advertising restrictions with much deeper skepticism. More and more, Blackmun's antipaternalist attitude is no longer leavened by an appreciation of government policies that require restrictions on advertising. Instead, once it is ascertained that the impulse behind any legislation is an effort to shield consumers from the effects of commercial speech, the government is deemed to behave in a paternalist manner and no consideration of the relevant government interest or the probable efficacy of the legislation is necessary. In this view, restrictions on private speech motivated by a desire to help consumers avoid bad decisions are always unconstitutional.

Modern commercial speech doctrine manifests this view in a variety of ways. First, some judges want to scrap the commercial speech test entirely, instead evaluating restrictions on advertising through the same strict First Amendment standard as government restrictions on political speech. Like a modern-day Cato the Elder, Clarence Thomas has added his own personal concurrence to multiple Supreme Court decisions, always urging the *Central Hudson* test's destruction. According to Thomas, courts should not defer to any legislation that restricts truthful advertising: "All attempts to dissuade legal choices by citizens by keeping them ignorant are impermissible."[75] In a case involving restrictions designed to shield children from cigarette advertising, he wrote, "I continue to believe that when the government seeks to restrict truthful speech in order to suppress the ideas it conveys, strict scrutiny is appropriate, whether or not the speech in question may be characterized as 'commercial.'"[76] Justice Antonin Scalia, once a defender of commercial speech restrictions, came to consider the *Central Hudson* test too lenient as well.[77] In legal academia, others have joined the chorus, calling for the end of special treatment for commercial speech.[78]

So far, other justices have refused to officially abandon the *Central Hudson* test. But they and their brethren in the lower courts have adjusted its three parts to reflect a more skeptical view of government restrictions on advertising. It has become more difficult to demonstrate a "substantial" government interest that can justify a limit on commercial speech. In contrast to earlier decisions, the Court now emphasizes that this part of the test "is not satisfied by mere speculation or conjecture."[79] Following this lead, one court found that the government failed to show a substantial interest in communicating the actual health risks of smoking to consumers of cigarettes.[80] Similar skepticism of legislative interests can be found in the litigation over the national Do-Not-Call registry. The first court to hear a First Amendment challenge to the registry declined to find a substantial government interest in helping citizens avoid annoying telemarketers, stating that any involvement of the government in "assessing the value of, and determining, what consumers should and should not hear" was "highly paternalistic."[81] A subsequent decision by a federal court of appeals reversed the lower court's decision, but the constitutionality of advertising limitations akin to the Do-Not-Call registry remains an open question.[82]

Courts have also become more rigorous in determining whether a commercial speech restriction "directly advances" the government interest or is "not more extensive than necessary." Instead of merely requiring a showing that an advertising restriction is a "reasonable" attempt to limit particular harms, the Supreme Court now requires proof that the speech limit "will in fact alleviate them to a material degree."[83] As a consequence, judges feel free to suggest alternative means for accomplishing legislative goals aside from commercial blockades. For example, attempts by regulators to minimize demand for certain unregulated drugs through advertising restrictions have been rejected as "paternalistic" because the government could simply regulate the controversial substances. Of course, this ignores the massive resources required for such an expansion of regulatory commitments, but the current judicial approach seems to value leaving the private expressive field to advertisers.[84]

Even compelled commercial speech is now looked on with alarm. With courts hostile to government efforts to restrict advertising in private spaces, government actors may need to enter these spaces themselves to get their competing message before consumers. If the government cannot designate certain areas as ad free, at least they can require advertisers to disclose certain information designed to help consumers make better, safer choices. In the earlier commercial speech era, even those concerned with the paternalist nature of advertising restrictions could support such disclosures as providing citizens with additional information. But in the current legal environment, even this avenue seems to be increasingly unavailable. Whereas government disclosures attached to commercial speech were once seen as enriching the marketplace of ideas, in an environment dominated by private, commercial appeals, these mandated disclosures are now treated as dangerous interventions in private territory.

Aware that attempting to match dollar for dollar the massive advertising budgets of big tobacco was a fool's errand, Congress targeted one particular advertising space, cigarette packaging, for the mandatory installation of "color graphics depicting the negative consequences of smoking."[85] Cigarette packaging already carries textual health warnings, but government health experts believed that compelling visual images, akin to the advertising employed by the cigarette companies themselves, would be a more viable means for communicating the health risks of smoking. Yet a deeply skeptical federal court found that mandating the visual warnings violated the First Amendment. It deemed the visual images "unabashed attempts to evoke emotion" undeserving of the normally lenient standard of review for mandatory commercial disclosures.[86] The same fate befell a San Francisco ordinance requiring cell phone retailers to post information about the energy emitted from such phones in their stores. Under the ordinance, retailers needed to hang a poster depicting simple graphics of human silhouettes holding cell phones alongside the energy absorption rates for different phones. The presiding judge objected to the poster, contending that visual images "are always subject to interpretation" and consumers could interpret them in different ways, including some ways that were not accurate. He also noted that the poster "would unduly intrude on the retailers' wall space."[87] An appellate court affirmed the judge's decision, tersely concluding that the compelled disclosures were "misleading and controversial."[88] In both instances of compelled commercial speech, the courts rejected the government's attempt to enter space controlled by advertisers to articulate a significant public health message.

In two particular ways, the latest wave of commercial speech cases represents a new, less permeable vision of the public/private distinction when it comes to commercial spaces. First, rather than grappling with the appropriate balance between listener autonomy and public policy, the new approach to commercial speech eschews study of advertising's consequences. The commercial speech doctrine was inaugurated not just in an effort to recognize the importance of consumer access to information but also with the recognition that the qualities of commercial speech made it more susceptible to government regulation than other kinds of expression. These qualities meant that the legislative desire to restrict advertising, quarantine it from certain areas, and attach additional information to it deserved a certain amount of judicial deference. The new nonconsequentialist approach contends that the restriction of commercial speech is inappropriate even when yoked to a demonstrated desire to protect consumers. Laws designed to improve public safety and conserve government resources become unconstitutional once a court concludes that they prevent consumers from being exposed to advertising messages. For courts deciding these cases, it did not matter that the government could point to evidence showing that the messages led to worse, not better, health outcomes.[89]

Second, these decisions reveal a double standard—an unwillingness to allow government to compete on the same terms as advertisers in private, commercial spaces. Government regulators were told that they could not compel advertisers to show colorful graphics or photographs to consumers because consumers might inaccurately interpret these communicative tactics. But, of course, the advertising relied on by private interests depends not only on visual imagery but also on unrealistic audience interpretations of that imagery. On one level, consumers may recognize that the NFL cheerleaders and pristine beaches featured in beer commercials won't be present when they consume the touted product, but these contextual cues and the aspirational goals they represent still influence purchase.[90] Of course, the government remains free to purchase its own advertising on the radio, television, magazines, and other media, and it sometimes does, but it is naive to expect these expenditures to even come close to corporate America's advertising budgets. By restricting government messages in retail environments, the courts are repositioning the public/private distinction, sealing off the boundaries of private, commercial speech from government interference.

Turning Public Spaces Private

While modern commercial speech doctrine seals off "private" areas from government intrusion, the number of public spaces that could counterbalance these commercialized spaces is shrinking. Instead, private spaces are replacing civic spaces as the primary forums for expressive activity. The normalization of commercial discourse causes the curators of civic space to actively welcome additional advertising incursions. Meanwhile, those few governmental actors still seeking to block or limit advertising in public areas are hamstrung by current judicial interpretation of the First Amendment.

Shrinking Public Spaces

Commercial targeting of civic spaces can be viewed as part of a larger movement toward privatization of traditionally governmental activities. Reduced public support for education, combined with an embrace of competition from private actors to improve public school performance, have expanded the number of quasi-public schools while decreasing the number of truly public ones. Privately run prisons, treatment centers, and hospitals have replaced what were once predominantly public institutions. This privatization of traditionally governmental functions narrows the number of public spaces where civic curators can assert their authority to keep advertising out the door.

Looking at the legal landscape, there are few legal mechanisms for resisting this privatization process. For the most part, advertising law relies on private actors, not public officials, to enforce its provisions. The existing private enforcement scheme for advertising law offers few avenues for challenging commercial encroachment on public spaces. The law on false advertising polices only false or misleading commercial claims; it does not address a desire to keep certain spaces ad free. In addition, false advertising actions can only be brought by competitors, not by consumers themselves. The same is true of trademark law. Understandably, competitors are unlikely to be troubled by the prospect of handing over governmental spaces to advertisers. If anything, business entities are united in their desire to open up previously ad-free territories to commercial appeals. It is no surprise that there have been few courtroom challenges to advertiser infiltration of public space.

Meanwhile, the response of legislators and regulators to advertising's colonization of public space has been muted at best. Some federal laws have been passed to restrict advertising in noncommercial spaces. The Telephone Consumer Protection Act of 1991 restricts telephone solicitations and has been interpreted by courts to apply to the newer technology of unsolicited cellular phone text messages. Another federal law requires commercial enterprises to give recipients a mechanism for unsubscribing from unsolicited commercial e-mails. But these initiatives focus on intrusions that offend personal privacy, not commercial culture's potential corruption of civic spaces. They do not provide a mechanism for retarding the spread of advertising in schools, public lands, or other public areas. Federal and state legislators have been largely silent when it comes to corporate efforts to gain access to civic spaces. There has been no real legislative reaction to opening up public lands to advertising or the monetization of municipal ad space. A comprehensive review of state-level school legislation reveals little traction behind proposals to keep advertising away from schoolhouse doors.[91]

The public regulators charged with policing advertising seem unconcerned by advertising in civic spaces. The Federal Trade Commission (FTC) tends to focus its efforts on deceptive practices rather than patrolling the line between public and private expressive space. Although the FTC also asserts its authority to stop unfair trade practices, this authority has been limited to cases involving monetary or physical harms to consumers, not the more intangible harms caused by the loss of noncommercial preserves.[92] Advocacy groups find the FTC and Federal Communications Commission unwilling to set limits on product placement in entertainment or even to require that most sponsorship arrangements be disclosed to audiences. State regulatory officials view their mandate somewhat more expansively, but still focus mainly on outright consumer deception rather than the need to safeguard the civic character of particular public institutions.

At the same time, technological change has done further work to convert public spaces to private ones. "Minds are not changed in streets and parks as they once were. To an increasing degree, the more significant interchanges of ideas and shaping of public consciousness occur in mass and electronic media."[93] As the Internet has become the predominant communications medium, it has displaced other speech conduits. In the past, these conduits—think telephone companies and the postal service—were deemed "common carriers" and prohibited from discriminating against different forms of content. But the new online mediums—cable broadband providers, Internet search engines, online payment services—have not typically been subjected to the same nondiscrimination requirements.[94] These new private entities have no compunction about injecting advertising into the user's communication experience. Many of them rely almost exclusively on advertising revenue for their existence. The Supreme Court has been unwilling, for the purposes of First Amendment doctrine, to adjust its definition of a "public forum" to cover the predominantly private entities that control the communicative spaces of the Internet. The result is a communications environment dominated by private intermediaries managing private spaces.

Erosion of Self-Policing

Many, if not most, of the problematic advertising initiatives described in this chapter have been ignored or even encouraged by government authorities. To the extent that the public/private distinction relies not just on judicial enforcement but also self-enforcement by civic gatekeepers, these entities are no longer up to the task. So to a large degree, the problem is not legal barriers so much as political will. But the evolution of legal doctrine is part of this story as well. The First Amendment provides cover for schools and municipalities that do not wish to do battle with commercial interests. The harms from advertising's expansion can be more safely ignored when legal precedent suggests that government efforts to prevent those harms would be unconstitutional.

The best way to observe the current apathy toward civic commercialism is to compare it to a historical benchmark. Both public lands and public schools were shaped out of an antipathy to marketplace influences. In the late 1800s and early 1900s, government actors created new public territories with legal fortifications designed to withstand incursions from private forces. During this period, America's natural wonders were placed under public control not just for purposes of conservation and public access but to draw a visible distinction between public and private space. A notorious advertisement for the patent medicine St. Jacobs Oil painted on a rock at Niagara Falls generated international opprobrium and led to the first successful legislation restricting outdoor advertising.[95] European criticism of coarse American materialism in scenic spaces like Niagara Falls stung. It motivated a national parks movement designed to communicate noncommercial aspects of the American identity. The unique quality of America's scenic spaces no longer seemed unique when combined with marketing messages evident in any other kind of space. Publicly held lands, quarantined from commercial forces, were created by Progressive-era legislators to "express the most noble aspects of the national character."[96] In sympathy with these legislators, judges found advertising in natural areas galling. Early twentieth-century judicial decisions upheld advertising bans in public parks, areas adjacent to parks, and even entire regions known for their scenic splendor, like the Adirondacks.[97]

Although advertising has been taking place in schools for nearly a century, it was never a commonplace practice until today. Instead, as with America's scenic wonders, political and educational leaders took periodic steps to restrict further commercial encroachment. John Dewey, the most important American theorist on education, articulated an explicitly civic rationale for public schooling that eschewed the intrusion of private values. According to Dewey, the running of the school was meant to serve as a civic, noncommercial example to students of the values necessary to their future lives as engaged political citizens.[98] In the 1920s, when in-school commercialism seemed positively benign compared to the modern era of drink sponsorship deals and school naming rights, the National Education Association formed a committee to study the phenomenon. This Committee on Propaganda in the Schools sounded alarms, particularly over the potential influence of commercial interests on curricular content.[99] Even as business-sponsored materials entered the classroom, professional educators organized to limit and manage their flow.[100] More recently, in the early 1980s, federal regulators limited the advertising and sale of foods of low nutritional value that competed with federally regulated school meals.[101]

The attitudes of today's civic stewards are far different. For example, under Chris Clark, commissioner of Georgia's Department of Natural Resources, the department entered into an agreement to recognize Verizon on its publicity materials. In return, Verizon provided supplies for cleaning up some of the state's waterways and trails. According to Clark, the Verizon deal is just the tip of the iceberg. "Every interstate has these huge brown signs that tell you 'Red Top Mountain State Park,'" he says. "And at the bottom, we'd love to have 'Chick Fil-A,' or whatever else, as a simple way of marketing."[102] In a similar vein, instead of concerning themselves with the corrupting influence of market-based appeals, national park administrators claim that there is no disconnect between commercialism and the public ideals on which the parks were founded.[103] To celebrate its centennial in 2016, the National Park Service (NPS) inked a multimillion-dollar branding deal with Anheuser-Busch, waiving a long-standing NPS ban on sponsorship arrangements with alcoholic beverage companies. Sounding more like an advertising executive than a civic steward, an NPS official championed the blend of natural treasures and Budweiser as a "critical tool . . . to connect with and create the next generation of park visitors."[104]

Meanwhile, school administrators actively solicit bids from advertisers. School commercialism provides surprisingly little funding, at least when compared to overall school budgets. So commercial infiltration of the schools is not simply a matter of cash-strapped administrators needing the money. Instead, it seems that school officials (and the voters who keep school board members in office) see little need to keep public and private spaces separate. In Colorado, the first state to allow school bus advertising, a school district spokesperson voiced excitement about the potential for even more advertising. "Ultimately we hope to have advertisements on every bus to maximize our income," she said.[105] Opponents of marketing to students sometimes point to potential safety hazards (e.g., distracted kids looking at bus-side advertisements when they are crossing the street), yet arguments over the need to quarantine commercial values from civic values are voiced less and less.

This failure to self-police the public side of the public/private distinction is complemented by the same changes in First Amendment doctrine that restrict regulation of advertising in private, commercial territories. As advertising in public schools and government-owned property increases, the current construction of the commercial speech doctrine poses problems for civic curators seeking to reinforce the public/private boundary. Past judicial interpretation of the commercial speech doctrine offered great latitude to public officials bent on restricting commercial expression. This latitude applied to government interference in both private and public spaces. For example, the trustees of New York's state university system adopted a resolution barring private commercial enterprises from operating in university facilities. Businesses claimed a violation of their First Amendment rights. The test case came from a corporation barred by campus police from demonstrating and selling housewares to small groups of students in university-owned dormitories. In 1989, the Supreme Court held that there was no doubt that these "Tupperware parties" represented commercial speech. Nevertheless, the Court found that the trustees were in their rights to deny these commercial actors entry to their facilities. It observed that the trustees' interests in "promoting an educational rather than commercial atmosphere" on its campuses, "preventing commercial exploitation of students," and "preserving residential tranquility" were all substantial government interests satisfying the first part of the *Central Hudson* test.[106] It is doubtful that today's courts would be so solicitous of these governmental justifications for restricting expression. Sensing a change in judicial attitudes, emboldened marketers have begun to sue public schools when denied the ability to advertise in their halls.[107]

Even local authorities that want only to be selective in their choice of private partners, and not entirely ban commercial expression in public spaces, could run afoul of the First Amendment. School boards currently worry over susceptibility to costly lawsuits if they spurn a particular advertiser.[108] Because the First Amendment prohibits "viewpoint discrimination," even in cases involving commercial speech, certain entities denied sponsorship rights might challenge their exclusion under the First Amendment. Imagine a hypothetical case of a merchant barred from participating in the sponsorship program of a local school district, perhaps because the district is worried about the effects of the merchant's product on student health. A lot of money is at stake here, and all sorts of advertisers are desirous of getting inside schoolhouse doors. A First Amendment challenge would require the school district to articulate a compelling reason for excluding a particular corporate suitor. This burden becomes all the more difficult to satisfy as schools become increasingly commercialized and acquire track records of less-than-discriminating corporate sponsorship. To take one egregious example, an elementary school in Polk County, Florida, accepted a $300 donation from the Rogers and Walker Gun Shop. In return, the gun shop's name was placed on the school's marquee.[109] Seventy percent of U.S. elementary and middle school students are already exposed to in-school food marketing, some students seeing ads for Pizza Hut and McDonald's on their report cards.[110] Once a school legitimates commercial speech involving guns or fast food, there are not many other businesses that would appear inconsistent with the school's educational mission.[111] Under current interpretation of the First Amendment, a court might examine a school's history of sponsorship deals and determine that efforts to discriminate against other merchants were not motivated by a legitimate government purpose.[112] The same concerns might apply to any local government entity that sold space to advertisers. Sponsorship deals may seem like an easy way for states and municipalities to generate revenue. Yet once the advertising genie comes out of the bottle, the First Amendment makes it hard to put him back inside.

The New Market Research

YOU'RE APPROACHED by the representative of a Fortune 500 company. The representative proposes that you and your family submit to an intensive investigation. Your every location will be tracked, your every keystroke and mouse click logged. Paid snoops from the company will rifle through your trash to try and determine your buying habits. Without your specific knowledge as to their whereabouts, listening and recording devices will be installed throughout your home and your vehicle, and they will be embedded in any new electronic devices that you purchase. This investigation will be of indeterminate duration—there's no telling when it might end. The information collected will be used for two broad purposes. First, the company will design individually tailored advertisements crafted to make you buy more of its products. Second, without telling you when and to whom (and without cutting you in on the profits), the company will sell this data to other, unrelated businesses that might employ it for new, currently unforeseen commercial uses. Would you agree to this offer? Probably not. The proposal sounds like a Kafkaesque nightmare, an invasion of the sanctity of the home and the familial relationship. But millions of consumers currently grant marketers just this sort of intimate access every day.

The previous chapter showed that advertising's colonization of new spaces should be cause for concern. By infiltrating once-ad-free zones, twenty-first-century advertising could be changing how we develop our own sense of self, and not for the good. Even those favorably disposed to commercial culture may brace at the thought of advertising playing such a starring role in the movies going on inside our heads. At least most of the activity described in Chapter 2 is visible—observable battles over territory between commercial and noncommercial forces. By contrast, another aspect of the new advertising relies on clandestine tracking to make advertising messages more powerful. With the increasing digitization of everyday life, corporate entities scrutinize our every move and then, typically without our knowledge, use that data to influence behavior at an individual level.

Some respond to commercial surveillance with a shrug. Sun Microsystems CEO Scott McNealy famously said, "You have zero privacy anyway. Get over it."[1] Or to paraphrase Google chief executive Eric Schmidt, data collection should bother you only if you have something to hide.[2] Observation by commercial actors is different and less cause for concern, some scholars say, than surveillance conducted by the government, which can result in criminal prosecution and potentially squelch political dissent. Supporters of the new market research highlight its ability to make advertising more relevant as marketers use collected information to generate product offers tailored to individual interests. Regulatory interference, they contend, would jeopardize the benefits of surveillance, forcing consumers to waste their time sifting through impersonal commercial appeals.[3]

Yet the efficiency gains from personalized advertising must be weighed against other concerns. Surveillance, whether practiced by private or public entities, means power. When companies know more about you, they can leverage that information to their advantage. Thanks to new technologies and techniques of surveillance, companies know a lot more about consumers than they did just a few years ago. A growing array of businesses, including advertisers, retailers, social media companies, and trade associations, maintain detailed files on almost every American. The average consumer profile maintained by data broker Acxiom contains thousands of pieces of information. One person who used European privacy laws to request his data from Facebook discovered that Facebook's digital dossier on him totaled 1,222 PDF pages.[4] This material may be used to serve up more individualized ads, but it can also be used for more nefarious purposes. Particularly egregious uses of this kind of information could include blackmail (e.g., threatening to reveal embarrassing purchases or travels to particular locations, both online and offline) or discrimination (e.g., adverse employment consequences thanks to a commercial data collector's revelation of a user's sexual orientation or undisclosed pregnancy).

Even when consumer data is used only to make advertisements more persuasive, it should cause concern. Most advertising is designed to persuade, not to inform, and thanks to the reams of unseen data that today's advertisers collect, persuasion becomes easier to accomplish. Digital profiling can be used not only to match goods and services to consumer preferences, but also to pinpoint individual cognitive failings and moments of particular receptivity to advertising. Even the worst salesperson becomes more effective when armed with a hidden list of your interests, relationships, past purchases, and financial records. If there is a balance to be struck between advertisers and consumers, the new market research is definitely tipping the scales in one direction.

The sheer comprehensiveness of the growing commercial spying apparatus also needs to be considered. Technology now mediates virtually every commercial exchange. This will only intensify as manufacturers embed data collectors into the next generation of homes, cars, appliances, and even clothing. And this technology is sticky: it leaves a trail of data no matter how small the transaction. What is the psychological toll of living in a world where all of us have to assume constant supervision? Surveillance, regardless of its ultimate purpose, ultimately treats its targets as objects, dehumanizing them and corroding the trust needed for cooperative social enterprise. The same technologies developed by advertisers to surveil consumers are subsequently used by the government to track its citizens and by individuals to spy on each other.[5]

This new world of selling and tracking turns reasonable expectations of privacy on their head, but this is not the first time aggressive advertising has raised privacy concerns. The legal response to past advertising innovations deemed violative of personal privacy is instructive. At the turn of the last century, the right to privacy was created just as mass marketing was beginning to take hold. Its creators designed the new right to provide a sanctuary from unwanted commercial attention. Today, however, the legal system seems largely content to force consumers to make their inner lives an open book for advertisers. Why did legal authorities agree to stop invasive advertising in the past yet have failed to counter the data collection activities of today? At least part of the failure to use privacy law to curb corporate surveillance can be traced to a mistaken reliance on contract law. In a perverse way, freedom of contract has been pressed into advertising's service to legally ratify a surveillance state run not by the National Security Agency but by Madison Avenue.

They Know Where, When, and What You Did Last Summer

It has always been in sellers' interests to know their customers better. Systematic efforts to track individual consumers in order to provide more effective promotional messages date back to the early 1900s.[6] Now, however, advertisers have much more consumer information at their disposal than their counterparts of a century or even a decade ago. The sheer volume of data collected by modern marketers leads to discoveries that would have been impossible to detect in the past. Thanks to the law of big numbers, holders of massive consumer data sets can identify once undetectable correlations and then use those insights to convert potential buyers into actual purchasers. The information can also be broken down into smaller and smaller subcategories, giving advertising that personal touch. All this data is collected through various means and devices. The examples that follow, while not comprehensive, demonstrate how commercial surveillance has woven itself completely into the fabric of everyday life.

When compared to the market research of the past, the amount of information collected on individual consumers is staggering. A few technological changes have made this possible. First, as the predominant site of commercial transactions shifts from physical locations to online purchases, more and more data is generated. In an offline retail world, advertisers had little information on consumer behavior besides some records of point-of-sale purchases and queries posed to a small sampling of consumers. Online commerce opens up new possibilities as a variety of technologies, including cookies, beacons, Web bugs, and digital fingerprinting, document consumer activity on Internet pages. This software records a website user's decisions on where to scroll, what to click, and what search terms to use. Retailers then take that information and recommend additional products—not just in the form of online ads but in more subtle ways, such as altering the results of future online searches. Even when consumers conduct online research for purchases that they will eventually make at a physical location, the record of this online activity is of immense value to advertisers. It can be used to determine areas of interest and likely times of advertising receptivity.[7]

A number of the electronic devices that have become essential ingredients in our personal lives—whether as means to communicate or as mechanisms for consuming media content—record information that can later be leveraged by advertisers. Relinquishing this personal data has become part of the price for online activity. This is the quid pro quo attached to the application software (apps) we install on our desktops and mobile devices. Most popular gaming applications for Facebook are designed to grab consumer data that will subsequently prove useful to advertisers.[8] Supposedly free apps for smartphones surreptitiously pull sensitive information off user phones and then provide that information to third parties. Your favorite phone app might send copies of your contact lists, text messages, Internet search history, physical location, and even camera phone pictures to a market research firm.[9] An app provided by Qantas Airways allowed the airline to monitor, in real time, posts made by its customers on social media platforms like Instagram and Facebook once they checked in to a Qantas airport lounge.[10] By installing the Bing search engine smartphone app, a user agrees to allow Microsoft to record audio, send e-mails to guests, and read the data on the phone, all without the user's knowledge.[11]

It is not just apps or retailer websites but personal devices themselves that catalogue user inputs for marketing purposes. Without downloading a single invasive app, today's devices can take your information and later use it for personalized advertising. Perhaps the most valuable information recorded by these devices is the individual user's location. Marketing studies demonstrate the value of using location information to create irresistible serendipity when sending advertisements to individual consumers. Just imagine how much more likely you are to respond to an advertisement for a restaurant when you receive the ad for the restaurant when you are just a few steps from its front door. Consumers targeted on the basis of their location exhibit greater attention, interest, desire, favorable attitudes toward the particular brand being touted, and, most important, greater intention to purchase.[12] Hence, designers of electronic devices implant locational tracking systems in their products.

In 2011, it was revealed that the iPhone, Android phone, and iPad all contained software that silently recorded user location. The phones tracked their
owners' whereabouts every few seconds and then transmitted that information
back to the company, where it was stored in a database. Perhaps even more
disturbing, the software was designed in a way that facilitated the unwitting
spread of this data to the hard drive of any computer synched to the device.
Although this particular software has since been removed, the Wi-Fi and Blue-
tooth capabilities of today's smartphones allow retailers to track customers as
they travel through their stores.[13] Meanwhile, wireless providers watch their
mobile subscribers as they traverse the web, implementing technologies that
override customer efforts to safeguard their digital privacy.[14]

Digital coupons represent another way to build up databases of consumer
information. These coupons offer convenience to shoppers who would rather
use their phone (an accessory they already carry at all times) than small slips
of paper to receive instant rebates on products. But unlike their paper counterparts, digital coupons can add personal information to advertiser stockpiles.
When a digital coupon code is scanned, a tremendous amount of data can be
released, including the coupon user's IP address, the date and time of both obtaining and redeeming the coupon, the store location where the coupon was
used, the search terms used to find the coupon, and even items written on the
user's Facebook profile. When Target scans the bar code of a coupon off your
phone, it not only collects this panoply of information, but also gets your tacit
permission to collect your cell phone number and cellular carrier and to share
this information with third parties. According to one expert, roughly fifteen
separate pieces of personal information are relayed to retailers through the use
of a single mobile coupon.[15] In parallel fashion, companies offering daily deals,
like Groupon and Living Social, collect information on user location, social
relationships, and online search history, and then share that data not only with
participating merchants but also third-party advertisers.[16]

The convenience of electronic books and online video subscription services produces a wealth of data for retailers. Most individuals would probably take great offense at the idea of third parties poring over records of what
they checked out of the library. Nevertheless, Netflix and Amazon aggressively track the video viewing habits of their subscribers. They keep a record
not only of what is watched but how it is watched, down to the devices used

and the individual decisions to hit pause and rewind. In the past, video rental services were obliged to obtain consent from the consumer every time they wished to share that consumer's rental choice with an outside party. Now, thanks to a 2012 law, video subscription services need only obtain a single generalized consent to share a subscriber's viewing history on multiple occasions with potentially thousands of outside parties.[17] Amazon and other e-reader device makers record user searches for reading material, the particular book passages that readers most frequently highlight, and how and when users choose to read the books they select. This holds true whether the user obtained the book from the device manufacturer (e.g., a book purchased from Amazon for reading on a Kindle) or another source. And according to most e-reader terms of service, all of this data can be shared outside of the manufacturer's or publisher's company, even if the consumer has not specifically consented to such sharing.[18]

Advances in computing power and storage allow even more traditional commercial technologies to deliver new insights on individual shoppers. Credit cards have been available in some form since the late 1800s, but with the insights of Big Data, today's credit card transactions can generate significantly more information on buying habits and behaviors than in the past. Walmart, for example, the nation's second biggest retailer, captures data from point-of-sale transactions and houses it all in a 7.5 teradata warehouse. With data profiles on over 145 million adult Americans, Walmart has the potential to develop the most comprehensive market research record of any retailer. The sheer volume of data it controls allows it to recognize correlations that may not be apparent to smaller stores. In a now widely discussed marketing insight, Walmart crunched its point-of sale-numbers to find that beer and strawberry Pop-Tarts were purchased in much higher numbers upon the arrival of inclement weather. As a result, Walmart more prominently displays these items and increases its in-store supply of them when forecasters predict severe storms. Walmart's giant data set also allows it to spot more individualized anomalies, that is, situations where certain consumers deviate from typical consumer behavior. It can then use that information to identify particular cognitive shortcomings and biases, and then exploit them through particularized advertisements and offers. Rational consuming behaviors can be compared against deviant ones, and individual consumer vulnerabilities diagnosed. Potential vulnerabilities surfaced through this process include higher-than-average propensities for addiction, sensitivity to stress, and imperviousness to price.[19]

Two additional things should be understood about the modern collection of consumer information. First, the more data about an individual consumer that can be combined from different sources, the more valuable that data becomes. The sheer number of transactions Walmart processes every day makes it a formidable source of consumer information. Walmart can also combine this pool of data from traditional point-of-sale transactions with additional information that it intends to collect by increasing its Web presence and encouraging customers to use new technologies in its stores. Walmart's privacy policy broadly explains that it has the right to combine any information that it collects with "other sources."[20] Its CEO cited the information it gleans from its Sam's Club membership program as well as the "traceable tender" from credit and debit card sales to illustrate a larger point about the value residing in the company's gigantic analytic stockpiles. He said, "If you take that [Sam's Club] data and you correlate it with traceable tender that exists in Wal-Mart Stores and then the identified data that comes through Walmart.com and then the trend data that comes through the rest of the business and working with our suppliers, our ability to pull data together is unmatched."[21]

Walmart is not the only business that can aggregate consumer information from a variety of sources to build up robust consumer profiles. In the ecology of the Web, thousands of unrelated websites all participate and share data in a single advertising network. Survey evidence shows that the vast majority of consumers do not understand that businesses track a person's entire online history as opposed to just transactions with one particular website. Most would be shocked to discover that retailers like Target and Amazon combine myriad bits of online data from thousands of sources to identify and predict the intimate details of their customers' lives, like their reading habits or an undisclosed pregnancy, all in an effort to make their sales pitches more effective.[22] Consumers may not think they are disclosing much personal information in individual transactions, but what they do not realize is that all these transactions add up and they are often accumulated into a single digital record. Businesses recognize the predictive value from such records and are investing heavily in greater data collection. As Twitter founder Evan Williams stated (or, more accurately, "tweeted"), "Many of the great businesses of the next decade will be about making information about our [consumer] behaviors more visible."[23]

Second, it is important to recognize that even when businesses are careful to keep individual consumer profiles anonymous, obscuring any personally identifiable information like name or address that might be collected, these profiles can still be used to deliver ads to one specific individual. The detailed records on individual shoppers maintained by data collectors are typically assigned an alphanumerical code instead of a name. But even without a name, a business can still use those records to diagnose predispositions and target consumers accordingly. As soon as a computer connects to the Internet, it provides an IP address, which is all the personal information a commercial data collector needs to match someone's current activities to records of his or her past behavior. Online exchanges allow businesses to buy and sell the right to reach a particular individual at a particular IP address at the precise moment that person decides to load a particular web page. Those engaging in commercial surveillance claim to keep those being surveilled anonymous. But this promise of anonymity means very little if businesses can continue to follow you online and send you communications based on your history.

Life inside the Big Data Panopticon

The other critical component of the new market research is its concealment. The covert nature of today's market research (in addition to its sheer size and detail) is what makes it so valuable. Any market researcher will tell you that information gained from a consumer unaware that she is being surveilled is worth a great deal more than research composed of self-aware answers to a researcher's scripted questions. Prior attempts to acquire customer information required active engagement of those willing to participate in polls or interviews. In the 1950s, when these sorts of efforts were just getting off the ground, customers were flattered to receive the attention of advertisers, and response rates to mailed market research questionnaires were extremely high. Yet even with consumers willingly providing information, marketing campaigns based on this data often fell flat. The Ford Motor Company's disastrous introduction of the Edsel in 1958 became a testament to failed market research. The Coca-Cola Company's launch of New Coke in 1985 bombed despite a battery of focus group interviews showing widespread approval of the new soda formulation. Respondents told researchers what they wanted to hear instead of offering insights into their true feelings about the new product.[24] Consumer surveillance that allows individual behaviors to be tracked invisibly and unobtrusively over time is a godsend for advertisers trying to unlock the real secrets to purchaser motivation. Even for consumers generally aware that online surveillance is taking place, it is much easier to let one's guard down when there is no visible reminder that someone else is watching.

But let's say that you are concerned about the Orwellian nature of consumer data collection and take dramatic action. You don't use a smartphone, clip your coupons the old-fashioned way, only see movies in actual theaters, and pay for your purchases with cash. Or you adopt technological solutions of your own, carefully deleting the cookies left on your computer and deploying ad-blocking software during your online browsing.[25] No matter. Digital technology is used in other ways that even the savviest consumer cannot possibly avoid. In addition to online surveillance, businesses record offline activities and use that information to tailor their appeals in more and more compelling ways. By expanding and shifting surveillance to new forums, advertisers obtain better results and obfuscate the new repositories of commercial power.

Shopping in the physical world will never go away completely. Clothes need to be tried on, produce needs to be inspected. But even these analog shopping experiences now create a rich data trail for advertisers. Your weekly trip to the grocery store may involve you as an unwitting subject for market research. Some supermarkets contract with an in-store monitoring company that digitally records customer conversations with store employees and then studies those conversations to detect recurring words or phrases. Even if you do not carry a GPS-enabled smartphone, shopping carts and baskets are now equipped with location-tracking devices to analyze in-store traffic patterns. Cameras compile information about which in-store displays cause shoppers to linger and for how long. They can also tell a retailer whether someone who walks into a store actually bought something.

But the technology used to survey real-world shopping tracks more than records of purchase or the duration of conversations with store employees. It used to be that you could assume that advertisers could not see your face while you viewed their messages. Aside from negotiating with a particular salesperson, consumers could process most commercial entreaties in relative seclusion. Radio spots and television commercials could be mulled over without the advertiser immediately gauging one's response.

New technology, however, makes advertisements act like a one-way mirror: we cannot see the face of the advertiser, but they can see us. Facial and voice recognition technology is increasingly becoming part of the market researcher's arsenal. Tesco, the world's second-largest retailer, has screens in stores and at gas pumps that scan customers' faces so as to deliver individually targeted ads.[26] A camera inside the screen examines the shopper's face. From this it can work out the shopper's gender and general age range (child, young adult, adult, or senior). The technology has reached the point where it will not be fooled by hats, glasses, or scarves and can distinguish between actual living persons and mere facsimiles, say, a life-sized poster of a real person. Companies can also use these recognition systems to find a match between the current image being processed and another image of the same individual, thereby removing the cloak of anonymity from previously anonymous consumers. These matching capabilities allow outside data profiles to be combined with the data recorded during the facial scan. If you wrinkle your nose at one type of product or advertisement, that information is valuable to businesses that want to sell you something else down the road. Voice recognition software performs a similar function, using vocal signatures to track consumers while intuiting their emotional state. Tesco is not the only retailer embracing these consumer surveillance tools. Companies plan to use the technology to expand their shopping profiles of individuals, using what works and what does not work on that person to fine-tune their next individual marketing appeal. According to the CEO of one company that makes the facial recognition screens, "It is time for a step-change in advertising—brands deserve to know not just an estimation of how many eyeballs are viewing their adverts, but who they are too."[27]

Aware that the use of these data collection technologies may offend shopper sensibilities, businesses are taking steps to mask their use. One strategy is to camouflage cameras so that consumers can't know they are being watched. Several national chains hide cameras in the eyes of store mannequins. Or, in a strategy straight out of *Minority Report*, some facial recognition devices are hidden in billboards gazed at by strolling consumers.[28]

Another strategy is to embed this technology in new electronic devices and social media sites, in effect building a Trojan horse for the capture of personal information. You don't even have to leave the house for your face or voice to become part of an advertising profile. Microsoft's Xbox One device has an internal camera meant to facilitate facial recognition targeted ads. Microsoft's patent application for the device asserts the right to use the camera to "assign emotional states to the users" and then employ an "advertisement engine" to select "emotionally compatible" advertisements.[29] Microsoft backpedaled from initially requiring the camera to be turned on for the gaming system to function. Now games can be played without switching on the camera. Nevertheless, consumers are steered toward surveillance as the Xbox loses a great deal of its functionality if a privacy-minded user elects to disconnect her camera.[30] Similarly, although one might expect prospective television purchasers to balk, marketers and manufacturers are seeking to place similar cameras inside new TVs, thereby allowing market researchers to count not only how many people are watching an ad at any given time but also how they are emotionally responding to it. Samsung's "SmartTVs" come equipped with voice recognition software that captures users' verbal commands, and, at least initially, they collected data from those commands even when users tried to opt out of the TV's voice recognition features.[31] Meanwhile, social media sites like Facebook and Instagram are turning posted photographs into faceprint data banks and investing heavily in making facial recognition technology more effective. Smartphones may make the collection of such faceprints routine. For every selfie taken and posted online, somewhere there is a grateful advertiser.[32]

In one sense, this sort of spying on customers is old hat. For years, ethnographers have been hired to study the "naked behavior" of shoppers. Even in the Mad Men era, anthropologists were on the staffs of major advertising firms to accumulate in-depth records of consumer practices. What is different today is the ease with which the new technology allows for an intimate record of everyone's daily life. Hiring ethnographers is expensive, and the pool of customers that can be surveyed is naturally limited. Facial and voice recognition technology, however, is becoming increasingly prevalent and may soon become a built-in feature of our televisions and phones. Human spies can provide detailed information on only a few shoppers, but the new market research portends a world where all shoppers have their every move, facial tic, and vocal tremor recorded for future commercial scrutiny.

Surveillance Harms

The vast amounts of data now available to marketers produce some clear benefits, and not just for the marketers. Personalized advertising avoids waste, whether in the form of consumers searching through irrelevant information or businesses blowing their budgets on useless ads. If a lower-middle-class married father of three now receives ads for minivans and family restaurants instead of luxury sports cars and online dating services, that can be a good thing. Widespread surveillance brings hard-to-detect inclinations to the surface, potentially satisfying an individual consumer's tastes and desires that she did not even realize she had. Law professor Eric Goldman makes exactly this point, describing the benefits of digital market research that can uncover and then fulfill "latent preferences" that the consumer is incapable of articulating herself. Regulators should be hesitant to interfere with this process, he stresses, given their inferior capacity to discern consumer wants and needs.[33]

The utility gained from tools meant to more accurately assess consumer preference should not be dismissed out of hand. But digital tracking might actually cause more wasted effort, not less. Law professor Ryan Calo suggests that as consumers become aware they are the target of nonstop commercial monitoring and profiling, they will take steps to mask their identities. For example, someone concerned about online surveillance could use different browsers to shop for the same item and then compare prices. Another approach would be to create a variety of fake identities to use at one time or another on the Web. The problem with this kind of subterfuge is that it takes a lot of time and effort. Searching for every product two or three times or maintaining a stable of different consumer personas is a lot of work. Such efforts represent an increase in transaction costs and a further tax on the resources of overburdened consumers.[34] In an only somewhat tongue-in-cheek example, one artist advocates creating an "antiface" to subvert facial recognition technologies. As suggested by the artist, use of facially obscuring hairstyles and makeup could allow individuals to hide themselves from commercial (and governmental) eyes. But it would also be incredibly inefficient for consumers to take these steps every time they enter the marketplace. The new market research is causing real harm if it forces us to wear actual masks just to go shopping.[35]

This resistance to surveillance may eventually die out, but an even greater concern than inefficiency is what behavioral targeting means for individual privacy. Neil Richards outlines two main harms that come from living under a regime of constant corporate surveillance. First, surveillance is a threat to what Richards calls our "intellectual privacy." Richards makes a normative claim that processes of thinking and making up one's mind about a subject fare best when performed free from outside exposure. To be truly valuable, thoughts need time to incubate in private before they are able to be expressed publicly. When other entities can see the books we read, the music we listen to, and the websites we consult, this intellectual refuge evaporates. By maintaining a permanent record of our intellectual inquiries, commercial surveillance invades our inner thoughts and the personal contemplations that make us different from one another. When those inquiries become transparent to outsiders, they can also be influenced by outsiders. For example, records of book selections and Web searches allow advertisers to pigeonhole us as a particular kind of viewer and narrow the range of showcased new choices accordingly. Surveillance may also cause consumers to stop making particular kinds of choices for fear of observation, thereby stunting potential outlets for intellectual discovery.[36]

Second, all of this data collection gives new power to entities, changing the dynamics between consumer and advertiser (as well as citizen and government). Using surveillance to tilt that playing field too far in one direction can cause problems. The easy and hidden way in which personal information can be collected opens up consumers to potential blackmail. In the wrong hands, evidence of embarrassing product proclivities could become a tool for extortion. A consumer may rightfully worry about an outside entity disclosing her choices of viewing material or travel history. For instance, car service app Uber records extremely sensitive information about its passengers' movements, including whether they returned to their home address after going out on a Friday or Saturday night.[37]

A related concern is that businesses will use all this information to unfairly sort consumers into different categories. The concern is not so much that businesses will tailor commercial appeals in a more persuasive, individualized manner but that when it comes to the actual terms of purchase and types of products available, Big Data will slot people into discriminatory tracks. When detailed behavioral and demographic information on consumers was hard to come by, such discrimination was more difficult to accomplish. But now, with incredibly detailed profiles existing for most potential customers, discounts and promotions can be offered to a chosen few while other groups with less purchasing power may be forced to pay higher prices or endure greater burdens when navigating the marketplace. Richards says:

> The power of sorting can bleed imperceptibly into the power of discrimination. A coupon for a frequent shopper might seem innocuous, but consider the power to offer shorter airport security lines (and less onerous procedures) to rich frequent fliers, or to discriminate against customers or citizens on the basis of wealth, geography, gender, race, or ethnicity. The power to treat people differently is a dangerous one.[38]

Even without outright discrimination or blackmail, the new market research greatly improves the ability of advertisers to persuade potential customers. Armed with secret knowledge of your visual and vocal reactions, actual location, and past purchase history, advertisers will find it easier to convince you to buy. Sometimes this persuasive potential will be used to satisfy intrinsic needs, but other times it will be used to manufacture desire, giving businesses a powerful tool to wield against the consuming public. In a sense, this concern with information generating power imbalances is at the heart of a century of advertising regulation that has struggled to create the right playing field between marketers and their targets. Too much personal information in the hands of advertisers threatens to slant that playing field in one particular direction.

Inefficiency concerns, threats to intellectual privacy, and abuses of power are not the only consequences flowing from life in a commercial panopticon. Knowing that information is being collected about you but without knowing the particulars is a recipe for psychological dysfunction. Just the thought of being observed, even if that observation is not actually occurring, produces feelings of insecurity. And given the technology in place and the legal system's failure to restrain it, who wouldn't rationally believe they are under constant surveillance? As one cultural critic presciently asked about an earlier wave of nondigital commercial surveillance: "What happens when the boundaries of time and place are erased? When anyone, anywhere, at any time, could be studying you to make a buck? When consumer savvy means mistrusting everyone?"[39] Trust breaks down when individuals believe that their personal information is being scrutinized and potentially being used to their disadvantage.

To some degree, it will be a good thing if consumer suspicion increases, but distrust of hidden corporate authorities could translate into distrust in other relationships. In a world where corporations routinely snoop on our activities, norms against surreptitiously investigating our partners and friends may dissolve. If faceless corporations can use our online data, what is to stop our friends, lovers, and family members from somehow acquiring this information, perhaps even purchasing it from those faceless corporations? In fact, this routinely happens. Those searching for prospective mates acquire credit reports before deciding to proceed in a romantic relationship. Facebook and other social media sites are used not only to communicate and strengthen existing relationships but also as a means for romantic partners to track their significant other's behavior. Employers use the same sites to keep tabs on their employees, thereby introducing greater mistrust into employment relationships. Once-innocuous physical objects like Barbie dolls and children's toothbrushes now come armed with sensors for parental monitoring.[40] Churches deploy facial recognition software to keep tabs on their parishioners.[41] A culture of surveillance erodes the trust necessary for valuable cooperative undertakings. At a certain point, a surveilled society is one where the social glue binding people together begins to dissolve.[42]

Where Is Privacy Law?

If the new market research portends a culture of constant surveillance, we might expect privacy laws to step in and prevent such activity. At least in the West, resistance to surveillance has traditionally been mobilized under the concept of privacy. But privacy law turns out to have little force when it comes to most commercial spying. To be sure, there are some regulations that govern the collection of personal information. The compilation and distribution of particular categories of information, like personal health histories or credit scores, are subject to various federal and state restrictions. Private recording of biometric data has begun to attract the attention of state regulators.[43] Yet aside from these very specific categories, advertisers have carte blanche to take the quotidian data of everyday life, bundle it into incredibly detailed profiles, and then use it to beam back advertising to us in virtually any setting. To understand why, it is necessary to know more about American privacy law, as well as another distinct legal concept.

The American right of privacy started with a law review article. As articulated by Samuel Warren and Louis Brandeis in 1890, the right of privacy was a necessary counterweight to a changed world where new phenomena like "instantaneous photography" and nationally circulated magazines offered opportunities for prying into the private lives of citizens.[44] Brandeis, who later became a celebrated Supreme Court justice, would call this right of privacy "the most comprehensive of rights and the right most valued by civilized men."[45]

Scholars have often described Warren and Brandeis as responding to a new sort of aggressive journalism, in effect, giving overzealous reporters of the late 1800s the credit for instigating Warren and Brandeis's innovative legal response.[46] But an equally valid way to describe the birth of the privacy right is as a reaction to new kinds of advertising. Early cases interpreting the new theory of privacy made this plain, invoking the privacy right to slap the hands of advertisers as well as journalists. An early case employing Warren and Brandeis's theory involved the unauthorized use of a person's photograph in a newspaper advertisement for life insurance. The advertisement involved one Paolo Pavesich, whose picture was featured in an issue of the *Atlanta Constitution* above the following caption: "In my healthy and productive period of life I bought insurance in the New England Mutual Life Insurance Co., of Boston, Mass., and to-day my family is protected and I am drawing an annual dividend on my paid-up policies." It turned out, however, that Mr. Pavesich never had a policy with New England Mutual and never authorized the use of his photograph. The Georgia Supreme Court deeply sympathized with Pavesich, describing "the humiliation and mortification of having his picture displayed in places where he would never go to be gazed upon" and theorizing that the advertisement would make him "contemptible" among his friends. It even equated a world where Pavesich could not prevent unauthorized use of his image by advertisers as enslavement to a "merciless master."[47] The Georgia court held that the life insurance company as well as the photographer who surreptitiously took Pavesich's photograph for the newspaper ad violated his right to privacy.

Around the same time, the New York courts had to decide whether to recognize Warren and Brandeis's new legal concept. The test case involved the
unauthorized publication of a photograph of a minor, Roberson, described by
the court as "a young woman of rare beauty." The publisher was Franklin Mills
Flour, an advertiser, not a media interest. Franklin Mills published twenty-five
thousand lithographs featuring the girl's photograph along with the slogan
"Flour of the Family," posting the advertisements in stores, taverns, and other
gathering places across the United States. The trial court found in Roberson's
favor; on appeal, however, New York's highest court declined to invoke the new
privacy right, citing concerns over press freedom. Although Franklin Mills was
clearly not part of "the press," the court fretted about how to distinguish a hypothetical future case involving a newspaper's unauthorized publication of a similar photo.[48] The court's decision triggered a public outcry, prompting the New
York legislature to swiftly respond by enacting a new privacy law abrogating the
Roberson decision. The legislature did not seem bothered by the court's anxiety over a slippery slope leading from advertiser to journalist. The law, which
prohibits the unauthorized use "for advertising purposes or for the purposes
of trade" of any person's "name, portrait, picture or voice," remains in effect in
New York State today.[49]

In time, other state courts and legislatures followed Georgia and New York's
lead. Lawmakers and judges recognized that the country had entered a new
age where someone's picture might unknowingly be taken and splashed across
newspapers, magazines, stores, and mass-produced products around the country. This was a sort of personal invasion that had never been practicable before.
The result was approval of Warren and Brandeis's newly created right, specifically pressed into service to combat invasive advertising. Several court decisions recognized these new rights and used them to protect individuals and
enjoin advertisers.[50]

The parallels between Warren and Brandeis's time and our own are striking.
At the turn of the century, advertisers adopted new technologies to make their
sales pitches more effective. Candid photographs of citizens gave supposed
product testimonials a new sort of authenticity. This innovative advertising was
more effective than the dense text advertisers in the past favored, but it also
raised the hackles of those who believed that individual citizens had "a right to
be let alone." The ability to distribute a person's image on a mass scale without

his or her approval represented an unprecedented threat to personal dignity and autonomy. Once someone's photograph was placed on the packaging of a national product or imprinted on an advertisement in a major newspaper or magazine, the relationship between that person's private self and public self would never be the same again.

The detailed tracking of consumers afforded by today's technology also implicates privacy interests. The new market research lets advertisers know the different physical locations we inhabit, our online movements down to the mouse click, and the different purchases we have chosen to make (or even just come to the verge of making). Admittedly, there are differences between the commercial appropriations that Warren and Brandeis objected to and today's digital surveillance. Early twentieth-century advertisers were spreading false information when their advertising campaigns turned individuals into unwitting product endorsers. Online tracking captures information consumers might want to keep secret, but it usually does not turn that information into outright commercial falsehoods. Nevertheless, like the surreptitious use of Paolo Pavesich's photograph, digital surveillance acquires something very personal to the individual without her awareness and uses it to create more effective commercial appeals. The data is collected in situations when we believe we are outside of the advertiser's scrutiny: on our home computer, in our car, or simply walking through a store. Lawmakers embraced Warren and Brandeis's theory and introduced measures to stop the invasive advertising cropping up in the early twentieth century. By contrast, the invasive data tracking of the early twenty-first century has been allowed to go largely unchecked.

In part, the failure to regulate the new market research reflects a concern with facilitating commerce. To some, disclosure of personal information is the currency that must be paid in order to promote innovation. Others attribute the current regulatory failure to a fatalist attitude. Modern advertising's very ubiquity breeds a resigned acceptance of its presence, and this may even apply to the hidden collection of advertising data. But this is not the only reason why online surveillance continues to spread. When asked, consumers do not wish to sacrifice their privacy in return for the advertising efficiencies possible through digital surveillance. Instead, surveys reveal widespread disapproval of the new market research and strong support for new laws to prevent it.[51] So why are advertisers free to insert themselves into so much of our daily existence?

Contracting Away Privacy

A major reason for the hands-off approach to consumer data collection and targeting is that most of it is arguably already governed by a long-standing legal framework: private contract law. The advertisers in the *Pavesich* and *Roberson* cases used individuals' personal images without any semblance of consent. By contrast, digital technology allows today's advertisers and media providers to secure permission in the form of an online contract before most surveillance and data sharing begin. The ability of online watchers to obtain consent before collecting personal information makes data privacy a thornier legal question than the advertising appropriations of a century ago. When we go online, we regularly click through legal boilerplate that assigns any rights in our personal information to another entity. Because their data collection is already covered by this separate legal regime, advertisers claim privacy law should have little to say about their market research methods. Although consumers are almost completely ignorant of the actual terms of these online contracts, a number of legal scholars endorse such private ordering as the primary means for policing the use of personal information.[52]

Better Choices Don't Always Lead to
Better Privacy Outcomes

The contractual approach suffers from two debilitating flaws. The first flaw is descriptive: when it comes to empowering consumers, a contractual approach to information privacy simply does not work. Structural defects prevent citizens from acting on their privacy preferences in the marketplace. A collective action barrier makes it extremely difficult for consumers desiring greater privacy protection to push online providers into offering more protective terms of service. Part of the problem is that individual harm from data collection is usually minimal or hard to measure, thereby making it unlikely that large groups of online consumers will band together to negotiate better terms of service. Moreover, data misuse often occurs without individualized consumer awareness. As a result, online entities may be concerned with their corporate reputations, but they also appear somewhat immune to public backlash over their use of personal data. For example, despite being viewed in many circles as a privacy scofflaw, Facebook has over 1 billion subscribers and enjoyed a historic initial public offering, reaching a market capitalization of over $100 billion. Most online providers typically confront their data subjects with a one-size-fits-all offer: give up your personal information or forgo the proffered online services. Given the importance of online participation, both socially and economically, in modern life, it is unrealistic to expect consumers to choose the latter option.

Even without these collective action problems, consumers would still have trouble evaluating proposed privacy terms. A consumer agreeing to disclose personal information has little sense as to the universe of third parties likely to also have access to this information. Greater transparency will not resolve these problems. Cognitive biases skew assessments of the costs and benefits of greater privacy protection. Even with more disclosure of where data goes and how it is used, consumers cannot accurately assess the risk of loss of personal information from participating in behavioral targeting (e.g., data breaches) and the magnitude of potential harms from such a loss.[53] Optimism bias tends to cause consumers to go for the immediate reward of an online transaction rather than look for alternatives with better privacy terms. We want more privacy but are unwilling to delay gratification in order to get it. At the same time, we minimize the costs of future harms from privacy violations. Thanks to these cognitive handicaps, even highly motivated consumers accidentally trigger undesired privacy settings when they navigate online interfaces.[54] Admittedly, online entities do make some efforts to compete by touting moves to protect consumer information. Yet the overall picture is one of a malfunctioning privacy marketplace.

Recognizing these difficulties, some advocate for a Do-Not-Track law with an online privacy default. Legal scholar Cass Sunstein, noting the cognitive challenges faced by commercial data subjects, proposes that either "personalized default rules" or "active choosing" be required so that consumers could forfeit their online privacy only on the basis of an explicit statement to the data collector.[55] The proposed Do-Not-Track default fits within a larger literature favoring the use of default rules to steer individuals into making optimal choices. Lawmakers and legal scholars have noted a marked jump in savings rates when retirement plans have automatic enrollment as their default as opposed to requiring employees to opt in and actually make an affirmative decision to take money out of their paycheck and contribute it to a defined benefit plan.[56] Just as individuals respond to the complexity of allocating financial resources for retirement by sticking with automatic deductions into a retirement account, it is argued that consumers would tacitly embrace default rules that safeguard their personal information.

Industry has voiced its opposition to a Do-Not-Track default, preferring instead that consumers be forced to opt in to privacy protections. Recent research demonstrates, however, that consumer behavior under a Do-Not-Track default would not look much different from the current contractual model that lets businesses dictate their own terms. This is because a motivated business can quite easily steer consumers into opting out of a default that is against that business's interests. As Lauren Willis has shown, various government-mandated defaults designed to nudge consumers into making particular choices, from checking account overdraft coverage to mortgage payments structured to reserve funds for property taxes, have largely failed. Instead of truly anchoring consumer behaviors and encouraging optimal decision making (or at least encouraging the particular decisions policymakers favor), these defaults have been largely overridden by the marketers of financial products who stand to benefit when consumers opt out of the government-mandated status quo. Willis shows that motivated firms can typically use advertising and ways of framing choices to override defaults and convince consumers to affirmatively opt out of the very default schemes that are meant to protect them.[57]

For example, in the past, banks typically permitted checking account holders to overdraw their accounts from an ATM or debit card transaction, then charged the account holder a fee. Banks liked to do this because the fees they charged were very lucrative, usually more than the amount the consumer actually borrowed. Seeing an abusive practice, regulators set a new default whereby banks cannot charge overdraft fees unless the account holder elects to opt out and join the bank's "overdraft coverage" service. The regulators seemed to think that most consumers would stay with the status quo and avoid overdraft coverage plans that typically were not in their best financial interest. In reality, however, consumers have continued to pay for overdraft coverage, affirmatively opting out of the regulatory default. Willis notes that banks, motivated to maintain their revenue from overdraft fees, made opting out of the default simple, using aggressive marketing and customer service techniques to get account holders to agree to the overdraft plans. Some consumers reported that they opted out of the default simply to put an end to the banks' overdraft coverage marketing barrage.[58]

The failure of overdraft protection reform suggests the difficulty in using a similar default to protect consumers from commercial surveillance. A highly motivated industry that can advertise to consumers, encouraging them to opt out of the default, in combination with a relatively complex or obscure choice, makes the default a minor speed bump rather than a major hurdle. Billions of dollars are at stake in the world of commercial surveillance, and advertisers are guaranteed to fight tooth and nail to nudge consumers out of a legislatively created default of no tracking. Just as with banks and their account holders, advertisers will have ready access to consumers, conceivably lobbying them every time they consult a particular website or launch a particular browser. Moreover, privacy choices are inherently confusing and difficult to evaluate, probably even more so than the choice between overdraft coverage and being limited to the funds within one's bank account. Stories of people unwittingly selecting privacy settings that are less restrictive than they would like are legion.

Policy analysts distinguish regulatory efforts involving default rules like those already described from legislation mandating more notice for consumers. Both legal reforms, however, take as a given that contractual arrangements between data collectors and their subjects are the primary way to maintain consumer privacy. Contract law is simply too malleable to alter the contours of today's commercial surveillance culture. Better notice is largely ineffective when it comes to stopping people from forfeiting rights in their personal information. Even consumers concerned with privacy are likely to overlook privacy notices. Studies demonstrate that the mere existence of any privacy policy, *regardless of its actual content*, tends to increase consumer disclosure.[59] Whether the law creates a default rule requiring consumers to affirmatively opt out of privacy protections or mandates beefed-up notice requirements informing consumers of what a company may do with their data, advertisers seem likely to surmount either of these legal hurdles with ease.

Government Paternalism and Privacy

The second problem with the contractual approach to privacy stems from its theoretical underpinnings. Most people seem to realize that online users don't read the fine print. So why has the debate remained so focused on the law of contract—notice and consent and privacy-friendly defaults—rather than on mandatory rules for what advertisers can and cannot do? Part of the debate may reflect the general neoliberal climate in which we live, where market forces are hypothesized to allocate resources in the most effective manner. When consumers are viewed as full participants in this market sorting process, letting them pick and choose among different privacy policies seems to make a great deal of sense. Both enhanced notice and privacy default rules can be categorized as soft modes of regulation that avoid the stronger form of antimarket paternalism inherent in flat-out prohibitions on particular business practices.

As discussed earlier, an antipaternalist impulse dominates much of the legal discourse on advertising regulation. Critics of advertising restrictions accuse would-be regulators of engaging in "an assault on reason."[60] If particular advertising methods are to be legislatively removed from the consumer experience, then aren't we depriving consumers of one kind of communication and merely substituting a governmentally approved message in its place? This kind of reasoning is evident in the Supreme Court's increasing skepticism toward government regulation of commercial speech. Embedded within the antipaternalist view is the belief that mere speech, unlike actual conduct, can simply be shrugged off by unpersuaded listeners or effectively countermanded by other speech. As a result, government restrictions on speech seem particularly offensive to notions of individual choice. As the Court explained in one of its recent commercial speech decisions, "the fear that speech might persuade provides no lawful basis for quieting it."[61] According to the antipaternalist view, it is better to regulate privacy through voluntary agreements rather than legislative fiat. Particularly in the online context, judges seem concerned only with some provision of notice to consumers, not with investigating whether true approval of the challenged terms actually occurred.

The Court has stretched the antipaternalist vision of the First Amendment to include data collection activities that some might argue have little to do with speech. A 2011 case before the Supreme Court, *Sorrell v. IMS Health*, illustrates this phenomenon. At issue was a Vermont law restricting pharmaceutical marketers' access to and use of prescription data for advertising purposes. Pharmacies sold prescribing records to marketers, which resulted in targeted sales pitches to doctors. Vermont passed the law to curb this practice and protect "the privacy of prescribers and prescribing information." Applying "heightened judicial scrutiny" to the law, the Court struck it down as an unconstitutional burden on protected speech under the First Amendment.[62]

Sorrell signals a potentially broad new restriction on government's ability to regulate certain business practices. Even accepting the premise that commercial speakers deserve First Amendment protection, one can still argue that data collection represents a nonexpressive activity deserving no free speech protection. Although subject to criticism,[63] long-standing doctrine holds that government regulation of speech receives First Amendment scrutiny, but government regulation of conduct does not. In addition, the Court has traditionally refused to label activities as "speech" when the activities have an attenuated relationship to subsequent expression. As the Court explained in another context, "We cannot accept the view that an apparently limitless variety of conduct can be labeled 'speech' whenever the person engaging in the conduct intends thereby to express an idea."[64]

In *Sorrell*, however, the Court failed to distinguish between Vermont's effort to restrict the transfer of prescribing information from pharmacies to others and its attempts to limit the use of that information for pharmaceutical marketing. The Court condemned a lower court, which had upheld a similar state law, for characterizing the prescriber-identifying information at issue "as a 'commodity' with no greater entitlement to First Amendment protection than 'beef jerky.' . . . " The better approach, the Court chastised, is that "the creation and dissemination of information are speech within the meaning of the First Amendment." Not only must the government be restrained from interfering with data-driven speech, but it also should be estopped from restricting the compilation and transfer of consumer data when those activities are motivated by speech-related goals. In the Court's view, Vermont's restrictions on data collection and sharing smacked too much of government paternalism. "That the State finds expression too persuasive does not permit it to quiet the speech or to burden its messengers," the Court explained.[65]

With legal pronouncements like this, it is no wonder that advertising's would-be regulators have moved to softer tactics like enhanced notice and optional default rules that businesses and consumers can transact around. These tactics also pay obeisance to individual control, a central component of the scholarly model of privacy law, at least when one looks at privacy law scholarship in the United States. This view can be attributed to the work of Charles Fried and Alan Westin. In now classic and routinely cited scholarship, Fried and Westin defined privacy in terms of individualized control over information. Westin defined privacy as "the claim of individuals, groups, or institutions to determine for themselves when, how, and to what extent information about them is communicated to others."[66] Fried explained that "privacy is not simply an absence of information about us in the minds of others; rather it is the control we have over information about ourselves."[67] Subsequent scholars and the Supreme Court have echoed this notion of privacy as control.[68]

Explaining privacy in terms of control makes consent an essential ingredient to investigating privacy's boundaries. After all, if a consumer agrees to grant access to her personal information, it would seem the "control" aspect of privacy is being recognized. One might argue that the reality of today's commercial surveillance practices means that individual consent and control are illusory. But supporters of the control model of privacy contend that these realities do not so much require an abandonment of notice and consent as a strengthening of corporate disclosures to make informed consent more viable. If privacy's core interest is individual control over personal information, then a contractual consent model (and the ability to opt in or opt out of privacy defaults) would seem to be mandatory for privacy regulation. Privacy scholar Daniel Solove has noted that the leading theorists in this field have been drawn to the notion of privacy as control over information and, as a result, frequently conceptualize it under the legal frameworks of property and contract.[69]

But the concept of control is not the only or even the most necessary ingredient to a meaningful definition of privacy. Robert Post, a legal historian and constitutional law scholar, contrasts a theory of privacy based on individual autonomy (which is closely related to control) with privacy interests rooted in human dignity:

> Autonomy refers to the ability of persons to create their own identity and in this way to define themselves. Dignity, by contrast, refers to our sense of ourselves as commanding (attitudinal) respect. Unlike autonomy, dignity depends upon intersubjective norms that define the forms of conduct that constitute respect between persons. . . . To equate privacy with dignity is to ground privacy in social forms of respect that we owe each other as members of a common community.[70]

A view of privacy rooted in dignity relies less on individual control and more on maintaining relationships between parties that observe an appropriate mutual respect based on social norms. This view of privacy will not apply in all situations. Post gives the example of historians who dig up unflattering personal information about people because they see historical figures as objects to be understood rather than independent entities deserving mutual respect. But in other situations, society has constructed customs that demand considerate use of information because of norms communicating respect for the other party.

Do consumers deserve to be treated with dignity by advertisers? In the early twentieth century, legal figures responded with a resounding yes. In the nineteenth century, P. T. Barnum was celebrated for the quote "there's a sucker born every minute," implying a world where the relationship between advertisers and consumers resembled predators and prey. But Progressive-era legal thinkers changed that view. Warren and Brandeis's right to be let alone was a call for dignity in a world where technology and new advertising techniques suddenly jeopardized social norms of respect for the boundaries between public and private life. It was less important to present choices to autonomous legal subjects than to make sure that advertisers and journalists properly observed their subjects' dignity. Warren and Brandeis saw the veil of domestic secrecy traditionally observed by commercial actors as "an aspect of the social order that had to be protected" and the maintenance of this secrecy "essential to human dignity."[71] Shortly thereafter, a nascent consumer movement cemented the idea that there were certain boundaries between advertisers and consumers that should not be crossed.

Data collectors might argue that giving consumers options is treating them with dignity. But this would disregard the maintenance of relationship norms at the heart of a dignity-based vision of privacy. It ignores the growing power imbalance, caused by surveillance, between advertisers and consumers that threatens to disrupt these norms. Consumers are not full participants when it comes to the marketplace for their personal data. Surreptitious data collection allows advertisers to have the upper hand in any negotiations with consumers over privacy. They make it their business not just to provide information but to exploit consumer weaknesses. As Professor Willis's research shows, even with the benefit of a legislative nudge, this power imbalance can still result in consumers being manipulated into poor decisions about privacy. Surveillance necessarily involves the gaining of power at the expense of those being watched.[72] It is unrealistic to suggest that the threat posed by data-collecting businesses can be addressed merely through government speech alerting consumers to undesirable collection practices or by giving consumers the ability to opt out of such practices.[73]

Law has the power to shape as well as confirm social norms. Introduction of the right to privacy stabilized older norms about when it was appropriate to use someone's personal information in the public sphere. Judges and legislators acted to protect individuals from advertising techniques that took what was personal and made it public. By contrast, the legal system's strictly contractual approach to today's commercial surveillance threatens to erode norms of consumer dignity. Past attempts to elevate contractual freedom over government efforts to improve the lives of its citizens have, with years of hindsight, come to look misguided and insensitive to social welfare.[74] Mere legislative nudges, requiring affirmative opt-ins to online tracking, will not solve the problem. What is needed is a recognition that stronger legal rules are required—rules that actually ban the data collection practices that most Americans, when polled, object to. But if the legal system stays in thrall to a notice-and-consent regime that routinely enables a vast commercial spying apparatus, nothing will change.

From Market Share to Mindshare

FROM SMALL BEGINNINGS, Arthur C. Nielsen built the largest market re search firm in the world. Nielsen, a former electrical engineer, leveraged new technologies to better record and understand the hard facts of consumer behavior. In 1923, Nielsen kickstarted his firm by borrowing $45,000 from college friends. He invested these funds in tabulators and calculators, state-of-the-art machines that could crunch reams of industry-wide sales numbers. Armed with these computations, Nielsen could calculate a company's sales share for an overall product category or, as he called it, the company's "market share." In 1955, he pur chased the UNIVAC I, the second commercial computer ever produced in the United States, to further analyze the streams of data pouring in from the company's various research arms. Nielsen also pioneered the use of the "audiometer," a mechanical device that tracked the listening behaviors of radio users and was later adapted for television viewers. Nielsen also used traditional focus groups to solicit customer opinion. In effect, consumers were voting every time they responded in focus groups, made purchases, decided to turn on or turn off their radios and televisions, or chose to tune in to particular stations. Nielsen then tabulated these "votes" and submitted them to his clients so they could make informed decisions as to the value of their advertising dollar. The Nielsen firm quickly became the top dog in market research, with sales figures that dwarfed its competitors. Today, the Nielsen Company continues to dominate the field, garnering billions of dollars in revenue each year from its corporate clients.[1]

In 2005, another former engineer, A. K. Pradeep, began a very different kind of market research firm. Headquartered in Berkeley, California, Pradeep's company, NeuroFocus, eschewed the kind of market research pioneered by Nielsen. For Pradeep, traditional focus group research was an anachronism and mass tabulations of sales and viewership not much better. Instead, he proselytized for studying brain activity, claiming such observations yielded better insights and led to more effective marketing results than any consumer survey. In effect, Pradeep proposed to replace Nielsen's focus on market share with a new ability to determine "mindshare." On assignment for Frito-Lay in 2008, Pradeep put his theory into practice by interrogating the neuroscience of Cheetos eating. NeuroFocus conducted brain scans on a small group of consumers. One area of the consumers' brains exhibited a surge in activity from the accumulation of orange cheese dust on fingers that comes from eating the popular snack food. When interviewed, a potential snacker might say that she did not like this messy part of the Cheetos eating process, but according to Pradeep, the "primal emotional responses" of the brain do not lie. NeuroFocus interpreted the scans as revealing a pleasurable sense of subversion in snackers' brains when the Cheetos orange dust hit their fingers. After seeing Pradeep's research, Frito-Lay revamped its advertising strategy and Cheetos sales jumped by $47 million. The Nielsen Company took note, acquiring NeuroFocus in 2011, retaining Pradeep, and giving him the title of "chief provocateur." The move suggests a new realization among advertisers of the importance of obtaining data from the one pure wellspring of consumer motivation: the brain.[2]

Better understanding of consumers' mental geography is a double-edged sword. Armed with neural data, businesses can target needs and desires that consumers may not be able to fully articulate on their own. As with online surveillance, the ability to better satisfy consumer preferences represents the chief argument in neuromarketing's favor. But the more we know about how the brain works, the greater the danger of interventions that impinge on free will. When advertisers can devise campaigns based not just on voluntary responses but on involuntary subconscious reactions, consumers lose some of their capacity for advertising resistance or, as the philosopher David Hume put it, "the power of acting or of not acting."[3] Theorists have long emphasized the distinctly human capacity for deliberative action, contrasting acts based on free will with the instinctual following of compulsive appetites. Neuroscience may give marketers the ability to design more appealing products and brands, but it can also reveal and activate the inner prejudices and evolutionary hardwiring for unhealthy behaviors that we might prefer to keep from view. If advertising shapes who we are and advertisers increasingly use these neural revelations to build advertising content, we may confront a commercial culture that increasingly celebrates the worst in us, not the best.

This chapter describes neuromarketing—a process by which advertisers use new insights into the functioning of the human brain to redesign the ads we watch, the marketplaces we frequent, and the products we buy. It scrutinizes marketers' own descriptions of how they intend to employ neuroscientific insights to build commercial goodwill, revealing the potential for marketing that clandestinely manipulates, discriminates, and blinds consumers to other, more optimal consumptive choices. It also describes the reactions of legal authorities to past attempts to leverage psychological insights in the service of selling. Psychologists have had a long relationship with advertisers, and their contributions to marketing research have influenced the shape not just of advertising but of advertising law. In many cases, judges and regulators welcomed the psychologists' expertise, but they also set boundaries. The battle for consumer mindshare needed to be transparent and open to competition. Lawmakers rushed to halt "subliminal advertising" techniques in the 1950s that seemed more like brainwashing than good salesmanship. Twentieth-century judges refused to enforce state bans on nonconfusing trademark uses, concerned that these new laws would inoculate commercial psychological messaging techniques from semiotic challenge.

These limits on the use of psychology in advertising are now being challenged by Pradeep and others who are blending commercial promotion with brain research. Nielsen's data collection efforts were transparent and represented a dialogue between consumer and market researcher. But instead of exchanging ideas with the public, neuromarketing focuses on communications outside the consumer's awareness, relying on indiscernible emotional appeals to build brand goodwill. Regulators tasked with rooting out "unfair" marketing practices or setting the ethical boundaries of academic research have turned a blind eye to the potential social costs of neuromarketing, allowing widespread emotional experimentation on unwitting consumers. Meanwhile, at the same time that brand goodwill is increasingly built on subconscious stimulation, new developments in trademark law censor activities that threaten to erode this goodwill, including activities that are nonconfusing and immaterial to consumer purchasing decisions. Some writers optimistically refer to the latest era of brain discovery as a "neurorevolution," but in the commercial context, this is a revolution where advertisers are moving forward and consumers are being left behind.[4]

Mad Men and Gray Matter

Corporate America has jumped onto the neuromarketing bandwagon feet first. Fortune 500 companies now retain a growing industry of firms that employ neuroscience to reveal the physiology of thought and then use that information to recalibrate advertising content. NeuroFocus (now part of Nielsen Consumer Neuroscience) boasts an impressive stable of corporate clients like Citi, Google, HP, McDonalds, Microsoft, and ESPN.[5] Advertisers typically try to keep their neuromarketing initiatives a secret, but there are now a number of documented examples, in addition to the Cheetos campaign, that demonstrate its growing influence. Jack Daniel's whiskey used neural imaging to learn that its younger consumers preferred commercials with images of nubile spring breakers to more classic advertisements featuring rugged, outdoor scenes (even though these same consumers claimed the opposite when questioned directly). Volvo studied electrical activity in the brain to change its design process and build "a more emotive connection" with its brand. Brain scans showed Procter & Gamble how to address women's anxiety over bad hair days in shampoo ads. Campbell's examined data on pupil dilation, heart rate, sweat levels, and changes in body posture to develop soup can labels with a more emotional impact. In 2013, business giants Unilever and Coca-Cola announced that they would use facial coding technology to measure the psychological impact of all of their advertising.[6]

Neuromarketing differs from other applied psychological research on consumer behavior in that it does not attempt to engage the consumer in a dialogue, that is, an exchange of written or spoken information. For decades, firms like the Nielsen Company have organized focus groups, solicited survey responses, and reviewed purchase data to take consumers' emotional temperatures. But there have always been accompanying accuracy concerns with this sort of research. Consumers lack perfect insight into their own thought processes and motivational structures. Even if we want to give market researchers the honest truth, we aren't able to. Because people want to believe they are not influenced by advertising, their reports to commercial questioners often underestimate the actual influence of marketing in their lives.[7] Neuromarketing avoids these problems by giving advertisers the ability to detect emotional responses in the brain, stimulate those responses, and segment consumers based on their emotional signatures.

Detecting Emotion

From university labs to corporate boardrooms, neuromarketers focus on one particular subject: the physiological signs of emotional response. By detecting emotion, advertisers can assess and recalibrate the affective strength and particularized meaning of brands. In describing their craft, neuromarketers frequently reference the work of neuroscientist Antonio Damasio. Beginning in the mid-1990s, Damasio used neuroscientific research to stress the centrality of emotion to human reasoning and decision making. According to Damasio, emotions, and the neural markers they create in the brain, guide our reactions and behaviors. Advertisers have long tried to play on human emotion in their messaging, but Damasio changed the narrative by cementing the importance of emotion to consumer choice. By touting emotion's role in efficient, welfare-enhancing forms of cognition, his work provided cover for marketers reliant on emotionally based appeals who once might have been charged with subverting the rational and deliberative faculties of consumers.[8]

Psychologists have long promised to unlock the keys to profitably deciphering consumer emotions. But this was a speculative and unverifiable enterprise, perhaps best reflected in the famous quote of department store magnate John Wanamaker: "Half the money I spend on advertising is wasted; the trouble is, I don't know which half."[9] Claims by marketing gurus to find the psychological roots behind brand loyalty—whether via survey data, theories on the hallmarks of emotional response, or "depth interviews"—required a great deal of faith in the marketer's individual interpretation of consumer representations. Ernest Dichter, the most famous of a group of 1950s marketing psychologists, told his client, Dial soap, after psychoanalyzing consumers, that they were afraid of the highly advertised deodorizing features that defined Dial's brand. Apparently they feared those features would cause them to lose the distinctive personal odors that represented their true identity. One can understand why Dial execu tives might have been skeptical of Dichter's analysis and ultimately decided to take their marketing strategy in a different direction.[10]

By contrast, neuromarketers point not to their subjective interpretation of consumer representations but to new technologies that allow real-time observations of the biology behind advertising effectiveness. Thanks to machines that can reveal a consumer's neural processes as they happen, advertisers for the first time now have a ringside seat to view the biological mechanisms that often precede and predict purchasing decisions. The technologies of neuromarketing can be divided into two main categories. First, there are techniques for detecting the electric and magnetic fields associated with neural activity in the brain. The most important among these is electroencephalography (EEG), which records the brain's electrical activity through electrodes attached to the scalp. This technology has been around for years, but has recently become vastly more valuable because of greater processing speeds that can measure the rapid neural changes that mark emotional response. Second, there are devices for measuring metabolic changes in the brain. Functional magnetic resonance imaging (fMRI) scanners can detect fluctuations in brain blood flow and oxygenation, thereby revealing which areas of the brain are activated by particular stimuli.

Also critical are supplemental ways of detecting neurological responses that do not involve specific recording of brain activity but reveal emotional reactions through other physiological correlates. These correlates are often used to confirm or refine EEG and fMRI findings relating to mood or emotion.[11] Extremely small, sensitive cameras can now measure eye movement with much greater detail than in the past, and these movements offer a window into individual thoughts and feelings.[12] Other devices detect nonvisible but measurable involuntary moistening of the eyes linked to emotional response.[13] Devices for tracking changes in voice and skin conductivity can also be used to assess mental state. Research on facial expressions reveals the presence of tell-tale "microexpressions" indicative of hidden emotions. These biometric technologies allow advertisers to "detect distinct emotional states and their corresponding distinct decision-making processes."[14]

A particular point of emphasis for neuromarketing is branding. By uncovering a brand's neural hallmarks, advertisers can better track the emotional bonds between trademarks and consumers. Studies reveal greater neural activation when a familiar brand is presented, particularly when that brand is presented under conditions of high uncertainty.[15] The best-known example of this kind of research came in a 2004 study where a Baylor University neuroscientist placed subjects in an fMRI scanner and asked them to take sips of Coke and Pepsi. At first, participants were not told which cola brand they were being served but were simply asked to rate the cola's taste. Overall, participants expressed a slight taste preference for Pepsi while the scanner revealed a corresponding response in a region of the brain that mediates reward when drinking the preferred beverage. Later, the same subjects were shown the brand name of the beverage before they took their sips. This resulted in a switch not only in preference (most participants now expressed a preference for Coke) but also in neural activity. Notifying subjects that they were drinking Coke prompted stronger neural responses in subjects than a notification that they were drinking Pepsi. The study proved that branding can not only change our reported enjoyment of a product, but it can actually change brain chemistry. It was widely heralded as proof of the ability of effective advertising to instill emotional memories that trump objective evaluation of the actual characteristics of a product.[16]

Researchers have built on the Coke study's findings in other contexts, pinpointing particular areas of the brain critical to successful branding and potentially making brand management less of an art and more of a science. Advertisers can now use neuroscience to determine brand strength. When a consumer is exposed to a strong brand, fMRI scanners detect activity in parts of the brain associated with value encoding. Researchers can now even identify the neural hallmarks of being someone's "first-choice brand."[17] Critical to branding is the ability to make a trademark serve as a signifier of status within the consumer's social group. Neuromarketers have diagnosed certain areas of the brain that show increased activity when a brand successfully signals status to a consumer.[18] Activity in other areas of the brain predicts how much brand associations will influence consumer judgment. Subliminal exposure to strong corporate logos influences the way the brain encodes perceived value, even for options unrelated to the brand, causing an emphasis on short-term benefits over long-term gains.[19] Other studies show a concomitant lessening of reflective thinking when subjects recognize one of their favorite trademarks.[20]

Neuromarketers currently face several limitations in their efforts to understand the relationship among branding, brain activity, and emotion. Although neuroscience reveals a wealth of information that was not available just a few years before, the psychological import of this information is not always apparent. There is a certain amount of subjectivity inherent in the reading of brain scans; it is not always clear how an influx of blood or electrical impulses to a particular neural territory should be interpreted. Mental functions rarely take place at only one location in the brain, making the detection of emotion a more difficult task than it might seem at first blush. While it is fairly clear that particular emotional responses (e.g., pain, fear, happiness) activate different parts of the brain in different ways, it is not so clear that when one of these regions is activated, a researcher can infer that a particular emotional state has been reached.

Nevertheless, it would be a mistake to dismiss marketers' attempts to read the emotional states of their target audiences. Regardless of their efficacy, those attempts are changing the nature of market research, altering how businesses design products and choose to interact with consumers. And even those skeptical of neuroscience admit that technology has opened up new territories for understanding the physiology of emotion. The brain's complexity suggests caution, but the ability to detect neurological reactions in the brain offers data that did not exist before, leading to hypotheses that can be tested in subsequent experiments. There is no doubt that researchers understand the neural geography of emotional advertising much better than they did just a few years ago. One might argue that this information provides advertisers a minimal advantage—they can observe our emotional responses toward brands, but they cannot control our thoughts and feelings about those brands. But, of course, neuromarketers are not only interested in reading our emotions, but in shaping them as well.

Planting Emotion

Neuromarketing does more than record emotional response. By revealing how stimuli trigger subconscious neural processes, it also provides a blueprint for seeding the mind with emotional markers. This campaign for emotional mindshare is critical to the enterprise of branding, and neuroscience makes it easier for brand managers to strike the appropriate emotional chord. Advertising practitioners increasingly recognize that brands are valuable for their emotional valences, not for their ability to communicate objectively verifiable information to the consumer. Neuromarketing promises to infuse brands with deeper and stronger emotional meaning in order to store desired brand meanings in implicit memory. It does this by deriving various methods for transmitting branding messages to consumers without triggering those consumers' conscious defenses or natural skepticism toward commercial appeals.

Much of the work of neuromarketing focuses on memory. Neuroscience demonstrates that instead of events leaving an indelible imprint in our minds, our memories can be altered and reconstructed by subsequent communications. According to Damasio, when individuals are exposed to a significant event or object, the brain (specifically the ventromedial prefrontal cortex) evokes a battery of feelings and sensations based on similar experiences in the past. This collection of emotional responses forms a "somatic marker" in our memory. When we remember a past event, the same somatic marker is activated and triggers particular feelings. In much the same fashion, when we experience a new but similar event, the somatic marker from the prior event will be brought up from memory and produce a similar emotional response. Borrowing from Damasio's theory, neuromarketers make it their goal to attempt to create or restructure somatic markers to tip the scales in favor of purchase.[21]

Brand managers are not shy about using neuroscience to play with our memories. Advertising that relies on "emotional deceit," according to one marketing expert, "represents an opportunity for marketers to erase consumers' bad brand memories with strongly positive emotions and experiences."[22] Advertisers are studying how to convince consumers of past pleasurable experiences with their brands, even if those experiences never actually took place. Neuromarketers even have a name for this phenomenon: "the false experience effect." Advertisements that retrieve previous positive somatic markers may produce a false memory, and these false memories can have a positive impact on brand attitudes. One study showed how advertising could implant false childhood memories of visiting Disneyland and shaking hands with Bugs Bunny.[23] Another revealed that advertising can alter our memory of a substandard experience. By exposing subjects to advertisements after they drank orange juice contaminated with vinegar and salt but before they were asked to recall their memory of the juice's taste, researchers caused an objectively substandard product to become more highly rated.[24]

Perhaps most important to the project of neuromarketing, advertisers can create new somatic markers without making the consumer aware of their creation. One key principle of neuromarketing, largely borne out by the science, is that messages can be lodged in consumer memory with very little active processing. Brain scans offer advertisers a road map for tucking certain branding messages into peripheral parts of the ad, thereby avoiding the conscious defenses or counterarguments that a consumer might construct.[25] For example, research reveals that even when a television commercial's brand message is fleetingly viewed during a DVR's fast-forwarding, this kind of unaware viewing is enough to strengthen brand preferences.[26] Similarly, by some measures, advertisements featuring celebrity endorsers have more influence when the viewer is vaguely familiar with but cannot specifically identify the endorser.[27]

Other research attempts to pinpoint how even shorter or more peripheral brand exposures affect consumers' brand attitudes and choices. Brand name and product can be communicated to a consumer in less than 100 milliseconds,[28] and "brand personalities can be automatically activated and assessed without the consumer's conscious awareness."[29] Moreover, this process of seeding the mind with brand-friendly somatic markers does not appear to be subject to the law of diminishing returns. The more ads we see, the less we pay attention to them, and, paradoxically, that can make those ads more effective. Although there may be some occasions when the sheer amount of commercial bombardment in a particular format causes audiences to look away, it turns out that the human capacity for registering advertising content is much larger than one might expect. As explained by a group of marketing and psychology professors, because "consumers process brand information relatively automatically," consumers still respond to peripheral branding even when deluged with thousands of brand images in the course of an average day.[30]

One vehicle in this process is priming: using particular cues to trigger neural changes that can shape purchase decisions. These cues can take the form of brands themselves. For example, unconsciously exposing research subjects to prestige brands such as Tiffany and Neiman-Marcus activated prestige goals that shaped the subjects' behavior. Exposure to prestige brands caused study participants to spend more out of a limited account to purchase a single higher-quality item instead of using the same resources to obtain more of a lower-quality item.[31] In another study, a brief flash of the Apple logo, so brief a flash that the logo was not consciously recognizable, caused people to become more impulsive when making financial decisions.[32] In other work, researchers have shown that consumers can be primed to feel disgust, and thereby become unknowingly drawn to images relating to cleanliness.[33]

Technology makes this priming easier to accomplish than ever before. As compared to once fairly static retail environments, today's shoppers confront a greater variety of customizable stimuli designed to trigger emotion. In marketing-speak, these customizable stimuli are referred to as "touch points,"[34] Take, for example, the in-store video screens that are mushrooming across the commercial landscape from gas station pumps to grocery displays to office waiting rooms. These screens provide optimal platforms for the kinds of low-attention cues that can get consumers to mentally rehearse the brand and its underlying message. Social media companies are constantly tinkering with ways to provide additional and more effective touch points for companies that wish to build up the emotional resonance of their brands. The most newsworthy attempt to clandestinely influence individual emotional state via social media was an experiment Facebook performed on over half a million unaware subjects in 2012. These Facebook users had their news feeds manipulated to change the number of positive and negative posts they saw as part of a study designed to show that emotions expressed by others on Facebook can affect our own emotional state.[35] The study did indeed reveal emotional contagion: when positive posts on users' news feeds were suppressed, the users produced more negative posts and fewer positive posts (and vice versa). Although designed by academics to test a psychological phenomenon, the study also testified to Facebook's ability to manipulate the emotional state of its users to better serve the interests of its advertisers.[36]

Emotional Segmenting

For decades, marketers have sought to segment consumers into different markets and target them accordingly. Segmenting not only allows for product differentiation that can make firms more profitable; it also facilitates more customized appeals that can produce greater yields per advertisement. The more a consumer can be segmented, the more predictable that consumer's behavior becomes. Neuroscience, as well as the data collection measures discussed in the previous chapter, allow advertisers to more fully refine this process. Neural technologies offer new opportunities for detecting emotional state and cognitive idiosyncrasies and then delivering corresponding content. Like a poker player eager to learn her opponent's tell, advertisers salivate over the prospect of a future where consumers can be sorted based on their inner-thought processes, not just their outward behavior.

Neuroscience allows for the identification of particular neural markers and physiological states that correlate with receptivity to certain kinds of advertising. fMRI results can reveal differences in individual capacity for self-control that would be masked by an examination of outward behaviors. Three consumers may all make the same buying decision, but one would do it impulsively, another would retrieve memories of past product experiences, and another would undertake a lengthy cost-benefit analysis. Parsing out these cognitive differences allows consumers to be categorized not just by the choices they make, but by the way they make choices. Some marketers already segment consumers on the basis of their resistance to stress, which can be measured with increasing reliability using EEG monitoring and eye tracking and matched with the nonphysiological data discussed in Chapter 3.[37] Another useful marker for distinguishing among consumers is their propensity toward narcissism. The narcissists among us may be unwittingly identified and then primed for purchase. One could envision advertisers subtly blending images of ourselves into customized ad content. Clothiers and eyeglass retailers already allow shoppers to upload photos of themselves to facilitate the creation of virtual fitting rooms before purchase. Soon, perhaps using the photos we have uploaded and been tagged in on Facebook, companies will create digital doppelgangers to help sell us their products.[38]

At this stage, technology imposes a significant limit on obtaining richer understandings of consumer mental state. Even if an fMRI machine could identify individual propensities for stress tolerance and narcissism, these machines are big and cumbersome, and it is impossible today for someone to have his brain scanned without his knowledge. On the other hand, insights from nonneural data collection can serve as proxies for the emotional signatures that scientists match to particularized marketing strategies. Businesses already take our emotional temperatures through analysis of eye movement, voice, and facial expressions. In 2014, Pizza Hut unveiled a new ordering system, what it described as "the world's first subconscious menu," relying on retinal scans to predict the ordering choices of its patrons.[39] Beyond Verbal, a company specializing in voice recognition software, claims to be able to extract a "full spectrum of human emotions" by building up a record of consumer conversations. Corporate call centers already use this technology not only to better serve customers but also to develop individual psychological profiles. Hershey's used facial coding technology in retail environments to identify particular emotional responses. If you smiled at a video display, the display dispensed a free chocolate sample.[40]

Moreover, thanks to nanotechnology, neural imaging will become relatively unobtrusive in the near future. Nielsen and other neuromarketing firms already have portable EEG devices that they use, along with eye-tracking equipment, to test consumers in the field. Soon it will be possible to screen customers as they enter retail environments and register their reactions to various marketing stimuli. In return for an initial discount, a consumer might agree to have her brain scanned, her dopamine levels checked, or her facial expressions coded. Armed with this information, marketers can adjust in-store advertising and sale strategies. After detecting a particularly desirable stress level or lack of self-control, the marketer might redouble efforts to close the sale or even raise the offered price if confident of an eventual purchase.

One might argue that consumers would never willingly subject themselves to such invasive techniques. But we have already seen a tendency for consumers to sacrifice their privacy for short-term gain. Neural privacy may simply become another casualty in a world of omnipresent commercial surveillance. As technology allows brain scanning devices to become smaller and less obtrusive, the temptation to submit oneself to neurological market research will just increase. Miniaturization allows advertisers to scrutinize emotional response without ever giving the subject a real sense of the scrutiny she might be under. Already, tiny hidden cameras can decode our facial expressions to reveal inner emotions.[41] One writer hypothesizes that future generations of the Nielsen ratings system will rely on these cameras to record not just channel choice but emotional response.[42] Video game makers are using EEG sensors, along with other sensors that record heartbeat, facial and voice expression, and gaze, to make the gaming experience more responsive to a player's affective state.[43] Meanwhile, technology companies are stockpiling patents that use the motion and voice recognition capabilities of smart devices to develop emotionally targeted advertising. Those using their smartphone's voice recognition technology might subsequently find themselves served with ads dependent on not only their word choice but the emotional timbre of their voice. Products like the Apple Watch offer the potential for constant streams of metabolic data to be fed to corporate entities. Some theorize that the next communications advance won't be a kind of phone or watch but an implant, maybe the i-Implant, that guarantees a continuous register of our individual physiology and corresponding emotional state.[44]

This Is Your Brain on Neuromarketing

Neuromarketing has a long way to go before it turns consumers into puppets dancing on advertisers' strings. But even if it is impossible for advertisers to fully control our emotional states, their increasing ability to influence human emotion represents a comparative lessening of human autonomy. Like guerrilla marketing and digital surveillance, neuromarketing is another strategy designed to shift the balance of power between consumers and marketers. If even a fraction of the neuromarketers' promises come to pass, there will be a seismic change in the ability of advertisers to influence consumer behavior. Along with this lessening of consumer agency, there will be a concomitant rise in the ability of advertisers to discriminate, to tap into the urges and emotions we would like to keep private, and to substitute emotional stimulus and response for actual investment in product quality.

Some contend that opposition to neuromarketing is misplaced because neural detection simply makes it easier for advertisers to give consumers what they want. UCLA neuroscientist Marco Iacoboni argues, "Mind control requires some form of manipulation. Neuromarketing does exactly the opposite. It reveals to consumers and marketers what people truly like. It makes consumers more aware of their own deeper motives—motives that . . . consumers cannot explicitly verbalize."[45] But this argument ignores what advertisers are actually doing with a better understanding of how our minds work. At the same time that advertisers ascertain emotional reception to their messages, they deploy that knowledge to better influence consumers. Studies pinpoint the ideal moments for stimulating particular affective reactions, as well as how long the affective itches marketers instigate should remain before they can be scratched. Because distraction has an impact on the encoding of memories, neuromarketers study how to create the optimal amount of distraction in the shopping environment.[46] Of course, consumers try to resist advertising, often taking steps to avoid commercial appeals or review them with a skeptical eye. And today's consumers are assuredly savvier than those in the past and more skeptical of advertiser claims thanks to decades of experience in an often untrustworthy marketplace. But neuromarketing's techniques are new and hidden. Rather than making each consumer's own desires more transparent, one of the central tenets of neuromarketing is to communicate in a way that does not trigger the consumer's conscious defenses. Because it is geared to cause involuntary affective responses, it is not clear that consumers could defend themselves against neuromarketing even if they knew more about it. As one expert in the field noted, "We are more vulnerable when we are only vaguely aware that our emotions are being influenced, and most vulnerable when we have no idea at all that our emotions are being influenced."[47]

Neuromarketing strikes at consumer agency in another way by silencing consumer representations about the products they buy and the ads they see. The raison d'être for neuromarketing is its ability to bypass messy discourses with consumers. But market research that relies on consumer representations serves an important, alternative role: it allows consumers to actively influence product design and marketing. People wanted to become "Nielsen families," by either having audiometers attached to their home appliances or volunteering to fill out paper diaries of their daily listening and viewing habits, so they could influence radio, television, and product content.[48] Since the latter half of the twentieth-century, American citizenship has been linked to the ability of individuals to express themselves through commercial choice.[49] Consonant with this attitude, the Supreme Court has explained that an average citizen's interest in commercial expression "may be as keen as, if not keener by far, than his interest in the day's most urgent political debate."[50] Part of the democratic promise of the marketplace lies in the belief that it is responsive to consumer voice, whether through consumptive choices or more particularized feedback through traditional market research.[51] By contrast, in a world where brain scans take the place of dialogue and opportunities for addressing corporate authorities diminish, consumers lose their capacity to consciously shape their commercial environment; in the process, the marketplace comes to seem less democratic.

By ignoring consumer communications and constructing marketing messages meant to avoid conscious defenses, neuromarketing portends a way to keep consumers from recognizing better experiences or value. Will brain mapping encourage investments in product quality? Under an optimistic view, brain scans will reveal the formulas for the tastiest soda, the freshest scent for detergent, and the kinds of financial services that make us feel the most secure. But when one looks at the neuromarketing literature, there is little talk of how fMRI data will make for better products. Instead, neuromarketers speak in terms of how neuroscience allows for maintaining only a minimum level of product quality while using emotion to lock in consumer preferences.[52] The takeaway from the 2004 Coke neuroimaging study wasn't that Coke actually tastes better than other colas, but rather that Coke's pervasive advertising has succeeded in linking its product with a belief that it provides a more satisfying experience than other soda purveyors. Similarly, researchers who scanned viewers of Super Bowl commercials concluded that powerful trademarks have the effect of overriding the area of the brain that evaluates product quality "uncontaminated by knowledge of the brand name."[53]

Some might argue that it doesn't matter why a consumer enjoys the brand as long as she enjoys it—the utility she gets from the product is the same. Businesses have long tried to infuse their brands with an emotional aura. Even if the business ends up investing in a product's intangibles, not its physical attributes, one could argue that this investment still redounds to the consumer's benefit. But do we really want the new wave of commercial communications to do nothing but encourage such false beliefs, untethered to product realities? If the neuromarketers truly are able to figure out ways to whisper emotional brand meanings into our subconscious, we might lose the capacity to switch to different brands that actually offer an objectively better experience. From an autonomy perspective, if Coke doesn't taste better than other drinks, it would seem important to preserve the opportunity for consumers to make such a realization. Even if the utilitarian stakes involved in subconscious soda persuasion might seem low, the same techniques can be used to get us to buy computers with inferior functionality, cars with less fuel efficiency, and investment vehicles with higher fees and lower returns. Neuromarketing will make it increasingly difficult for better, more objectively satisfying products to dislodge the psychological hold of brands that cling to market share only through emotional appeal.

The potential social utility that could come from businesses gaining a better understanding of their customers should not be cast aside lightly. The problem is that neuromarketers not only purport to uncover consumer preferences but also to create exogenous preferences through primes and the implanting of false memories. If individuals acting to satisfy their own preferences make for efficient markets, behavioral strategies that manipulate individuals to act according to advertiser preferences signal market failure.[54]

Even if one is willing to accept a future where our tastes are shaped by emotional brand implants and not real sensory engagement with actual product attributes, another aspect of neuromarketing should give pause. Swapping dialogue with consumers for physiological measurements also makes it more likely that commercial appeals will be based on socially deleterious messages. Market researchers tout neuromarketing's ability to avoid the problem of consumers filtering their responses based on what they think is socially acceptable.[55] Long before neuromarketing, advertisers came under fire for emotional appeals insensitive to questions of race, gender, sexual identity, and body image. But in the absence of an actual dialogue with consumers, there is an even greater likelihood that marketers will change their communications to respond to some of our worst instincts. Someone who has learned not to disclose racial or gender prejudices in public will not be able to keep these things secret when his involuntary emotional responses are being catalogued. Advertisers will not be able to resist using this information, particularly when techniques are available to signal such prejudices without triggering the audience's overt recognition that the commercial communication contains a discriminatory message.[56]

Trading focus groups for brain scans will do more than highlight our prejudices. Some of the dialogue between consumers and advertisers in focus groups and surveys reflects a desire to better ourselves, to exhibit the self-control that is the ideal and not the actual. But an unvarnished look at the brain's physiological responses may play down these consumer aspirations. For example, Frito-Lay used NeuroFocus's findings to develop an ad campaign that revolved around antisocial behavior, all egged on by the Cheetos mascot. In one ad, the protagonist purposely used the orange cheese puffs to ruin another person's dryer load of white laundry. In another, a puff is nihilistically mashed into the keyboard of a tidy coworker. When directly questioned, sample viewers did not approve of the campaign, finding the depicted actions off-putting. Outside commentators deemed the ads' embrace of vandalism "cynical and disgusting."[57] Brain scans told a different story, however, and convinced Frito-Lay to proceed with the campaign. Perhaps this sort of neuromarketing is harmless, creating unrealistic characters to make us laugh and providing viewers with a temporary release from the bounds of social norms. But one could envision many similar alterations to advertising content that eventually would not just reflect our inner thoughts but shape our behavior. Ads filled with social transgressions may eventually fuel those social transgressions.

This is not the first book to raise concerns over marketers' use of psychological research. In the 1950s, Packard's *The Hidden Persuaders* sounded a clarion call against the use of Freudian psychoanalysis to understand consumer behavior. Two decades later, sociologist Wilson Bryan Key purported to expose an array of sub-liminal codes in advertising, mostly involving (supposedly) erotic imagery. More recently, Naomi Klein lamented a postmodern turn in marketing that switched from touting individual product attributes to "a psychological/anthropological examination of what brands mean to the culture."[58] Someone familiar with this recurring pattern of alarm against advertisers' use of psychological techniques might contend that neuromarketing is simply another marketing fad that merits little attention. If society hasn't collapsed from these other commercial persua-sion initiatives, then it probably won't collapse now.

But it would be a mistake to dismiss critics of neuromarketing as so many anticommercial Chicken Littles. Packard erred by taking the claims of marketing firms and the psychologists they hired at face value. Exposing the use of Freud-ian psychoanalysis on consumers made for good copy, but this kind of psycho-logical market research wasn't necessarily effective. One doesn't have to make the same mistake with neuromarketing. Although the hype of neuromarketing does not always match current reality, researchers have been able to document advertising's ability to alter memories, including memories that shape attitudes toward brands, and to pinpoint individual mental susceptibilities to advertising. Neuromarketing's ability to substitute real-time physiological records for con-sumer dialogue, along with its more granular capacity for triggering emotional response, renders it a different sort of psychological technique than the strate-gies criticized by Packard, Key, and Klein. In the past, advertising's imprecision and dependence on consumer representations helped shield its targets. Now with a more targeted attack, resistance to commercial epistles will become more difficult. Once repeated measurement and analysis of our brain activity becomes the new normal, extracting this data for advertising will seem less shocking. So far, neuromarketing's potential regulators have stayed on the sidelines. To un-derstand why, it is helpful to take a look at the historical interface between law and advertisers' use of psychological techniques.

Law, Psychology, and Advertising

Much of the history of advertising regulation can be viewed as the history of interactions among three groups of professionals. Advertisers joined forces with psychologists to reach consumers more effectively in the early twentieth century. This symbiotic relationship deepened over time. Lawyers, in turn, have reacted to this combination, sometimes with support, at other times with alarm. In the early twentieth century, courts gave their blessing to this relationship, altering the contours of trademark law to better reflect the insights of psychology while at the same time legitimating the marketing that used those insights. But there were limits to this embrace. Some fusions of marketing and psychology triggered a backlash from legal authorities. At points, advertisers' attempts to win mindshare by eliminating dialogue—whether by blocking access to competing voices or masking their own commercial appeals—met with a stern legal rebuke. More recently, however, judges and other potential regulators have ratified neuromarketing techniques that lack transparency and eschew conversations with consumers. Under the current legal paradigm, the law provides increasingly robust legal protection for the meanings engineered by advertisers for their corporate brands. At the same time, marketers have better tools for shaping these positive brand valences in our minds than ever before.

Advertisers and Psychologists Join Forces

In the early twentieth century, advertisers and psychologists entered into a powerful marriage of convenience, blessed by legal authorities, that strengthened over time and eventually led to the alliance between neuroscientists and marketers we see today. In the late 1800s, advertising was not meant to trigger an emotional response in prospective consumers. It was primarily informational, describing a product's attributes, composition, and availability. This kind of copy could be written by anyone and, consequently, there was little need for advertising specialists. Relatedly, trademarks had a limited role in this period, particularly for a largely rural population that bought goods produced in the same areas where they lived and that could rely on conversations with local merchants and craftsmen to assess product value. Unable to claim possession of an exclusive skill, marketers were viewed as mere hucksters with no specialized training or knowledge that made them different from anyone else. As a consequence, advertisers found themselves several rungs below elites like lawyers and doctors on the professional ladder.[59]

This began to change in the early 1900s. An urbanizing American population, along with advances in manufacturing and transportation, led to a nationwide distribution of consumer goods and a concomitant explosion in the number of products competing for consumer attention. Instead of simply communicating the informational attributes of content and availability, advertising now needed to stimulate demand through emotional appeals designed to differentiate similar products. Ivory and Lifebuoy soap did the same thing, but marketers labored to give each its own separate emotional meaning. This kind of copy couldn't be written by just anyone, it was argued, but rather only by those with a particular expertise in arousing consumer desire. At the same time, trademarks took on increasing importance as brands, infused with the emotional messages crafted by advertisers, became repositories of customer goodwill, replacing the local testimonials and neighbor-to-neighbor commercial relationships of the past. By staking claim to a unique skill set, advertisers set out to prove that they deserved professional status.

To claim this particularized skill set, advertisers welcomed any association between their craft and something that boasted a scientific pedigree. In the 1920s, the J. Walter Thompson advertising agency hired psychologist James B. Watson, putting his expertise to work on publicity initiatives for retail giants like General Motors and Procter & Gamble.[60] Other ad agencies followed suit, and by doing so, they adopted a calculated air of exclusive knowledge like that of other professionals such as doctors and lawyers. One practitioner of the time wrote, "The wonder is that the advertiser who has not had a thorough scientific and mathematical training can know anything about his business."[61] Psychologists engaged in quite a bit of self-promotion themselves. Columbia University psychology professor Albert Poffenberger credited the sudden popularity among Americans of mouthwash and toothpaste to his discipline's "strokes of genius in the control of behavior."[62] Similarly, psychology professor Walter Dill Scott maintained that human behavior could be controlled to a degree previously thought impossible by using advertising that followed scientific principles.[63]

Judges were not immune to the scientific sell of early twentieth-century advertising. They formed a new appreciation for advertisers, acknowledging the efficacy of the psychological techniques now central to their craft. In sharp contrast to the prior perception of advertisers as unskilled hacks, judges now gave credence to the idea that "mastery of the psychology of advertising" produced results in terms of gains in market share and brand goodwill.[64] The courts began to accept evidence of a business's expenditures on advertising as proof of secondary meaning (i.e., when the public associates the trademark with a particular provider of goods or services). Proof of secondary meaning was often necessary to begin an infringement suit, at least for suits involving trademarks that were merely descriptive of the underlying product. For example, to state a claim for infringement against a company that sold brushes embossed with the words "Set in Rubber," the owner of the mark for Rubberset brand rubber brushes had to demonstrate secondary meaning in the word Rubberset. Historically, courts had construed the secondary meaning requirement strictly, deeming these kinds of words too important for competition to permit them to be trademarked. But by the early twentieth century, a mark holder could prove secondary meaning largely by demonstrating that it had spent large sums of money on advertising. The Rubberset court, for example, impressed by the plaintiff's extensive advertising expenditures, not only found secondary meaning but ventured that another finding was impossible, "knowing as we do the effect of modern advertising."[65]

Judges also took a hard look at their ability to reach into the minds of the average consumer, ceding some of their own authority to the psychologists retained by advertisers. For decades, judges had evaluated trademark infringement claims by channeling the average consumer and assessing whether that consumer was likely to be confused by the defendant's actions. Reformers called for replacing this ad hoc "judicial estimate of the state of the public mind"[66] with psychologist expert testimony.[67] In response, judges moved to shore up their analysis by admitting in as evidence surveys of consumer confusion conducted by psychologists.[68] Ultimately, this made confusion easier to prove as the psychological research of the time emphasized consumers' limited intellectual capabilities. Judges ended up trading earlier views of a cautious and logical consuming public for a description of that public as "that vast multitude which includes the ignorant, the unthinking and the credulous, who, in making purchases, do not stop to analyze, but are governed by appearances and general impressions."[69] These changes in legal doctrine, spurred by an embrace of the science of psychology and an increasing appreciation for the specialized knowledge necessary to modern marketing, strengthened the hand of advertisers. By making it easier to assert trademark rights in merely descriptive terms (like "Rubberset") and to demonstrate that consumers would be confused by alternative uses of those terms, courts turned trademarks into more powerful business resources, encouraging further investment in psychological techniques designed to burnish their emotional resonance with consumers.

Preserving Consumer Free Will

By the 1950s, the symbiotic relationship between psychologists and advertisers had reached new heights. Motivational researchers, employing Freudian theories of the operation of the subconscious mind, became staples at advertising agencies. Market research continued to be performed the old-fashioned way by tracking sales numbers and polling potential purchasers, but now this was complemented with in-depth psychological profiles of consumers. This new market research stressed the importance of reaching consumers at an emotional, instinctual level. This was particularly needed in the 1950s, many argued, as consumers had begun to get wise to advertising claims that often fell short of their explicit promises. Better to subvert brewing consumer skepticism with new techniques meant to slip past conscious defenses undetected. Courts and regulators were not willing, however, to ratify every psychological technique pressed into the service of branding and promotion. Two historical episodes from this period offer useful points of comparison for understanding the legal reaction to neuromarketing in our own time. Discovery of subliminal advertising campaigns ignited a public firestorm and triggered a strong response from regulators. Meanwhile, new antidilution laws designed to inoculate the brand meanings that advertisers planted in consumers' minds from nonconfusing alternative messages met with stern judicial resistance. What both of these midcentury legal controversies have in common is an antipathy to attempts to use psychology in a way that would circumscribe dialogue with consumers. Marketing techniques calculated to produce particular emotional responses were acceptable, but not at the cost of consumer free will.

News of subliminal advertising first leaked out sometime in late 1956, but it really began to attract public attention in 1957. In that year, James Vicary, a Manhattan marketing executive, claimed to have successfully screened an "invisible commercial." During screenings of the movie *Picnic* at a New Jersey movie theater, Vicary inserted the messages "Drink Coca-Cola" and "Hungry? Eat Popcorn." These messages flashed at the audience for only one-three-hundredth of a second, not long enough to actually be perceived by consumers or register in their consciousness. Nevertheless, Vicary claimed these subliminal ads sparked a marked increase in audience purchases of popcorn and soda at the theater concession stand.

Vicary was not the only marketer at this time experimenting with subliminal ads. A Los Angeles television station hired Precon, an aptly named company, which specialized in subliminally inserting corporate trademarks into films. Precon claimed that such a technique created instant brand goodwill as audiences transferred the pleasure they felt from being cinematically entertained to the corporate symbol. The company also marketed a device meant to be placed on retail counters. The device blinked subliminal messages at consumers at the point of sale, reaching them just as they opened their purses and took out their wallets.[70]

Public reaction to these techniques was swift and condemning. Marketers tried to justify subliminal advertising as a win for consumers who could trade the annoying interruptions of commercial breaks for exposure to imperceptible embedded ads. If advertising was inevitable in modern life, why not make it unnoticeable and allow consumers to enjoy films and television without perceptible commercial interruption? But subliminal advertising's promise to elude conscious processing threatened a radical loss of individual control to unseen forces. Instead of embracing its convenience, subliminal advertising's targets feared brainwashing at the hands of hidden corporate (and perhaps later governmental) interlocutors. *Brave New World* author Aldous Huxley found the new advertising technique alarming and suggested that its wide implementation would subvert human free will.[71] One critic described subliminal advertising methods as a potential "rape of the mind."[72]

Noticing the public's disquiet, politicians and regulators stepped in to stop subliminal advertising before it could really get started. Congressmen proposed legislation calling for fines and jail time when broadcasters aired subliminal messages. At the urging of Senator Charles Potter and Representative William Dawson, the Federal Communications Commission (FCC) considered an outright ban on the practice. Vicary was summoned to demonstrate his invention before members of Congress as well as federal regulators. Meanwhile, individual states joined the antisubliminal push. Bills to block such practices were introduced in the New York, California, and Texas legislatures. Seeing the handwriting on the wall and aiming to stop a growing public relations nightmare, the three television networks, as well as the National Association of Radio and Television Broadcasters, banned their member stations from using subliminal advertising. Years later, the FCC warned broadcasters tempted to end the old embargo against subliminal ads that "such techniques are contrary to the public interest . . . and intended to be deceptive."[73]

The ironic thing about this public and political reaction is that, at least in its 1950s incarnation, subliminal advertising did not work very well. Vicary's attempt to recreate his experiment in front of politicians and regulators failed. Years later, Vicary admitted that his original experiment was a fraud cynically calculated to garner publicity for his marketing consultancy. But perhaps more important than the efficacy of 1950s subliminal advertising was the legal system's response. Subliminal advertising threatened prevailing notions of individual autonomy and free will. At a time when average Americans feared brainwashing by Communist foes, the notion of advertisers holding the strings while consumers danced unawares was too much to take. As a result, when federal regulators and legislators acted quickly to curtail subliminal advertising, advertisers and their mass media partners had to back off, abandoning an advertising technique before it had a chance to get off the ground.

Another legal limit on the psychology-advertising alliance began to form around the same time. Shortly after World War II, state legislatures started to pass antidilution statutes, eventually enacting them in thirty-eight of the fifty states. Instead of focusing on the transmission of reliable information from advertiser to consumer, dilution law, according to its originator, was explicitly meant to safeguard the "psychological hold" that successful advertising had on the public. In contrast to previous trademark protection laws, dilution laws were not designed to prevent consumer confusion. Instead, a trademark holder needed only to show that the defendant's behavior would cause its mark to lose "its arresting uniqueness." The owner of Blue Goose oranges could use a dilution claim to enjoin another company from selling Blue Goose fountain pens simply by demonstrating a probable reduction in the capacity of the Blue Goose mark to identify oranges. Such a claim would succeed even if consumers were unlikely to believe that the fountain pen maker was affiliated with the company that sold oranges. The real harm that antidilution law was meant to protect against was the "gradual whittling away or dispersion of the identity and hold upon the public mind of the mark."[74]

Judges asked to enforce these new laws balked. They apparently saw little need for additional safeguards above and beyond the existing prohibition on confusing uses to protect a brand's "psychological hold" on the public. There were some exceptions, but by and large, courts ignored the plain language of the dilution laws and refused to implement them. Judges often denied dilution claims simply because the plaintiff had failed to prove likelihood of confusion even though the applicable laws clearly eliminated confusion as an element of the dilution cause of action. Some courts held that dilution claims were precluded when the parties were market competitors, reasoning that dilution laws should not be allowed to alter the competitive balance forged through traditional trademark infringement law and its likelihood-of-confusion test. Both approaches represented strategies to strangle dilution in its cradle before it could emerge as a powerful new weapon to protect advertising interests.

Why the antipathy to dilution law, a legal innovation meant to strengthen advertising's project of infusing brands with emotional meaning? Judicial willingness to protect advertisers rested on a belief that advertising's influence in the competition for mindshare was short-lived. Even as courts recognized that psychological advertising techniques influenced consumers, they also believed that consumers were fully capable of shrugging off one emotional appeal for another. Judges viewed consumers as susceptible to emotional advertising, but at the same time, they refused to believe that the conditioned reflex created by advertising would be permanent. In a 1942 case, the Supreme Court described the goodwill built up in a trademark not as a "psychological hold" but as a "psychological current," implying that a consumer could leave this current and drift away on another advertising stream at a subsequent time.[75] Judges accepted that consumers behaved somewhat irrationally and that modern advertising sought to capitalize on this insight, but they did not believe that advertising's emotional appeals left a permanent mark. In the face of better products, declining brand quality, or more compelling advertising, consumers would break free of advertising's spell.

Dilution laws, however, threatened to make the consumer mindshare secured by emotional appeals last forever by placing it in a legal lockbox. Unlike actions for trademark infringement, an action for trademark dilution did not require a likelihood that consumers might be tricked into purchasing the wrong brand. Instead, dilution merely required some action by the defendant that weakened the emotional signal being broadcast by the trademark holder. Although, as compared to their early twentieth-century predecessors, courts were taking an increasingly broad view of what sorts of uses might be considered confusing, they refused to abandon consumer confusion as the touchstone for trademark protection. In judicial eyes, business activities involving unauthorized uses of another party's trademark that did not confuse consumers should not be actionable. But under a dilution regime, any weakening of the bond between consumer and advertiser became actionable, even if there was no potential for confusion. This was too much for most courts, and as a result, they brazenly misinterpreted dilution statutes to neutralize what they perceived as anticompetitive effects.[76]

Letting in the Hidden Persuaders

The responses to subliminal advertising and antidilution laws revealed a discomfort with two particular aspects of the use of psychological techniques in advertising. First, commercial messaging that elided conscious perception struck regulators as a sort of mind control that deserved condemnation regardless of the scientific study or expertise required to pull it off. Second, to the extent that advertisers could use their psychological know-how to more transparently annex space in consumers' heads, their rights to that space were limited. The law would prevent mistaken information about brands from being communicated to the public; otherwise, the battle for mindshare had to be free and open. This is not to say that late-twentieth-century advertisers never engaged in covert or deceptive marketing techniques or that legal officials always intervened to block these techniques. But the reactions to subliminal advertising and dilution laws did place real limitations on the ability of advertisers to use some psychological techniques in the service of selling. Recent actions by legal authorities suggest an abandoning of these limits, leaving neuromarketers free to hone their skills on unwitting consumers. Potential regulators have chosen to avoid review of neuromarketing methods kept hidden from their targets. Meanwhile, courts have altered trademark law to give brand owners greater power to impose semiotic discipline on competitors and consumers.

Abdicating the Regulatory Role

By diagnosing individual mental susceptibilities and designing advertising content accordingly, neuromarketing triggers many of the same autonomy concerns that motivated the legal response to subliminal advertising in the 1950s. Neuromarketers take great pains to distinguish their own work from

techniques like Vicary's. Subliminal advertising does not require human perception, they argue. Instead, although it may be used to trigger subconscious
desires, neuromarketing is typically operationalized in a way that requires
some minimal amount of consumer awareness.[77] The distinction between ads
that require human perception and those that do not is not so meaningful,
however. Calculated incidental exposure to brands and brand messages is very
similar to subliminal advertising in terms of its purposes and ultimate effects.
What matters, regardless of whether the ad is technically perceived by the consumer, is that neuromarketers, like those engaged in subliminal advertising, attempt to manipulate consumers through hidden techniques. As one prominent
law firm acknowledged in a white paper detailing potential legal challenges to
neuromarketing, "At its core, neuromarketing involves an effort to influence
consumer decision-making at an unconscious level."[78]

Nevertheless, in stark contrast to the uproar over subliminal advertising,
the legal response to neuromarketing has been muted at best.[79] The problem is
not a lack of regulatory authority. Admittedly, no specific federal law prohibits
neuromarketing (the same goes for subliminal messaging). But these psychological techniques do seem to be within the purview of at least two kinds of regulators: the Federal Trade Commission (FTC) and institutional review boards
(IRBs). The FTC has broad authority to investigate and prohibit "unfair" trade
practices. It has taken pains to define unfairness (and its resulting regulatory
powers) broadly, explaining that a trade practice is "unfair" if it injures consumers, violates public policy, or is otherwise unethical or unscrupulous. Consumer
injury results when a seller "unreasonably creates or takes advantage of an ob-
stacle to the free exercise of consumer decision-making."[80] It is not a stretch to
argue that neuromarketing, by bypassing a consumer's conscious defenses, prevents the free exercise of consumer choice and falls within the FTC's purview.[81]

Yet neuromarketing has received little attention from this legal watchdog.[82]
Part of the problem is a matter of legal emphasis. Neuromarketers concentrate
on unlocking the secrets of emotion because it is becoming increasingly evident from the work of Damasio and others that emotion drives all behavior,
including consumer decision making. But for the advertisers, their focus on
emotion has the additional benefit of falling into a legal blind spot. In general,
legal authorities and theorists have been hesitant to interrogate human emotion, instead counterposing a view of law as reliant on unemotional, analytic

reasoning.[83] Because its messages are typically not factual, neuromarketing seems to be getting a free pass, so far falling outside the ambit of "unfair" advertising as defined by the FTC.[84] An example is an action that a consortium of consumer groups filed with the FTC in 2011. The groups accused a maker of high-fat snack foods of using neuromarketing "designed to trigger subconscious emotional arousal."[85] Rather than denying the use of neuromarketing, the snack food company's chief marketing officer unabashedly touted the value of brain imaging tests to his company's bottom line.[86] Yet the complaint failed to gain traction with the FTC, which has preferred to focus its attention on demonstrably false factual statements, like unproven weight loss claims, bogus environmental pedigrees, or violations of a company's own privacy policy.

For their part, IRBs are charged with monitoring and reviewing research involving human subjects. Unless the research falls under a particular exception, IRBs require researchers to obtain the informed consent of their subjects. This includes providing subjects with a description of the proposed research, disclosing "any reasonably foreseeable risks or discomforts," and offering an opportunity to opt out of the experiment. Although U.S. law mandates IRB approval only for federally funded research, several states mandate IRB approval regardless of funding source. One might contend that advertising should not be considered "research" and, hence, not subject to IRB review. But as we have seen, neuromarketers rely heavily on human experimentation to determine advertising content. These experiments would seem to be research and, hence, deserving of IRB review and necessitating informed consent.

Neuromarketing successfully skirts this regulatory blockade as well. Here, the problem is not so much a refusal to consider emotional messaging as a serious consumer threat as it is a willingness to abdicate responsibility when private commercial enterprises have a hand in generating psychological data. Admittedly, most applied neuromarketing research has to be done with its participants' knowledge because at this point in time, it is hard to put someone in an fMRI machine without that person knowing it. But some psychological experiments meant to improve advertising effectiveness can be performed without their subjects' awareness. For the Facebook news feed study, researchers from Cornell University tinkered with the emotions of over half a million subjects, arguably making some people (at least for a time) sadder and some people happier than they would have been otherwise. The study's authors did go before Cornell's IRB, but the board declined to review the study, apparently reasoning that Facebook, not Cornell's researchers, was responsible for manipulating the news feeds. This was patently untrue: the study's authors admitted that they themselves structured the changes in news feed content rather than simply analyzing some old data that Facebook had retained. The Cornell IRB seemed to believe that it was off the hook because its researchers had partnered with a private entity, but the proper response should have been the opposite.

Facebook contends that all of its users consent to this sort of digital manipulation when they agree to its terms of service. Because the study's participants had already agreed to subject themselves to experimentation while on Facebook, there was no need for the IRB to scrutinize the study. Taking this argument to its full conclusion, market researchers are free to engage in any sort of manipulation on social media so long as the private entity running the social media site has already forced its users to agree to terms of service that include human experimentation. This argument sounds ridiculous. *South Park* even devoted an episode to mocking terms of service that could subject consumers to horrific medical research.[87] Yet these kinds of human trials are being run on online consumers all the time, the authority to run them arguably contained in capacious terms of service.[88]

Protecting Neuromarks

At the same time that regulatory authorities have been ignoring neuromarketing, judges have changed trademark law to strengthen the hand of advertisers wishing to leverage neuroscience to boost brand goodwill. They have done this in two chief ways. First, the initial judicial resistance to dilution law has been overcome. Dilution law now serves as a viable cause of action, giving famous brand owners the ability to shut down opposing commercial discourse even in the absence of consumer confusion. Second, an expansion of the definition of actionable consumer confusion provides advertisers with broader control over their emotional messaging. Neuromarketing's effectiveness can be blunted by the actions of others competing for mindshare. Research shows that as a brand name becomes attached to a variety of goals, the association between the brand and any particular goal will be diminished. As a result, unauthorized uses of marks—by competitors and consumers—act as a counterweight against the carefully constructed emotional messaging of neuromarketers. But when this semiotic competition is restrained through legal means, the ability to use neuromarketing to shape preferences increases. Brand managers, well aware of this, attempt to identify the neurologically critical parts of brands and then use legal strategies, like claims of dilution, to control unauthorized communications surrounding these same critical areas.[89]

Perhaps eventually worn down by legislators intent on crafting laws protecting famous brands, courts have shed some of their initial antipathy to dilution law. In 1995, Congress passed the first federal dilution law. Just as they had with the state dilution laws of the past, courts examined the legislation skeptically, questioning the need for protections against nonconfusing mark uses. In a 2003 decision, the U.S. Supreme Court held that "actual dilution" needed to be proven for a federal dilution claim. This threatened to eviscerate the potential for successful dilution claims. After all, dilution is a gradual process. How does one prove that there has actually been a slow "whittling away" of the signaling power of a famous brand in the consumer's mind? By requiring proof of actual dilution rather than evidence suggesting a mere likelihood of dilution, the Supreme Court attempted to circumscribe the ability of brand owners to use the new federal cause of action.[90]

The Supreme Court decision represented, however, the last prominent moment of judicial resistance to the dilution cause of action. Congress quickly moved to rebuke the Court, passing a new law affirming that only a "likelihood" of dilution was necessary for a successful claim. Soon after, in contrast to their willingness to ignore the plain language of past dilution laws, courts acknowledged the significance of Congress's amendment. For example, noting that the amendment "significantly changes the meaning of the law," a federal court in New York concluded that a one-second display (in a thirty-second television commercial) of a basketball emblazoned with a faux Louis Vuitton logo was dilutive. Even though the ad portrayed several humorous examples of misplaced luxury—policemen eating caviar in a patrol car, an inner-city basketball game being played on a marble court with golden hoops—that were meant to highlight the contrasting fiscal soundness of buying a Hyundai, a court concluded that Hyundai was illegally "borrowing equity" from Louis Vuitton in violation of the new dilution law. It did not matter that Louis Vuitton could provide no proof of actual dilution from the commercial, that is, that there had been a diminution in the signaling power of the luxury handbag maker's logo. In fact, a survey of viewers of the ad revealed that not a single person believed that the Hyundai ad had made them think less favorably of Louis Vuitton. Nevertheless, under the new standard, the court was willing to infer dilution based on the one-second display. The result: brand owners are free to influence consumers with split-second displays of their trademarks, but dilution law prevents their rivals from doing the same.[91]

New doctrinal developments have made it even easier to bring dilution claims. When lingerie maker Victoria's Secret sued a Kentucky lingerie shop under the federal dilution statute, it managed to convince the court not only that the name "Victor's Little Secret" *could* be dilutive, but that for any sexualized derivation of its name, dilution *should* be presumed. In the words of the court, "Any new mark with a lewd or offensive-to-some sexual association raises a strong inference of tarnishment."[92] Other courts have implicitly come to the same conclusion, finding dilution from sexualized uses of a famous mark with little proof that such uses actually reduce the mark's signaling power. By some accounts, 20 percent of all advertising features sexualized content.[93] Hence, these judicial decisions dramatically expand the ability of trademark owners to censor competing expression that implicates their brand.[94]

Even without the sea change in judicial attitudes toward dilution, advertisers would have another legal weapon to safeguard their brands' emotional meanings from competing messages. Over time, courts have expanded what kinds of consumer confusion can be countenanced for purposes of trademark law.[95] "Confusion" once referred to confusion as to the source of origin of the goods at issue by actual purchasers. This has changed. Courts now recognize confusion not just among actual purchasers, but among mere bystanders. They also prohibit not only confusion as to source but as to "sponsorship or affiliation," or even what some courts have tellingly labeled "subliminal confusion."[96] As a result of these changes, actionable confusion now includes situations when there is no real harm to the mark holder from the defendant's activities and whatever "confusion" exists is immaterial to the consumer's purchasing decision.[97] In a relatively recent spate of university merchandising cases, universities sued to block businesses from selling T-shirts that feature their traditional colors and make reference to the school's athletic teams. In these cases, it is not at all clear that consumers believe that the university endorses the activities of the T-shirt maker or would care if it did. Nevertheless, courts have deemed such designs to create "an [actionable] link in the consumer's mind between the t-shirts and the Universities."[98]

These legal changes particularly aid those businesses most likely to use neuroscientific insights to surround their brands with an emotional aura. Dilution law protects only "famous" brands and even statutorily defines what it means for a trademark to be famous.[99] In contrast to small market share brands that need to communicate factual information to prospective consumers, well-known brands rely on emotionally charged advertising, knowing that the basic functionality of their products has already been established with the public. Hence, dilution law favors businesses most likely to use neuromarketing to trigger emotional responses in consumers.[100] It also helps businesses like cigarette makers, pharmaceutical firms, and oil companies that need to rely on particularly opaque, atmospheric appeals without overtly acknowledging their true identities.[101] By expanding the definition of confusion to encompass merely mistaken "affiliations," courts give advertisers greater control over their message, thereby strengthening the emotional hold of their brands over consumers. Many trademark suits are filed not against genuine competitors, but against businesses in other industries or even nonprofit groups attempting to use a corporate logo to make an expressive point.[102]

Confusion and dilution are legal concepts that judges apply with reference to precedent and statutory text. But these legal forces also need to be responsive to the state of the art in psychology and advertising. Neuroscience has changed things. By better understanding how our minds process, store, and emotionally respond to stimuli, advertisers can infuse brand names with qualities of their choosing. Particularly valuable are individualized understandings of consumer psychology, which may soon be realized through technologies allowing unobtrusive recording of the biomechanics of emotion. As it stands now, neuromarketing's methods for acquiring mindshare have been left uninterrogated by regulators and bolstered by new legal rules protecting an advertiser's emotional messaging from semiotic resistance. Brain science has the potential to find cures for neurological disorders and, by better understanding cognitive functions, a more humane framework for meting out criminal justice.[103] But it is also creating neuromarks that occupy more space in our minds whether we want them to or not.

Sellebrity

CAN YOU QUANTIFY the price of fame? Kim Kardashian thinks so. To work your way up to Hollywood's A-list, she proposes a ruthless prowling of the Los Angeles social scene, auditioning for any and all opportunities to increase personal visibility. For Kardashian, dating, going to parties, and communicating the right message for corporate brands on social media are all part of an overall scheme to seize the brass ring of celebrity. The tasks on Kardashian's quest for fame might be a little tongue in cheek—these examples come from the "Kim Kardashian: Hollywood" app, a game that lets users mimic the famous reality star's own expertise in grabbing the spotlight. But they are also tied to a real price tag. The app made $1.6 million in its first five days on the market, with Ms. Kardashian netting almost half of the profits.[1]

Celebrity marketing is yet another technique used to discipline consumers in a variety of ways and locations. It runs through each of the phenomena described in prior chapters. Public schools serve lunches branded with the names of television chefs.[2] Online surveillance companies like Brandwatch and KnowYourFollowers dissect digital chatter for celebrity mentions.[3] Neuromarketers probe test subjects' brains to see how they react to the presence of famous spokespersons in new commercials.[4] Celebrity marketing differs from some of the other techniques of the new advertising, however, in that it offers a very human example to follow. Celebrities are a kind of brand. Like the famous trademarks discussed in the previous chapter, their public appearances are deployed to trigger emotional connections with audiences. Yet celebrities can determine how much of their activities occur before the public. This capacity to distance one's self from commerciality distinguishes celebrities from other commercial symbols. It helps explain their potency as a model for consumers engaging in their own efforts at self-presentation.

Using modern celebrity messaging as a model for fashioning the self has pluses and minuses. Some psychologists maintain that the parasocial relationships formed with pop divas and sports stars bring tangible psychic benefits. Gossiping about celebrity missteps can serve an important purpose, binding relationships through a clarifying discussion of the metes and bounds of social norms. More generally, celebrities provide useful fodder for interpersonal communication, an alternative lingua franca that stands outside of what was once deemed worthwhile "news" by privileged white men.[5]

But there are costs to the growing celebrification of everyday life. Behaving like a celebrity means exposing yourself, offering up personal disclosures to sustain fan interest. Similar to Kardashian's game, we attempt to win over online followers through calculated confessions and score our popularity through the modules handily embedded in social media's architecture. In some ways, this is empowering. Today, even the nonfamous can behave like celebrities by taking payouts from marketers in return for endorsing a chosen product to their online acquaintances. The public's choice to emulate celebrity example should not be dismissed out of hand. But when the metrics for scoring one's social influence are controlled by private media companies and their affiliated marketers, we need to ask just how much of the quest for online visibility actually benefits its participants.

It is not just technology but law that encourages the link between visibility, commerciality, and social standing. In Kim Kardashian's Hollywood app, there is no discussion of law or lawyers. They might take some of the fun out of the game. But the evolving law of celebrity fuels tendencies toward more disclosure, more self-branding, and more celebrity advertising. This chapter focuses on one particular legal construct, the right of publicity, that reinforces the importance of visibility as a measure of status and has taken on new prominence in an era of instant audience quantification. Ms. Kardashian sued Old Navy for infringing her right of publicity when it aired a commercial featuring an actress that resembled her. Old Navy agreed to settle the lawsuit, and although the settlement remains confidential, reports were of an agreement between $15 million and $20 million.[6] Decades ago, such a lawsuit would not have passed muster, judges being loath to stop others from using celebrity images for their own expressive purposes.[7] Over time, however, the commercial value of visibility came not only to be recognized by the legal system but deemed to be "property," meaning it can be exchanged, transferred to others, and even legally protected beyond death. The question is whether average citizens benefit from the propertization of audience attention. This chapter suggests that they do not, that the law of celebrity promotes a culture of disclosure that hurts everyday participants while playing into the hands of advertisers.

Stars In Our Eyes

Linkages between celebrities and advertisers are nothing new. Stars of stage and screen, famous inventors, and record-setting athletes have lent their names and likenesses to marketing testimonials for decades. But the sheer amount of celebrity content in today's commercial culture represents a step change from prior use of famous faces in advertising, another example of adcreep like online surveillance and marketing in civic spaces. Meanwhile, more precise measures of audience engagement have heightened fame's rewards. In keeping with these cultural and technological shifts, the modern right of publicity reinforces visibility's increasing importance as a marker of social standing, encouraging noncelebrities to emulate the attention-seeking behaviors of the famous.[8]

Celebrity Everywhere

Once a citizen could avoid exposure to celebrity messaging, at least for a day or two. This is now impossible with the proliferation of programming formats and digital communications platforms that are part of life today. Old analog platforms—films, television, magazines—continue to do a brisk business reporting the activities of screen idols and media-savvy athletes. Compared to just a few decades ago, when American television viewers had only a few channels to pick from, there has been an explosion of viewing possibilities on various cable networks and online streaming sites. Media companies now use celebrities as part of a calculated, synergistic, and cost-effective strategy to differentiate their products. Time Warner can employ the same celebrity for its motion picture, television, and publishing arms. Disney grooms a famous face like Selena Gomez for its broadcast and cable networks, its record label, its films, its magazines, and its theme parks. Adding to this trend, the forces of globalization place a premium on finding personalities that can translate content across different communications platforms and cultural environments. The result is a culture infused with more celebrities and more media launching pads designed to make them visible to consumers.

Turning off your television, staying out of movie theaters, and avoiding magazines won't give you a celebrity-free existence. Modern life necessitates the daily traversing of a virtual red carpet. Everyday activities now require interacting with notorious celebutantes, headline-grabbing criminals, pop star divas, and teen heartthrobs. If you go to Yahoo to check your e-mail, you will have to at least glance at a list of what is "Trending Now." And most of what is trending are people we already know or who have momentarily seized the spotlight of our tabloid culture. Checking the *Huffington Post* for news headlines means viewing a prominent column of faces breathlessly captioned with provocative titles like "Marilyn Manson Got Punched in the Face at a Denny's" and "Jon Cryer Still Hopes to Speak to a Sober Charlie Sheen."

You might characterize resources like Yahoo and the *Huffington Post* as entertainment destinations that we should expect to be filled with celebrity content. But all of the dominant guideposts for navigating the Web reflect the same celebrity-crazed sensibility. Old journalistic lions like the *Washington Post* and the *New York Times* pepper their Web pages with "Trending Topics" and "Watching" stories, typically posts aggregated from other content providers and often featuring celebrity names and faces, a strategy that owes more to Perez Hilton than Ben Bradlee. Google fills in our partially typed search requests with celebrity names, scrutinizes our e-mail accounts to target us with ads featuring celebrity endorsers, and releases an annual report on the most-searched-for people. News and discussion site Reddit may provide a home for narrow Internet subcultures, but it also hosts popular AMA (Ask Me Anything) sessions where celebrities generate an atmosphere of intimacy while using the platform for self-promotion. Many online entities depend on celebrity social media messages to fill their pages. The largest online study resource, SparkNotes, tells students to "Take a Study Break!" by clicking on celebrity publicity materials. Notations on *Hamlet* are mixed with the publicist-approved images posted on the Instagram accounts of Rihanna and Justin Timberlake. Celebrities generate the bulk of the messages shared on Twitter. As described by *Forbes* magazine, "Twitter, at its heart is where Lady Gaga, Ashton Kutcher and Kim Kardashian talk to their millions of fans."[9] The operators of the portals we use to search for information, check our e-mail, and share our discoveries constantly remind us of society's most visible, enticing us to click, learn more, and make them even more well known.

Blurred Lines

We owe the supersizing of our diet of celebrity content not only to the creation of new media platforms, but also to the erosion of boundaries that once restricted the spread of celebrity publicity. Tensions between commerciality and artistry cabined celebrity efforts to capitalize on fan recognition. Popular narratives emphasized the corruptive effects of high visibility on artistic integrity. In an influential essay published in 1947, Tennessee Williams described celebrity renown as a "Bitch Goddess" that produced spiritual alienation while removing the striving and social connection necessary for personal creativity.[10] Films like *A Face in the Crowd* and *A Star Is Born* trafficked in similar themes. Commercial visibility also threatened the ethereal images cultivated by those falling into celebrity's highest castes. Well-known radio and television personalities agreed to become commercial pitchmen, but Hollywood stars typically refused, concerned that shilling for consumer goods or raising the curtain too far on their personal lives would tarnish their larger-than-life images. Audiences were recognized as essential to celebrity success, but they needed to be kept at a remove lest they topple the celebrity's artistic underpinnings or destabilize her carefully crafted public persona.[11]

In the late twentieth century, boundaries between celebrities and their audiences began to fall away. This erasure occurred for numerous and complex reasons, including the demise of the Hollywood studio system and the rise of cinematic realism. Meanwhile, as it became commonplace for people to express their individuality through the purchase of consumer goods, it became more acceptable to expressly attach one's famous persona to particular products. No longer raising the suspicion it did in Williams's time, advertising has become a conventional outlet for celebrity messaging as most stars have come to invite commerciality, not reject it. Celebrities, including Hollywood's A-list, dominate the perfume industry. Fashion houses simultaneously recruit highbrow authors like Joan Didion, respected politicians like Mikhail Gorbachev, and reality TV-stars-cum-models like Kendall Jenner. Once concerned with "being tagged a sellout, or looking desperate, for doing commercial work," prominent actors now flock to opportunities to voice television commercials.[12] There is still a distinction between different kinds of famous individuals and the kinds of marketing opportunities deemed appropriate for their overall schemes of publicity management. Superstars like George Clooney and Angelina Jolie may stick largely to overseas commercials and the talk show circuit, while reality television stars leverage their familiarity through more intimate online presentations. But by and large, thanks to the variety of platforms available for celebrity visibility projects and the related ability of advertisers to target particularized audiences, virtually any celebrity from any social group is invited to commercialize his or her persona in some form.[13]

As the divide between art and commerce narrows into insignificance, new technologies transform celebrity private lives into commercial platforms. Publicity has always been needed for celebrity; one cannot be famous without being known. But when yoked to social media, celebrities now find themselves constantly forced to up the ante to maintain their fan followings. Because the tweets and posts of the highly visible come in the same format as communications from our own friends and family, celebrity messages come to seem more intimate, and fans in turn have come to expect more personal celebrity revelations. Communications, particularly ones proffering some sense of personal unveiling, just like the candid photos snapped by paparazzi, are needed to keep the publicity machine going and online followers engaged. In a calculated strategy, celebrities offer intimate disclosures in the form of pictures (the racier, the better) and confessions to attract friends, followers, and retweets. In 2014, Kim Kardashian posted professionally taken nude photographs on Instagram in a self-proclaimed effort to "Break the Internet." Ashton Kutcher infamously tweeted a photo of his then wife Demi Moore's bikini-clad posterior with the caption, "shhh don't tell wifey." Natural attributes may have started Chrissy Teigen's modeling career, but she is best known for posting descriptions of drunken escapades and intimate Instagram photos of herself and celebrity husband John Legend. Moves like these, bypassing traditionally private boundaries, have netted Kardashian, Kutcher, and Teigen millions of social media followers.

These disclosures are not the product of a few particularly exhibitionist celebrity entrepreneurs. All social networking sites have specific departments devoted to inciting celebrities to post more and more captivating content online.[14] Publicists guide this process, offering disclosures that a single celebrity might not have the time or inclination to provide herself. As a publicist to pop stars Britney Spears and will.i.am explains, "It can get really busy if you're doing interviews on the red carpet, and it's just nice to have someone with you who can say, hey, you should take a picture with your other-famous-person friend right now. Here you go, now you should tweet it."[15] Various websites make it their business to document celebrity conspicuous consumption while providing ready online conduits to purchase the consumer goods they have endowed with the glamour of high visibility. Of course, stars have always calculated when to let audiences in on an emotional reveal to draw their interest. But today, intimate revelations and performances of emotionality are so accessible to consumers, easily circulated online and promoted through social media, that they have become an expected part of celebrity image management. These communications uproot prior norms against the mixing of the private and the commercial, allowing celebrity narratives to flood into new territories, enhancing visibility, promising intimacy, and selling merchandise.

Quantifying Celebrity Influence

Celebrity advertising has changed not just in scope and form but also in the measurement of its effects. A vibrant marketplace exists that ties numerical influence to social media endorsement deals, some deals explicitly calibrating payments to the size of a celebrity's online following. Followers on Twitter and Instagram, likes on Facebook, and reblogs on Tumblr can be cashed in for advertising dollars. After forming an alliance with Adly, a firm that plays matchmaker between businesses and celebrities willing to post favorable content on social media, Charlie Sheen successfully pledged to gain over 1 million Twitter followers in a single day. Shortly after reaching the million-follower milestone, Sheen agreed to tweet for a start-up called internships.com, reportedly receiving $100,000 for doing so.[16] Kim Kardashian's legions of Twitter and Instagram fans netted her $20,000 for every post she made describing EOS lip balm or Midori liquor. Little sister Khloe's somewhat smaller audience garnered her $13,000 per tweet.[17] In 2015, sports marketing experts estimated the value of a single sponsored tweet from NBA superstar LeBron James at $126,000.[18] That same year, *Adweek* breathlessly noted nineteen-year-old model Gigi Hadid's 2.5 million followers on Instagram and 2.8 million followers on Twitter, placing her in a group of so-called Instagirls—fashion models with large online followings. These numbers led to contracts with Victoria's Secret and Maybelline and even more visibility.[19]

The quantification of celebrity popularity via social media provides information not just about potential endorsers but also about their audiences. Maintaining celebrity status now not only demands more intimate revelations from celebrities themselves but the ability to prompt and monitor personal disclosures from digital fans. A panoply of entities now offer the ability to break down information on celebrity followers to better woo them in the future. KnowYourFollowers provides the country, state, gender, marital status, employment, and location of a star's online fans as well as who else they follow. BumeBox, a Facebook marketing platform that runs question-and-answer sessions between celebrities and their fans, explains, "We monitor the engagement of every event: who's participating, what they're excited about, and how much influence they have. Our natural language processing helps find that sweet spot and tells you exactly what people want to know."[20] IZEA, which provides an auction-style platform for connecting advertisers with celebrities and other social media influencers, touts its proprietary algorithm for tracking the sharing of celebrity-sponsored content across the Web. In similar fashion, Adly and Brandwatch license their fan surveillance capabilities, charging publicists and advertisers for their views of how a pop star's paid-for Twitter posts flow across social media. For WhoSay, a company originally built to allow the clients of Creative Artists Agency to push home-grown branded content out to larger venues like Facebook, Instagram, and Tumblr, its ability to track means that "no online or offline data is off limits, which means WhoSay can now create highly tailored audience segments in real-time, enabling advertisers to achieve significant audience engagement and drive ROI."[21] Evidence of a celebrity's following on social networks provides two important marketing resources: proof of celebrity visibility and individual audience disclosures that can be repurposed for targeted advertising. But what does this new environment of ubiquitous and quantifiable celebrity visibility mean for the rest of us?

The High Cost of Micro-Celebrity

Celebrity-infused advertising works. The presence of a celebrity in an ad causes the ad to be read more shallowly and with less resistance.[22] Our natural inclination to want to know more about the well-known can turn into a cognitive bias, causing viewers to fixate on the celebrity endorser and tune out objective product information. Even advertising that only obliquely triggers association with celebrity, as with a celebrity voice-over that the hearer cannot quite place, is still deemed more credible than equivalent advertising without a celebrity voice.[23] No wonder that 17 percent of all ads feature a celebrity, and in the United States that number is even higher.[24] Like online profiling and neuromarketing, famous personalities are yet another resource, deployed through new technologies and infiltrating once commercially resistant spaces, designed to convince us to consume.

But there is more going on here than just effective advertising. Thanks, at least in part, to the combination of a pervasive celebrity publicity machine and a communications landscape dominated by social media, everyday actors now adopt the techniques of micro-celebrity: the use of social media to attract and maintain audiences, just like the pop divas and reality stars who preach to us online. Friends are viewed as fans to be stimulated and managed. For the micro-celebrity, greater visibility equates to greater social status. Online representations of the self are constructed in ways that resemble celebrity images, with provocative disclosures designed for audience consumption and response.[25]

Modern self-presentation is too complicated and evolving to attribute simply to celebrity messaging. But the parallels between celebrity advertising and online self-branding warrant a close look because engaging in these celebrity behaviors comes at a price. There are some perks. Noncelebrities can now monetize their own recognition within a relatively small social circle. And for a select few, micro-celebrity can translate into actual celebrity as disparate online communities unite to discover someone worthy of their attention. But building followings through personal revelations can also backfire on individuals lacking the public relations resources of the famous. Digital architectures celebrating authenticity and individualism efface the labor needed to manage the online self, normalizing online surveillance by valorizing visibility. Friends and family can now knock on virtual doors and lobby us to buy products, but unlike the door-to-door salesmen and Avon Ladies of the past, they can keep their commercial allegiances hidden. As celebrity and self-definition become more and more intertwined, we need to take note of what is being lost when the Kardashian model of visibility and disclosure displaces other modes of navigating the social.

Visibility Games

The quest for visibility, the urge to display, to reveal, and to curate to satisfy an online audience does a lot for Facebook and Twitter. These companies are always hungry for more personal content that can attract new viewers and be filed away for market research. But bad press sometimes results when social networking sites adopt new policies that remove privacy protections without permission. So it is all the better when disclosures are made voluntarily. Social media companies adopt a variety of strategies to place the costs of heightened visibility on users, not the online businesses facilitating their displays.

One strategy is to use game-like mechanisms to incent personal privacy leaks. On Facebook and Instagram, more updating earns more coveted "likes" from friends and family. Posts on BuzzFeed win different "badges," as assigned by internal algorithms factoring in the number of reactions a post gets and its viral traffic. Reddit users can boost the "karma" score attached to their user name by submitting more links that receive more votes from more viewers. Meanwhile, social media companies make sure their users are always aware of their numbers, automatically tallying up and displaying not only lists of overall friends and followers, but the number of people who retweet a post or acknowledge a user's birthday or anniversary on Facebook.

Another strategy relies on inculcating an ethic of authenticity in social media users. Of course, what is considered authentic is relative. Nevertheless, the particular norm of authenticity fostered by social media companies demands glimpses of the personal and unique. As one study of celebrity presentation on Twitter noted, "Celebrity practice that sticks to the safe and publicly consumable risks being viewed as inauthentic, while successful celebrity practice suggests intimacy, disclosure, and connection."[26] In other words, part of being authentic means disclosing things about yourself. Social media communicates this vision of authenticity to all of its users, not just celebrities. Instagram describes itself as "a fun and quirky way to share your life with friends through a series of pictures."[27] Facebook rechristened its requirement that users employ their real names in their profiles as its "authentic" name policy.[28] According to the operators of social sharing sites, authenticity also means the instantaneous and constant release of personal information. Instagram contends that it was built "to allow you to experience moments in your friends' lives through pictures as they happen," using technology to avoid the inefficiencies typically involved in taking and sharing photos.[29] Facebook not only records typed but never posted status updates and comments, but also labels such considered choices not to post as "self-censorship."[30] These narratives and practices suggest that online revelations are not constructed—they are simply released from within with a minimum of work. Instead of actively managing the projection of ourselves online, we are merely "lifestreaming," effortlessly discharging an effluvia of data and emotional outbursts that tell our audiences exactly who we are.

In reality, projecting authenticity takes effort. Individual consumers are performing a great deal of labor for free when they emulate celebrities in their online presentations. They are obliged to create a persona, calculate the right amount of personal information to disclose, and construct a kind of intimacy even with those they are only dimly aware of in online space. And it is not like when this personal product is rolled out, all work is done. Instead, micro-celebrity demands constant product testing and evaluation, tweaks and adjustments to maintain market share, and additional disclosures to retain followers and ensure that one's profile appears "authentic." There is the construction of content, the checking of responses, and the weighing in on other posts to reflect your own sensibility but also to trigger a quid pro quo so your next post will be "liked" as well. Moreover, the omnipresent nature of social networking means that we perform this labor at all hours: at work, at home, in the not-so-spare moments when we might be present and engaged in other activities. One study contends that the average British woman will spend 753 hours of her life taking, retaking, deleting, and touching up selfies.[31]

This is where the alliance between celebrity and social media does the most work. Celebrity presentations provide a natural model for their online viewers to follow. According to youth researcher danah boyd, celebrity publicity practices "influence [today's teens'] understanding of how to navigate attention and status," and they mimic these practices by "us[ing] social media to drum up attention for themselves and shower attention on others."[32] Social media companies also make the parallels between everyday profile work and celebrity visibility explicit. Facebook's advertising slogan—"Be Connected. Be Discovered"—suggests an equivalence between the rewards of online visibility and the way in which an aspiring actor might hope to be "discovered" by a Hollywood talent scout. Twitter emphasizes its ability to connect users to celebrities, at one point describing its service as "instant updates from your friends, industry experts, favorite celebrities, and what's happening around the world."[33]

The link between celebrity presentation and everyday self-performance effaces the labor involved in projecting an "authentic" identity online. One does not think of celebrities as laboring to manage their audiences. In Marxian terms, the careful production of celebrity visibility is concealed as the famous are fetishized and their value described as a natural occurrence instead of a socially and economically constructed phenomenon.[34] Anthropologist Charles Lindholm describes a modern suspicion of the constructed nature of consumerism, which prompts concerns over using consumer products to configure one's own unique identity. Advertisers combat these concerns by stressing the authentic, individualized nature of particular product offerings. The more individually tailored a commercial offering seems, the more authentic it appears and the more suitable as a raw material for configuring one's identity.[35]

In a similar way, celebrities promote the personal, offering up themselves as totems for consumer self-fashioning and attempting to erase consumer skepticism by suggesting that consumers are seeing the real them instead of a symbol constructed by a larger publicity apparatus. In their online communications, celebrities promote illusions of immediacy, masking the role of public relations gatekeepers, highlighting the quotidian nature of their interactions with others, and supposedly offering backstage glimpses of their lives as they happen. Whether on reality television or Twitter, celebrity authenticity is communicated through emotion, ideally letting millions of viewers see supposedly unguarded and spontaneous moments of affectual response.[36] These tactics and points of emphasis obscure the process behind celebrity self-presentation. As a result, when we self-identify with the celebrities in our Twitter feeds, we see ourselves as free entrepreneurs, branding and revealing ourselves by choice to succeed in a marketplace whose currency is visibility. When others complain, perhaps about privacy policies that seem to change on a whim or about the forced necessity of participating in these privately controlled spaces, we feel less sympathy. Labor is for losers; we, like the celebrities we follow, are management.

The Downsides of Disclosure

In one sense, all this online identity work is a con game; Facebook is like Tom Sawyer granting us the "privilege" of whitewashing its digital fence. But there is nothing inherently objectionable about micro-celebrity's focus on visibility or tactical displays of the self online. Many, if not most, of our leisure pursuits offer some benefit to corporate forces whether we see it that way or not. Sports team fandom and video game playing can become all-consuming and profit outside entities, but these activities, like performing on social media, are usually thought of as recreation, not work. Moreover, strategically presenting a particular face to the outside world is far from unusual. In his pathbreaking study of human social interaction, *The Presentation of Self in Everyday Life*, sociologist Erving Goffman showed that calculated self-performance is a critical part of social life and an essential tool for self-development. Goffman described how humans pay constant attention to their representations to others, in effect performing like an actor in a play, in an attempt to structure social situations to their liking. In engaging in this changing performative process, individuals simultaneously shape their own sense of self-awareness and tailor their outward appearance to their audience. In a way, there is no self without someone watching. Goffman was writing in 1959, but his revelation of the highly constructed nature of our dealings with others reflects truisms about human behavior not rooted to any particular time or place.[37]

Personal disclosure in online environments is not problematic in itself. The problem lies in the particular system for self-exposition constructed by social media companies. A closer look at the requirements for navigating this system reveals a false equivalence between celebrity self-promotion and everyday online identity work. Social media users must forfeit control of their constructed revelations to false friends, hostile outsiders, and, most important, the social networking platform itself. For everyday users, the stakes for each self-performance rise as online barriers stymie attempts to discard old personas and experiment with new ones. By contrast, celebrities possess unique tools to manage their disclosures and monitor their audiences.

Celebrities routinely upload risqué photos on their social media accounts and make provocative posts. But patterning one's style of self-presentation on the stars of social media is misleading because celebrities possess special resources for image management. Social media platforms create elite pathways for celebrity online damage control and audience surveillance. For example, Facebook gives the famous their own unique tools to track online commentary and then place their own well-timed ripostes on individual message boards.[38] Other services allow celebrities to share their images through channels unavailable to the average user and thereby preserve their ability to use copyright law to block unauthorized appropriations.[39] For the right price, reputation management firms will bombard the Internet with positive posts and profiles to push a celebrity peccadillo onto the second page of Google's search results.[40]

The famous also possess human capital in the form of publicity professionals who calculate optimal amounts of revelation and respond quickly to manage the media when the public's reception to a disclosure takes a negative turn.[41] When Ashton Kutcher sent out an ill-advised tweet criticizing the firing of Penn State football coach Joe Paterno for his role in a sexual molestation scandal involving an assistant coach, Kutcher quickly turned over management of his Twitter account to a public relations firm. The damage control seems to have worked: Kutcher remains one of the most popular celebrities on Twitter, with over 17 million followers.[42] It also helps that today's media institutions are starved for celebrity content, readily opening up their doors for celebrities seeking to spin a particular revelation in a new direction. Admittedly, a celebrity's presence in the public eye also heightens attention to any revealed personal failing. Yet in another sense, celebrities have their own "right to be forgotten" as they can use unique visibility resources to repair the damage from tone-deaf revelations and at least partially erase the past.

The rest of us are usually not so lucky because of social media's structural choices. Without celebrity resources for image management and audience tracking, everyday users must present themselves to "superpublics," audiences created by digital architectures that are assumed but not completely known to their speakers.[43] Studies show that users routinely miscalculate the size of their social media audiences. Social media platforms do offer some limited tools for limiting audience size and maintaining privacy. But even technologically savvy individuals can have difficulty navigating these tools, routinely finding themselves broadcasting over a site's default public settings.

Revelations can be repurposed by their recipients—sometimes in an effort to gain more followers themselves, sometimes in an effort to seek revenge against a past lover. There are many examples. Noe Iniguez posted a topless photo of his ex-girlfriend on her employer's Facebook page, along with messages calling her a "slut" and a "drunk" and encouraging her firing.[44] Marianna Taschinger discovered that an ex-boyfriend submitted a nude photograph of her from when she was eighteen years old to a so-called revenge porn site, along with her home address. Concerned with what unidentified online viewers might do with this information, Taschinger told a reporter, "I don't want to go out alone, because I don't know what might happen."[45] In some other highly publicized cases, pressure on teenage girls to share sexual images to curry favor with a partner or peer group led to suicide once those images were disseminated before a larger audience.[46]

Businesses routinely rely on social media and the reactions of superpublics to make employment decisions. Take, for example, the case of Lindsey Stone, a thirty-two-year-old Massachusetts woman who visited Arlington National Cemetery. While standing next to a sign that asks for "Silence and Respect," she pretended to scream and extend her middle finger while a friend snapped a picture and posted it to Facebook. Stone and her friend had a running joke about disobeying signs, but the larger public did not know this context, pouncing when the picture came to light. A "Fire Lindsey Stone" Facebook page appeared that quickly had its desired effect: Stone lost her job at a program for developmentally disabled adults, then suffered through bouts of posttraumatic stress disorder and depression.[47] In a similar episode, shortly after a horrific church shooting in Charleston, South Carolina, East Texas firefighter Kurtis Cook was fired after posting on a Facebook thread: "This person ought to be praised for his good deed." Cook claimed he was making a reference to someone earlier in the thread who had donated money to the shooting victims, not praising the shooter.[48]

Less sensationally, but perhaps more systemic and widespread, social media companies and their marketing partners use our attempts to engineer greater visibility for their own alternative purposes. Our posts provide content that attracts new users, personal data that can be monetized through targeted advertising, and photos that can be used in corporate advertising campaigns and faceprint databases.[49] The information we discharge when we communicate on Twitter and Instagram can be picked apart by sentiment analysts and used to determine moments of emotional susceptibility. Records of Facebook likes offer a better blueprint of our personality type than any market research, particularly as the number of likes in the sample size increases.[50] Businesses purchase and use this information to determine creditworthiness. According to the chief executive of one of the nation's largest credit rating companies, "If you look at how many times a person says 'wasted' in their [Facebook] profile, it has some value in predicting whether they're going to repay their debt."[51] One might argue that social media users are acting as "venture consumers," willingly accepting these appropriations of their online performances in exchange for the possibility of online attention. Public opinion surveys reveal widespread disapproval of this kind of corporate surveillance, however.[52] In addition to the influence of celebrity example, it seems likely that online self-revelation is propelled, at least in part, by a combination of impenetrable privacy settings and cognitive biases that weigh the potential for short-term rewards more heavily than long-term privacy consequences.

At the same time that the structure of social media permits these reappropriations, it blocks attempts to distance oneself from regrettable disclosures. Goffman's view of social life was one where we try on many different social masks in our dealings with others, a world where experimentation and contextual appropriateness are privileged over consistency. He noted how self-presentation at a cocktail party fluctuates depending on which of several conversational subgroups a participant finds herself in at any particular moment.[53] Yet the modern system for online self-presentation discourages this kind of performative fluidity. Onerous terms of service make efforts to reclaim regrettable posts difficult, if not impossible. Audience quantification measures discourage the maintenance of multiple profiles lest the popularity of one profile siphon support from another. According to Mark Zuckerberg, "Having two identities for yourself is an example of a lack of integrity."[54] In keeping with Zuckerberg's views, Facebook actively prevents users from maintaining multiple accounts.[55]

This stands in contrast to the Internet's earlier days when online participants could afford to strike more playful notes in their communications with others and to try on different personas without worrying about inconsistency. Sherry Turkle's study of mid-1990s real-time multiplayer computer games showed college students simultaneously adopting different personalities through different characters of their own creation in multiple games.[56] In a more recent example, the virtual world *Second Life* encouraged the creation of fantastical avatars bearing little relationship to the user's actual corporal body. Lindholm celebrates these virtual environments as ones where multiple selves can be made, where "an imaginary identity can be tried on and then shed like a set of clothes."[57] But as interest in Twitter and Instagram surged, corporate advertisers fled *Second Life*, concerned that there were too many discarded avatars on the site for them to engage in successful targeted marketing.[58] Meanwhile, new gaming apps pressure users to log in to their social media accounts, tying their virtual avatars to their real-life personas (and attached commercial profiles). The online identity experimentation of the past has been replaced by the more permanent self-branding of the present.

The problem is not so much with celebrities or digital communication per se, but with a system that goads users into personal disclosures, then strips them of control over those disclosures after they take place. People have been trying out modes of self-presentation based on celebrity models for decades, but when we do this in the current online environment, it is like putting our hands in wet cement. Soon the medium hardens, fastening our choices into place. In the past, we may have modeled ourselves on many and felt free to abandon these choices when the fit just didn't seem right. But now we are increasingly locked into our initial forays at self-construction. The consequences of the false starts and wrong turns that are a natural part of identity formation are greater than in prior eras and destined to become a part of our permanent record.

The Price of Fame

Modern fame's data-driven character has other social consequences. There are good things about the trend toward greater quantification of audience engagement. Social media users take solace in the tangible evidence that their communications are finding followers, potentially reducing feelings of loneliness or disconnection. Knowing audience numbers helps activists tailor their messages in ways that can galvanize supporters. But the numerification of social influence should also be investigated for what it is pushing aside.

In his book *The Daily You*, Joseph Turow reveals quantification's destabilizing consequences for journalism, consequences that have impoverished public discourse as they have strengthened advertising effectiveness. For a long while, measurement of advertising's success in newspapers and magazines was woefully imprecise. As a result, marketers had to place their faith in editors, giving journalistic entities a certain amount of freedom to write stories they themselves thought were important, not ones that had been subjected to online focus groups. The quantification opportunities afforded by digital advertising changed the equation. Being able to measure the value of the banner ads attached to journalistic content through metrics like click rates wildly depressed the prices newspapers could charge for advertising. Thanks to online tracking, marketers could finally piece together which stories attracted attention and which did not. Building a more efficient and precise advertising regime may have benefited advertisers, but it has cost journalists dearly. Traditional journalistic entities were forced to consolidate, with those left standing increasingly trading expensive investigative reporting for the celebrity stories peddled by publicists.[59]

Technology writer Evgeny Morozov notes the disruptive effects of audience quantification in a variety of domains, not only journalism. Digital tabulations seem democratic in that they offer a mechanism for wresting editorial control from media mandarins, but the supposed efficiencies these calculations created have displaced the civic, noncommercial purposes that once influenced media gatekeepers. Audiences may vote with their clicks and keystrokes for more celebrity content, but it is not good to turn everything into an online popularity contest. For Morozov, we are in danger of becoming a nation of sheep, counting numbers on Yelp to decide where to eat, on Amazon to decide what to read, and on Facebook to decide who to friend.[60] This is not to say that the costs of quantification always outweigh their benefits. Yelp offers information for consumer choice where little to no information existed before. Even as Amazon's predictive technologies might displace more serendipitous discoveries, they also make it much easier to unearth relevant resources and find reading materials matching personal tastes. But numerification can also transform environments in unpredictable ways, and in the social media context, that transformation needs to be examined instead of assuming that greater datafication is always an unmitigated blessing.

By quantifying the value of online relationships, social media makes possible a marketplace where once uncommodifiable social bonds can now be reduced to exchange value. "Buzz marketers" recruit individuals—sometimes through outright payments, sometimes through free samples—to proselytize for particular products in their social networks. Thanks to the surveillance measures built into social media, our relationships with others have become increasingly transparent and, hence, susceptible to outside evaluation. Advertisers do not have to take our word for it; the worth of our social contacts is now on view. Twitter, for example, tells marketers they can target the right influencers with the data it pulls from the bios and social graphs of its users. Instagram's Popular Pays app lets users post about brands in return for giveaways or cash, but screens out those with fewer than five thousand followers. Facebook's social graphing features allow businesses to profile potential influencers, weeding out the connected from the unconnected, before approaching them.[61]

As a result, businesses now make online word-of-mouth marketing a priority. Corporate expenditures on word-of-mouth marketing, defined as "a marketing method that relies on casual social interactions to promote a product," rocketed from $300 million in 2003 to $1.5 billion in 2013.[62] More than 85 percent of the top marketing firms deploy some form of word-of-mouth marketing, and 70 percent of corporate marketing professionals polled in a 2014 survey expected to increase their spending on social media marketing.[63] It is not hard to see why buzz marketing is appealing to advertisers. Instead of relying on traditional, discernable modes of persuasion that might trigger consumer suspicions (e.g., a radio jingle or newspaper ad), they can generate word-of-mouth sales pitches unlikely to be treated with the same skepticism. Word-of-mouth marketing campaigns have been around for long while, but social media makes it possible to design such campaigns on a simultaneously massive and more personal scale.

Buzz marketing relies not only on technological change but celebrity example. The foot soldiers in buzz marketing campaigns are motivated by both tangible rewards and the ability to act like the famous. Often the quid pro quo for a sponsored Instagram post is no more than a parking space or free cup of coffee.[64] But endorsing something to others, even within a relatively narrow social network, also rewards chosen influencers by letting them emulate celebrity behavior. Communications scholar Michael Serazio quotes the head of IZEA as saying that those chosen to monetize their social media outbursts are driven by "a sense of celebrity."[65] Similarly, online reviewers vie for markers demonstrating their own high visibility, competing for entry into Amazon's reviewer "Hall of Fame" or Yelp's "Elite Squad." The criteria for induction into these societies are kept purposely opaque, but in a way that encourages prospective recruits to view them as badges of celebrity.[66] IZEA warns those who want to get paid for their tweets that "celebrity status is granted at the discretion of IZEA," enticing prospective influencers to cultivate online audiences in a way that will let them join the famous personalities they see online.[67]

By providing a way to seek a return on investment from our friendships that did not exist before, buzz marketing turns a traditionally noncommercial sphere of activity into a commercial one. In her analysis of digital privacy, Helen Nissenbaum assesses the costs of technological disruption by looking at the social expectations embedded in different milieus.[68] In the context of our personal relationships, existing norms suggest a bias against commercial advocacy. Personal relationships may have structured business transactions in an earlier, more localized age, but in modern life, friendships and family ties typically provide at least some respite from being sold to. Theorists describe the workplace and the home since the Industrial Revolution as belonging to "two different countries" with clashing views as to "what constitutes acceptable behavior."[69] One axis of difference is the acceptability of commercial persuasion. We expect to be bombarded with product pitches in the marketplace, but as evident in public support for the FTC's Do-Not-Call registry, we are more likely to bristle when advertisers want to enter more personal territories.

This is not to say that the boundaries between work and home are impermeable or that personal relationships have never been targets for commercial transactions. Children sell commercial products to their neighbors to raise funds for after-school activities. Organizations like Mary Kay and Amway, where the sales force acts as independent contractors in direct contact with consumers, instruct new recruits to target friends and family.[70] Yet overall, this kind of hard sell in personal space has been the exception rather than the rule. Moreover, whether trafficking in Girl Scout cookies or cosmetics, those who would sell to their friends and neighbors typically need to be somewhat transparent about their motivations. Disclosing economic motives aids school-age sellers who rely on prospective purchasers' desire to support a cause more than the actual qualities of the product being sold. A certain kind of transparency also helps multilevel marketers, particularly when their compensation can be tied to drafting new parties to sell these same items. When it comes to our personal relationships, guards can be generally relaxed and information processed in a less skeptical manner, at least when compared to the commercial blandishments we experience in other arenas.

This may change as buzz marketing causes economic motives to play a greater role in shaping the information exchanged between friends and family. A first concern is deception. For buzz marketing's chosen influencers, disclosing corporate affiliations hamstrings their persuasive potential, creating an awkwardness in conversations that are meant to seem natural. As a result, most of the incentives line up behind a failure of paid influencers to acknowledge their commercial motivations or at least an effort to minimize the use of required disclaimers as much as possible. Such undisclosed sponsorship distorts consumer decision making, compounding the informational asymmetries between advertisers and consumers. Consumers normally consider the source when evaluating the merits of a proposed commercial transaction. We know not to take everything promised by a used car salesperson or a realtor at face value. By contrast, buzz marketing has the potential to camouflage commercial motivation by dressing up Madison Avenue appeals in the guise of organic commentaries from members of our social circle. Advertisers provide chosen influencers with product talking points, but, of course, the scripted nature of this exchange is never revealed.[71] By hiding the true motivations behind commercial speech, buzz marketing threatens to cross the line from persuasive advertising meant to engage our deliberative faculties to manipulative advertising meant to broker buying decisions for the wrong reasons.

At a minimum, buzz marketing should make us more skeptical about our online conversations, potentially jeopardizing the formation of the interpersonal bonds that were social media's raison d'être in the first place. As chronicled by law professor Ellen Goodman in an earlier study of covert marketing practices, communications motivated by undisclosed sponsorship corrupt public discourse, sapping the vitality of discursive spaces meant to be separate from the market and central to democratic debate. Buzz marketers are paid to promote not just products for manufacturers but news stories for publishers wishing to build online traffic.[72] Over time, people will become more alert to the presence of buzz marketing. But this is not necessarily a good thing. As Goodman writes, "*Caveat auditor* helps to inoculate against deception, but too much *caveat auditor* degrades a communications environment in which participants are unnecessarily disbelieving."[73]

Not everything about buzz marketing is bad. Buzz marketing appears more democratic than other modes of commercial persuasion. It alters the tradi-

tional top-down relationship between advertiser and consumer, allowing us
to discuss consumptive experiences with our friends rather than being told
what to buy by faceless corporations. Even if the financial rewards for chosen
influencers tend to be extremely small, there is still some value for individuals who can leverage their online contacts for financial gain, a sort of micro-
finance based on advertising to one's social circle that was not possible before
the quantification of online relationships. But these gains need to be weighed
against buzz marketing's sometimes deceptive premises, its potential to breed
skepticism in our personal relationships, and the informational advantages it
provides advertisers.

Regulatory authorities have made some attempts to police buzz marketing.
FTC rules require endorsers to acknowledge compensation they receive in return for favorable online commentary, so in theory, buzz marketing's paid influencers must reveal their corporate allegiances before buttering up potential
prospects. Indeed, most advertising agencies officially ask their hired influencers to disclose the sponsored nature of their posts, and the FTC has brought
a handful of buzz marketing enforcement actions, including one against an
agency that instructed its employees to post favorable commentary for a client
on their personal social media accounts without revealing their employment
status.[74] Nevertheless, buzz marketing's influencers are largely free to engage
in persuasive strategies as they see fit. Resources do not exist to monitor even
a small fraction of the conversations on Facebook or posts on Instagram that
could potentially be labeled buzz marketing. A significant cost of measuring
and monetizing our online visibility in the same manner as celebrities is the
formation of this rogue marketplace where the line between genuine sociability
and economic predation is hard to detect.

Celebrity, Property, and Status

What can judges and legislators do about the relentless commercial narratives
pouring out of Camp Kardashian, the digital carpetbombing conducted by
LeBron James, and the brand shoutouts transmitted by Justin Bieber? In general, legal theorists have eschewed the study of celebrity, sometimes viewing it
as a distasteful phenomenon, and one far removed from the heady concerns of
legal argument. Celebrity advertising might seem just like the air we breathe,

an unchangeable part of the cultural ether. Legal regulation may seem even more irrelevant when it comes to the self-branding mind-set produced by these commercial narratives, one that causes citizens to cultivate their own social media audiences through a stream of increasingly intimate disclosures.

Law does have an important role to play here, however. It can either further or restrict particular social comparisons. Desire for power and prestige is part of the human condition, making social comparison a natural part of existence. But if status races are unavoidable, the particular subjects of those status races are not. Thanks in part to modern celebrity advertising and its digital partners, there is a new emphasis in today's culture on status through visibility. The rest of this chapter describes how an intellectual property right—the right of publicity—amplifies the importance of visibility as a badge of social difference. The right of publicity is not responsible for today's celebrity culture or even buzz marketing. But it does reinforce visibility's value, and this valuation is difficult to justify on grounds of legal logic. Given the harms described in the previous section, legal actors should consider whether they want law to encourage our quest for online attention or instead channel our natural tendency toward status seeking into other avenues.

Propertizing Visibility

The right of publicity is defined as "an individual's right to the exclusive commercial use of his or her name and likeness."[75] By providing those with commercially valuable personalities the ability to block unauthorized use of their personas, the right reinforces the economic and social value of visibility. If someone uses Taylor Swift's name without her agreement to help sell a product, Swift can use her right of publicity to halt such use and seek damages. Unlike a trademark infringement claim for unauthorized use of a business's trademark, the right of publicity does not require onlookers to be confused by the defendant's use. Instead, merely employing some aspect of a celebrity persona without permission and in a commercial fashion is enough to trigger liability under the right of publicity. First recognized in a decision of a federal court of appeals in 1953 that gave baseball players the ability to prevent unauthorized use of their images on trading cards,[76] the right has become a potent tool in the arsenal of the famous. By assigning a property right to audience attention, the law helps celebrities monetize their visibility, encouraging revelations meant to build fan followings.

Since 1953, almost every state considering the issue has elected to recognize the right, whether through legislative enactment or common law judging.

Courts and legislators were initially reluctant to confer legal rights on the basis of visibility. Before 1953, celebrity litigants wishing to block unauthorized commercial use of their personas had to allege violations of the right of privacy originally articulated by Warren and Brandeis in 1890. For most celebrity plaintiffs, however, their efforts to halt such uses fit awkwardly into the standard account of the right of privacy. As articulated by Warren and Brandeis, the privacy right was designed to protect dignitary interests, not economic ones. As a result, remedies in privacy cases necessitated a showing of emotional distress. But rather than being emotionally harmed by having their image thrust before the public, celebrities actually labored for just that result, as evidenced by their public performances. As a result, courts in the first half of the twentieth century held celebrities' visibility against them. Denying relief, judges reasoned that well-known plaintiffs needed and wanted the public to be aware of their personas; hence, they could not be emotionally harmed by unauthorized use of their images.[77] Celebrity plaintiffs were directed to trademark law, which prevents confusing uses not just of words but also "symbols." But this route was unsatisfactory for some because trademark law offered no remedy for unauthorized but nonconfusing use of a celebrity's name or likeness.[78]

Even when the right of publicity was established, giving celebrities the ability to block even nonconfusing use of their images, courts limited the right in various ways, thereby lessening the potential financial rewards of visibility. Before the 1980s, celebrity visibility appeared too abstract and too dependent on shifting cultural tastes to warrant protection as a type of property. Just a few years after giving birth to the right in 1953, the same court determined that band leader Glenn Miller's publicity rights, when sold by his widow to a movie studio, did not represent "property."[79] Another court explained that the right was legally inferior to personal property, instead being more like "titles," "offices," "trust," and "friendship," "attribute[s] from which others may benefit but may not own."[80] In this period, judges often described the right of publicity and the personal right of privacy in the same breath. Privacy rights were not recognized as property. Rather, they were dignitary rights that resided with the individual and could not be exchanged with others. Just as the right to privacy was not meant to last after death and was not considered property, neither was the right of publicity. This was evident in judicial refusals to recognize post-mortem publicity rights. The right to bequeath one's property at death has been described by the U.S. Supreme Court as "one of the most essential sticks" in the bundle of property rights.[81] Yet courts in the two most influential jurisdictions for celebrity rights, New York and California, both concluded that the right of publicity died with the celebrity.[82]

Courts also limited the early right of publicity to unauthorized appropriations of name or likeness. They considered other aspects of the celebrity persona, even if extremely visible and well known to fans, beyond the right's scope. Thus, when Nancy Sinatra sued Goodyear Tire for airing radio and television commercials featuring a singer hired to imitate her own singing style, a federal court of appeals rejected her claim, suggesting that Sinatra's voice was not distinctive enough to deserve protection.[83] In a similar case involving actress Shirley Booth, the court expressed concern with recognizing publicity claims against mere imitators given "persuasive reasons of public policy."[84] In drafting right-of-publicity statutes, legislators strictly limited the law's reach to appropriations of a celebrity's name or likeness, and sometimes her actual voice, but not a vocal imitation.

Courts changed their views toward the end of the twentieth century. No longer were the "personal" right of privacy and the right of publicity mentioned in the same breath. Instead, as one court explained, there was a clear "distinction between the personal right to be left alone and the business right to control use of one's identity in commerce."[85] This "business right" was now referred to as a "property" right, signaling greater control for artists and athletes over their public personas. Affirming the right of the estate of Elvis Presley to control use of his persona, the Tennessee Court of Appeals labeled the right a "species of intangible personal property."[86] Similarly, the estate of the actor who played Spanky in the *Little Rascals* films was allowed to proceed with its right-of-publicity suit because the court deemed the right to be a property right and, hence, descendible under New Jersey law.[87] State legislatures followed the same propertization path, enacting laws in the 1980s and 1990s that explicitly marked the right of publicity as a "property right."[88]

"Property" is not merely a legal label. Characterizing something as "property" can trigger analogies to rights in land and personal property, which courts are hesitant to balance against competing concerns. For example, First

Amendment doctrine considers restraints on speech more justifiable when speakers attempt to use someone else's property to express themselves.[89] Concomitant with the property designation is the expectation that the property's owner can dispose of it as she sees fit. Some limits on the alienability of property do exist, but in general, legal theorists tend to assume that these limits are the exceptions rather than the rule.[90] As a result, the decision to deem the right of publicity a property right led to determinations that it should be freely transferable to others, even after death. As one state court explained in its decision to recognize postmortem publicity rights, because the right of publicity was "property," its holders possessed "the unrestricted right of disposition."[91]

Once visibility came to be conceptualized as a property right, judges came to view all aspects of the visible persona as protectable. They chose to make voice, like name or likeness, part of the celebrity property right, even if the secondary use was only a close imitation. In 1988, the same court that had ruled against Nancy Sinatra found that Bette Midler had a viable right-of-publicity claim against Ford Motors for using an imitation of her voice. The court explained that "to impersonate her voice is to pirate her identity."[92] Four years later, the same court affirmed a jury award of over $2 million for Frito-Lay's impersonation of singer Tom Waits's voice in a commercial. "A well-known singer with a distinctive voice has a property right in that voice," the court stated.[93] A related line of cases held that using actors bearing a striking resemblance to a celebrity in commercial activities violated the right of publicity, precedents that helped Kim Kardashian extract her hefty settlement from Old Navy. Courts have even recognized claims based on the use of objects associated with a famous person as when game show hostess Vanna White successfully sued Samsung Electronics for an advertisement featuring a robot dressed in a blond wig, gown, and jewelry standing next to a letter board resembling the one used on *Wheel of Fortune*.[94] Another case found that depicting a baseball pitcher's distinctive throwing stance in an advertisement could be the basis of a publicity rights lawsuit.[95]

These legal innovations made celebrity visibility much more valuable. Enlarging the scope of the right past mere name and likeness allowed celebrities to more effectively internalize the benefits of their fame, shutting down a greater array of unauthorized commercial references to their persona. Likewise, making the right descendible greatly strengthened the economic power of celebrities trying to trade on their fame. If celebrity can become monetized only within a famous person's life span, this diminishes the value of visibility. Under the old right-of-publicity framework, merchandisers and licensees could never be sure when their exclusive rights would run out (i.e., when the celebrity at issue would die). When courts and legislators changed their position and concluded that the right of publicity should be descendible, they turned visibility into an asset that could be managed for more than just short-term gain. This allowed a secondary industry of celebrity licensing companies to develop. These companies transacted with famous personalities so that they could manage a broad portfolio of valuable identities, diversifying their risk and strengthening the overall value of their visible assets. The celebrity rights management industry quickly became a political force as well, translating its nascent economic clout into sophisticated lobbying campaigns. These campaigns produced even more favorable changes in the contours of the right of publicity. Across the nation, new laws like California's Astaire Image Protection Act and Texas's Buddy Holly Bill lengthened the terms for postmortem protection to fifty, seventy or even one hundred years past the celebrity's lifetime and retroactively applied the right to celebrities who had passed away decades before.[96]

The right has developed in such a way that the monetization of one's identity is not only expected but demanded of publicity rights holders. Because the law views well-known personalities as alienable commodities, it is possible for a person who never chose to use his visage for advertising purposes to suddenly have a personalized ad campaign forced on him when property rights must be split in divorce or assigned in a bankruptcy to creditors.[97] Some celebrities still resist the call to lend their personas to marketing campaigns. Yet even the rare celebrity who elects not to commercialize her identity may have her publicity rights assessed at a high value at death, triggering tax consequences for her heirs that necessitate the licensing of her persona for advertising.[98] Trusts and estates scholar Ray Madoff describes the law's assumption of commercial motivation built into the right of publicity jurisprudence aptly, saying the "system . . . is incapable of recognizing the validity of the decision to not treat celebrity status as a commodity."[99] In this way, the right represents another force that encourages the commercialization of once noncommercialized arenas. One can see a parallel between the buzz marketing campaigns that turn once noncommercial online relationships into sites for commercial transactions and the right of publicity's commoditization of what might have been intentionally un-commodified personal attributes.

One cannot lay all the blame for today's environment of pervasive celebrity endorsement, or the parallel techniques of micro-celebrity practiced by non-celebrity consumers, on the right of publicity. Technological and social change play the starring role. But the right of publicity is an important supporting actor. The right's metamorphosis into a muscular property right has created a vibrant marketplace for commercialized celebrity images, heightening visibility's value. Judges and legislators interpret the right to spur the commercialization and the circulation of famous personas in advertising. The next question is why this is so.

"A Right in Search of a Coherent Rationale"

If you ask legal academics, nobody cares much for this particular property right. They complain that the right of publicity just doesn't make sense when considered in light of the main theoretical justifications animating property rights in general and intellectual property rights in particular. One writer describes the right of publicity as "a right in search of a coherent rationale."[100]

Judges and legislators, however, contend that the right of publicity simply represents a rational tool of intellectual property protection, just like patents, copyrights, or trademarks. Perhaps the most common argument for publicity rights is that they incentivize the creation of captivating celebrity personas. As one federal court of appeals explained, "The reason that state law protects individual pecuniary interests [through the right of publicity] is to provide an incentive to performers to invest the time and resources required to develop such performances."[101]

But it seems unlikely that actors and athletes would select different career paths if told that others might make unauthorized use of their visibility. Some are born with all of the tools in place for celebrity and do not need to be incentivized to change their behavior. It was serendipity more than anything else that brought Jim Thorpe and his athleticism to the attention of football coach Pop Warner and eventually led to Thorpe's national renown. Similarly, a talent scout happened to discover Natalie Portman in a Long Island pizza parlor. Individuals are often motivated to become celebrities for nonmonetary reasons. Many seek fame out of competitive zeal or a desire to leave a lasting historical memory. For those motivated by money, even without enjoying the remunerative potential of commercial endorsements, celebrities receive generous financial incentives in other forms, including performance fees.[102] Given these alternative incentives, motivations, and paths for superstardom, publicity rights are probably not needed to encourage the development of entertaining personas.

Others suggest that the right comports with the Lockean view of property rights naturally accruing to the fruits of one's labors. According to Locke, by mixing their labor with external objects, individuals become entitled to assert claims of ownership that give them the freedom to live independent lives. Under this reckoning, celebrities can claim legal title to their visible status because of all the work they put into making themselves visible.[103] But there are problems with this rationale as well. For one thing, many celebrities, particularly in a digital age, are accidental. The routine posting of hunky hoodlum Jeremy Meeks's mugshot on the Stockton, California, police department's Facebook page suddenly catapulted the previously unknown Meeks to international attention, winning him agency representation and a modeling contract.[104] Lockean labor theory would suggest that Meeks should have no legal claim to the rewards of his new-found fame. The theory awards property rights on the basis of purposeful effort, not an inadvertent stumbling into the media spotlight. Moreover, a host of other individuals, such as directors, producers, writers, and publicists, are responsible for the celebrity images we see on our television screens and smartphones. Awarding publicity rights in an on-screen personality to a single person ignores the productive labor of all these other parties.[105]

Finally, some would justify the right as preventing consumer confusion. One can see how an advertisement falsely implying celebrity endorsement would sow confusion in prospective purchasers. But if consumer confusion is the main concern with unauthorized use of celebrity images, trademark law arguably already does an adequate job of policing such behavior. In fact, celebrities routinely use this branch of intellectual property to protect their personal brands, often submitting right-of-publicity claims simultaneously with claims for trademark infringement.[106] Unlike trademark protection, the right of publicity lets celebrities police nonconfusing use of their personas, but it is not clear why this added protection is necessary. In sum, the right of publicity cannot be justified as a means for incentivizing creative activity, a natural right to the fruits of one's labors, or a tool for consumer protection. One must look not to legal logic but to changing definitions and perceptions of celebrity to explain the right's relatively recent embrace by lawmakers.

Making Celebrity Politically Palatable

Judges and other elites once castigated celebrity publicists as "flimflam" men and "ballyhoo" artists.[107] Supreme Court Justice Felix Frankfurter described these publicists as "professional poisoners of the public mind" who exploit "foolishness and fanaticism and self-interest."[108] Unlike other elites that judges could identify with, publicists seemed reliant on subterfuge and lacked a method of licensure or ethical code to guide their profession. Legal commentators placed quotation marks around the word *professional* when describing public relations analysts.[109] The most famous celebrity publicists of the day were known more for their stunts—like the dramatic staging of screen idol Rudolph Valentino's funeral—than any sort of specialized knowledge or training.

But just as an alliance with psychologists helped professionalize the advertising industry in the early 1900s, joining forces with social scientists helped spruce up the image of celebrity publicists. Psychologists and anthropologists began using their disciplinary insights to create models for evaluating the effectiveness of celebrity endorsements. This made celebrity management appear more systematized and rationalized, winning over legal elites. Welcomed into court, the heads of celebrity licensing agencies offered expert testimony as to the commercial value of particular famous personalities.[110] The courts' increasingly warm reception to such evidence reveals not only a greater affinity with the celebrity industry but also a greater willingness to propertize celebrity visibility. Rights considered vague are not treated as fully alienable and inheritable under the law. But as celebrity marketability became susceptible to more meaningful measurement in the 1970s and 1980s, it also became easier to accept its legal protection.

Legal and political elites now adopt the techniques of celebrity visibility themselves, abandoning an earlier disdain for celebrity culture and the public spotlight. In the past decade, the visibility of Supreme Court justices has increased dramatically, their growing number of public appearances chronicled by the media and their images sometimes packaged for commercial gain.[111] Online legal "halls of fame" and law-themed gossip blogs award judges and lawyers celebrity status. Many television shows revolve around celebrity legal troubles, and cable news invests heavily in legal questions, simultaneously turning the parties and their attorneys into media sensations. Meanwhile, legislators increasingly adopt the same publicity strategies as famous actors and athletes, paying greater attention to the construction of images and personal narratives and relying on social media to reach voters. Rather than preempting visibility status races, today's legal actors are full participants in them. Individuals who invest effort in a particular metric to improve their status typically believe themselves to be engaging in activities that are of unquestionable merit.[112] Hence, backers of the right of publicity simply assume that visibility should be an important marker of status and afforded according legal protection.

Meanwhile, a new, broader view of celebrity has taken hold and made special legal protections for celebrities politically palatable. Until the last part of the twentieth century, fame remained tied to some form of greatness in the popular imagination. In his description of early accounts of Hollywood celebrities, sociologist Joshua Gamson writes that the greatness necessary for stardom involved "virtue, genius, character, or skill that did not depend on audience recognition."[113] In other words, the greatness linked to fame relied on special qualities inherent in the celebrity herself. Film stars from this era were described as "royalty." Even as Hollywood began to present more inclusive descriptions of celebrity in the 1950s and 1960s, there was still a sense that the talent necessary for celebrity was innate. One could not plan or strategize fame. Instead, "Fame, based on an indefinable internal quality of the self, was natural, almost predestined."[114]

Lawmakers acted in the context of this restrictive view of what it meant to be famous. Not everyone could be great, not everyone had equal access to the spotlight, and this caused reluctance in awarding special legal protections to celebrities. Occasionally judicial concern over the antidemocratic implications of celebrity rights rose to the surface. In a case involving postmortem protection for the persona of Elvis Presley, a federal appeals court articulated several reasons for why the right of publicity should not survive a famous individual. Most troubling for the court was the thought of the rewards of celebrity visibility being passed on from generation to generation. It explained that in the past, "the law has always thought that leaving a good name to one's children is sufficient reward in itself for the individual."[115] Placing the economic rewards of fame "in the hands of heirs," the court maintained, "is contrary to our legal tradition and somehow seems contrary to the moral presuppositions of our culture."[116] Similarly, in a 1979 case involving the descendability of the publicity rights of famed horror movie actor Bela Lugosi, the California Supreme Court rejected a legal regime where a celebrity's heirs "are the only ones who should have the opportunity to exploit their ancestor's personality."[117] In this earlier time, legal protection for the rewards of visibility, separate from any underlying achievement, struck judges as inequitable.

By the 1980s, however, the understanding of fame as dependent on achievement had changed. Although narratives discussing a celebrity's destiny or inner talents still existed, greatness in large part was no longer a prerequisite for celebrity. Examples of famous artists and athletes who had actually achieved little in their particular fields began to multiply. Madonna, the quintessential 1980s celebrity, became known for self-promotion, not her talents as a singer or actor. As media outlets proliferated, particularly with the introduction of cable television, more and more celebrities were needed, generating high visibility for individuals with little claim to fame. Even the increasing use of the word *celebrity* reveals the heightened importance of visibility. Before, the term *star* had been favored. *Star* suggests a connection to the individual's profession, whether as an actor, an athlete, or something else. *Celebrity* represents the popularized version of the individual regardless of her professional standing.[118] With celebrity no longer tethered to narratives of inner greatness and outside accomplishment, there was a sense that anyone, not just the talented, could become a celebrity.

More recent celebrity narratives reinforce this modern divorce of fame from talent. As Graeme Turner notes in discussing reality television, "Public visibility per se is offered as an achievement to emulate and desire; little wonder that it is pursued with such tenacity and at some personal risk by a large number of people."[119] Contests for the spotlight now include not just a select few but almost everyone as the tools of social media offer celebrity potential to all. We all have access to Facebook, Twitter, and Instagram. Contrast this to a pre-Web celebrity culture that relied on highly restricted communications vehicles such as films, radio, magazine interviews, and talk show appearances that everyday fans had little hope of commandeering themselves. The very idea of celebrity has mutated from a rarified, innate condition to one that almost seems to be a reasonable expectation for everyday citizens. Public opinion surveys demonstrate a dramatic increase in the number of people who think that they themselves will someday be famous. Not everyone can be great, but everyone has a chance to be a celebrity.[120]

Perhaps as a consequence of this changing view of celebrity, judicial decisions now presume visibility's value rather than forcing plaintiffs to prove that value. Instead of requiring a plaintiff to demonstrate previous commercial exploitation of her identity, most courts have switched to a presumption that sufficient economic value in the identity exists if it has been commercially exploited by the defendant.[121] One court deemed the visibility of noncelebrity individuals to their Facebook friends as sufficiently important such that the individuals could sue Facebook under California's right-of-publicity law for sharing their "likes" without their permission. The court even characterized Facebook users as "celebrities within their own Facebook social networks."[122] Another court embraced the same logic, finding that all names have "concrete value in the marketplace" when "those names are used to endorse or advertise a product to the individuals' friends and contacts."[123] Of course, part of the reason these names have "concrete value" is because the legal system chooses to recognize that value. This is a change from how the right was conceptualized in the past, when noncelebrities, rather than being awarded a property right in their personas, would have been routed to the privacy protections first articulated by Brandeis and Warren over a century ago. As one litigator comments, "Before the social media invasion, it is unlikely that any of us who practice in this area of law would have conceived of a case wherein the plaintiffs are average citizens trying to prevent others from commercially exploiting their identities."[124]

The decision to treat visibility as property is a mistake. Even if lawmakers have accepted a democratized view of fame and social media platforms make it technologically feasible to use images of ordinary persons for targeted advertising campaigns, there still needs to be a compelling reason for using the law to protect a person's personal audience share. Again, as a matter of legal logic, there is no convincing justification for a property right in personal visibility. False advertising and trademark law already protect against uses of personal images likely to confuse consumers. The right of publicity's defenders maintain that the right is needed to encourage individuals to pour their energies into attracting an audience. But there is no evidence that visibility for visibility's sake is an area where status-seeking efforts should be focused. Instead, individuals practicing the techniques of micro-celebrity, seeking to attract and manage their own online audiences through a steady stream of intimate disclosures, are playing into the hands of social media companies and their associated advertisers. These entities have created a commercial proving ground where they set the terms and conditions, yet, thanks to celebrity example, consumers are happy to enter. Efforts to mimic the celebrities operating in this space simultaneously commercialize discourse and make the commercial motivations behind that discourse less transparent. "See me!" we tell our quantified audiences, driving changes that corrode social trust and encourage deception.

Stopping Adcreep

AT A TIME when a panoply of new marketing techniques is changing human behavior and eroding consumer agency, the legal system has stood still. I have argued in previous chapters that a large part of the problem is the sheer ubiquity of commercial appeals in modern culture. By taking over domains that were once ad free, advertising's influence has swelled. When one domain becomes colonized by marketers, the colonization of other domains becomes more likely. Adcreep manifests not only in the intrusion of advertising into new physical spaces. It also manifests in the surveillance of once-private activities, the exposure of once-internal thoughts, and the commodification of once-uncommodified aspects of human identity and social relations.

All of these trends are related, the sum of them greater than their individual parts. Acting in combination, the techniques of the new advertising make consumer resistance more difficult. At the same time that targeted advertising relies on hidden informational asymmetries, businesses catch consumers unawares by entering previously commercially resistant spaces. Neuromarketing prioritizes biological snapshots over consumers' conscious responses, while online surveillance and social networking facilitate the unwitting production of "data exhaust" to be mined for marketing gold. The simultaneous arrival of all of these techniques, somewhat paradoxically, makes advertising less objectionable. Advertising's growing presence numbs onlookers to commercial persuasion, immobilizing mental defenses. It also facilitates the internalization of advertising's precepts. My objection is not so much to the actual content of these precepts—building the self through consumption, focusing on the individual over the collective—as the crowding out of alternative discussions. The danger is that these new selling techniques, and their concomitant philosophy of human flourishing, will become ingrained, normalized to the point of invisibility, and the power to change them lost.

There is still time to chart a different course. This chapter offers some tentative prescriptions for change. My goal here is to think creatively about potential legal responses, not to present a complete framework for resolving all of the problems posed by modern marketing. There are no simple solutions to the problems of adcreep. The historical parallels detailed in this book's preceding chapters are relevant because they reveal the possibility of resistance to marketing encroachments, not because they offer perfect analogies to the new sales techniques of today. No exact blueprint exists for determining where commercial freedom ends and consumer protection begins. Deciding when commercial speech can be restricted, when consumers should be allowed to transact away their privacy, and when intellectual property protections for celebrities and advertisers should yield to the expressive appropriations of others is not easy. But the social costs accompanying the new advertising argue for doing more than standing still.

Building a New Consumer Movement

Most of this book has emphasized the culpability of legal actors in allowing advertising's advance. But adcreep is due not just to legal lethargy, but to our own failure to skeptically review transactions in an era of point and click. Instead of protesting, the public acquiesces to new forms of commercial messaging and market research, seemingly accepting their presence as the price to be paid for subsidized public infrastructure, free online content, and celebrity connection. Legal actors take their cue from the public and will not restrain the new advertising on their own initiative. To a large degree, the problem of adcreep requires behavioral changes, a willingness to personally protest new advertising encroachments whether in the form of buzz marketing or advertising in schools.

Some of the new advertising is being contested. Fed up with constant commercial proselytizing and concerned about data privacy, some are moving to new platforms, using anonymous search engines, or taking sabbaticals from social media. Citizens fight back with technological resources like ad-blocking software and antitracking apps. Resistance to targeted advertising also takes the form of bogus online aliases and the use of multiple profiles designed to fool online surveillors. Corporate campaigns inviting user-generated content sometimes become sites for citizen resistance as well. In 2012, when McDonald's paid for the privilege of having the hashtag #McDStories promoted on the Twitter home page, it had to abandon the campaign within two hours. Consumers immediately seized on the Twitter handle to vent their objections about the fast food giant, and even today, the ill-advised hashtag still serves as an online repository for anti-McDonald's tirades.[1]

Such individual acts of contestation are important, but there is also a need for coordinated action. Structural and cognitive barriers make the problem of adcreep too big for individuals to solve on their own. Advertisers, increasingly savvy in their deployment of user-generated content, have learned to co-opt semiotic resistance and use new tools for herding online sentiments into desired forms. The communications marketplace periodically offers alternatives to portals that depend on online tracking. But advertising-dependent giants like Facebook and Google use their immense resources to buy out start-ups that are promising less commercially intrusive experiences.[2] And even if the marketplace did offer a more robust set of private, commercial-free communications tools, human nature makes it hard to resist pushing the buttons that allow us to get to promised digital territories. To a limited degree, our minds can be trained over time to become more aware of advertising. But we also have finite reserves of mental energy and cannot be perpetually vigilant.[3] Exposés of various data breaches, hidden surveillance techniques, and advertiser reappropriations of personal content attract flickers of public attention. But the attention quickly dissipates, rarely translated into tangible, corrective action. For there to be any prospect of real reform, these episodes need to be tied to a larger narrative and resistance channeled into a broader movement.

Framing and Legal Change

Sociologists studying the evolution and efficacy of collective social movements point to framing processes for an explanation. Like the frame around a picture, activists choose a vocabulary to focus the attention of their audiences and convince them of an injustice. The frames negotiated among movement members and with policymakers and even movement adversaries help to organize experiences and guide action.[4] Successful movements can promote conversations that disrupt settled legal understandings. From voting rights to gay marriage to affirmative action, courts react to these conversations, producing new doctrine responsive to public discourse. For example, LGBT rights advocates deployed a frame of inequality to demonstrate the shortcomings of civil unions and domestic partnerships, propelling not just a successful litigation strategy but an essential precursor to that strategy: a change in the public conversation surrounding gay marriage.[5] Framing theory's chief insight is that social movements are shaped not just by political circumstances and material resources, but also by the interpretative package that surrounds a plea for collective action.[6]

Of course, not all efforts at prompting collective action succeed. "Even when oppression is intense or when leaders' tactics open up clear opportunities for action, individuals must be convinced that an injustice has occurred, persuaded that collective action is called for, and motivated to act if a social movement is to occur."[7] The study of social movement framing has focused mostly on descriptions of frames and framing processes instead of investigating their relative strength or causal effects. As a result, at least for those looking to build on this scholarship to develop strategies for reform, social movement framing can be a bit of a black box.

Nevertheless, sociologists agree on at least two framing strategies essential to movement success. First, successful social movements must refute or at least neutralize the opposition's own arguments and symbols. Those protesting the Pinochet regime in Chile used mothers of "disappeared" citizens to rally support for their cause. The mothers proved a particularly potent symbol given the regime's self-depiction as a protector of the family.[8] A study of different frames surrounding women's suffrage shows that a "reform" frame, which linked women's supposedly more nurturing and morally pure nature to specific political reforms, succeeded where other suffragist frames did not. The reform frame openly addressed antisuffragist arguments about gender differences, turning what opponents portrayed as a weakness into a strategic advantage.[9]

Second, successful frames rely on the familiar. Frames are crafted not out of thin air but from existing cultural materials. In Poland, the Solidarity labor movement borrowed heavily from the symbolism of the Catholic Church, venerating slain workers as martyrs and displaying portraits of the Virgin Mary and Pope John Paul II on factory walls. Martin Luther King Jr. used the language of the Bible to convince the public of the need for black equality. Often this reliance on the familiar means creating a frame that invokes memories of past social movements. The "rights" frame that anchored the black civil rights movement was subsequently deployed in collective movements in support of women, Hispanics, and gays. The feminist movement for reproductive freedom used the tagline "a woman's body is her own" to echo previous discourses regarding individual autonomy unrelated to abortion rights.[10] Stopping adcreep requires a similar mobilization of socially resonant frames that can be yoked to legal reforms.

Frames for the Future

From a rational cost-benefit perspective, active participation in a movement to stop adcreep seems not worth the effort. According to one analysis, "the individual benefit of joining in collective action to pass consumer protection legislation is likely to be less than the cost of joining and supporting an interest group."[11] Nevertheless, the historical episodes highlighted throughout this book, which produced the current advertising regulatory structure, reveal once-resonant frames that may again appeal to modern consumers. Over the history of advertising regulation, consumer activists battled with advertisers and their allies over three central issues: they debated the ability of consumers to keep pace in a changing commercial world, the government's competence to police that world, and the impulses that drive marketers to construct that world. Narratives that implicate these interrelated themes—consumer capability, government competence, and advertiser motivation—may provide schemas for changing the conversation about advertising.[12]

The rest of this chapter offers three potential narratives to organize a new wave of consumer activism: complexity, private paternalism, and brand tyranny. Like all other social movement frames, these narratives provide a limited and strategic interpretation of phenomena, not a complete or nuanced description. As one legal scholar wrote forty years ago, "There is no 'whole story' that can be told about anything, especially anything as socially, economically, literarily, anthropologically, philosophically, legally, historically, and politically complex as advertising."[13] Instead, the hope is that these frames can rally citizens to respond to a critical social challenge. They can also suggest avenues for legal intervention.

Complexity

In the mid-2000s, a Harvard law professor began a crusade to reform the consumer credit industry. The industry was a rigged game, she complained, lamenting "a growing number of families who are steered into over-priced credit products, risky subprime mortgages, and misleading insurance plans." The stark consequences of this game were "wiped-out savings, lost homes, higher costs for car insurance, denial of jobs, troubled marriages, bleak retirements, and broken lives." The professor blamed the sheer complexity of these financial vehicles and the finite ability of consumers to understand their functioning: "Consumer capacity—measured both by available time and expertise—has not expanded to meet the demands of a changing credit marketplace. Instead, consumers sign on to credit products with only a vague understanding of the terms." The other problem she identified was advertising that overwhelmed individual buyers into signing on to risky credit vehicles they could not hope to understand. "Aggressive marketing," she prophetically diagnosed, "almost non-existent in the 1970s, compounds the difficulty, shaping consumer demand in unexpected and costly directions."[14]

This argument was one that future U.S. Senator Elizabeth Warren would repeat many times. It eventually bore fruit, leading to the creation of the federal Consumer Financial Protection Bureau (CFPB), although corporate lobbyists and political opponents managed to nix calls for the controversial Warren to head the new agency herself. The CFPB regulates the offering of consumer financial products and services, using its authority to reform mortgage lending rules, prosecute deceptive credit card marketing, investigate the student loan industry, and respond to thousands of direct consumer complaints. The discourse surrounding the creation of the CFPB reveals framing that produced legal change. Warren positioned the issue as one of hopeless complexity that necessitated regulatory intervention. As she put it, "The time has come to put scaremongering to rest and to recognize that regulation can often support and advance efficient and more dynamic markets."[15]

Some heralded the creation of the CFPB as the beginning of a new consumer movement, but that seems to have been premature. In the wake of the subprime mortgage crisis, even policymakers skeptical of advertising regulation became temporarily willing to restrict the sale of consumer financial services. Yet leaving the marketing of financial services aside, the predominant discursive framework surrounding modern advertising remains that of a sovereign consumer that can successfully navigate the marketplace on her own.[16] This view of consumer capacity minimizes the complicated and opaque nature of commercial transactions in today's marketplace. After offering a more realistic vision of consumer capability, this section explores how First Amendment doctrine could be reconceived for an increasingly complex commercial world.

It's Complicated

From a historical perspective, assessments of consumer capabilities fluctuate. Some cultural moments emphasize citizen self-reliance, others the influence of outside forces. Right now, the view seems to be that consumers can handle a lot. The concept of the "venture consumer" has taken hold. This consumer navigates the marketplace with great dexterity, negotiating trade-offs between privacy and desired services with awareness. Complication and obfuscation are reinterpreted as options to accept or reject, a rhetorical move that seems to have sapped the vitality of consumer activists. The narrative of the venture consumer reflects a decades-long trend. Since the late 1970s, advertisers have largely succeeded in depicting ordinary, individual consumers as capable of making their own choices in the marketplace, defining attempts to limit these choices as unnecessary and elitist interventions.[17]

In keeping with this narrative of the venture consumer, the discourses favored by the media and the legal system celebrate consumers' rational capabilities and downplay the complexity of the marketing techniques they face. *Sorrell v. IMS Health* is illustrative. In that case, the Supreme Court struck down Vermont's attempt to limit the use of drug prescription records in detailing, that is, face-to-face marketing between pharmaceutical reps and physicians. The Court described the detailing process as unsophisticated and benign, never mind that the pharmaceutical industry spends more on detailing than any other marketing instrument.[18] The Court ventured that the state should have little role in preventing consumer items (like brand-name pharmaceuticals) from becoming "popular" through detailing or other marketing techniques like "impressive endorsements or catchy jingles."[19] By equating detailing to advertising through obvious endorsements and snappy tunes, the Court belittled detailing's potential cognitive challenges to doctors or, by extension, their patients. In reality, rather than being an unsophisticated process, detailing relies on sophisticated data analysis and hidden informational advantages to influence physician behavior.[20] More generally, the Court's simplistic portrait of modern marketing seems far removed from a world where advertisers can access an array of inputs—from heart rate to facial expression to everything we have ever said on social media— to determine when we are most susceptible to a commercial appeal.

Like the Court, the media tend to minimize power differentials between buyers and sellers. This is not to say that the media celebrate every new marketing technique. The press provides some critical commentary, particularly when it comes to commercial surveillance. Nevertheless, a pro-technology bias shapes coverage of advertising initiatives. For example, the *New York Times*'s technology columnist lauded moves by ad-blocking software companies to allow in "acceptable ads." Google and other businesses pay these software companies; in return, their ads get to bypass ad-blocking software. The columnist explained that these arrangements represented "firms trying to create an ecosystem that provides better ads."[21] That seems like a charitable interpretation at best. "Better ads" may seem less annoying than the flashing click-bait that ad blockers screen from our eyes, but more subtle commercial representations still influence consumer behavior. The columnist failed to acknowledge consumers' need to defend themselves from a never-ending sea of ads targeted to their online activities, not just optically annoying ads. Likewise, the *Wall Street Journal*, reporting on Facebook's agreement to host articles from the *New York Times*, the *Atlantic*, and NBC News on its mobile app, only noted how the arrangement would allow articles to be uploaded faster than the current norm, thereby pleasing impatient smartphone users. The report ignored another consequence: Facebook's mobile app prevents readers from using ad-blocking software.[22] These initiatives designed to neuter the effectiveness of ad-blocking software represent yet another boundary being overrun, a breach in one of the few defenses consumers retain against the increasing complexity of online space. Yet that is not how they are typically described in public discourse.

It is important for the next iteration of the consumer movement to refute the narrative of the freely choosing consumer by highlighting the complexity of today's advertising environment. The movement needs to stress that exercising choice in the modern marketplace is not as simple as the legal establishment and media currently portray it. One source of complexity is contextual variety. Consumers confronting just a few arenas for sales pitches—radio, print, and television—faced a less demanding marketplace than the one taking shape today where any context can serve as a marketing resource. Madison Avenue can rely on much more than "endorsements or catchy jingles" to lure today's customers. Commercial missives come in all sorts of different individualized styles now as a result of targeted advertising and can be found in a host of terrains from gas pumps to social media posts. Behaviors that were once sufficient to deflect entreaties found in television commercials and print ads do not always work in these new advertising spaces.

The situation is even more complicated given the lack of transparency that is intentionally part of many of these new advertising initiatives. For campaigns built around biometric analyses and buzz marketing, invisibility enhances their persuasive capability. Negotiating commercial entreaties becomes much more difficult when the subject of that entreaty does not even realize that a corporate influencer is acting behind the scenes. Surveillance allows for the typical consumer's intersection with ads to seem serendipitous when it really is the product of an electronic stakeout. Data collection also arms sellers with reams of information that the buyer has no evidence of and can only guess at. Relatedly, the massive amounts of information collected on virtually everyone supply businesses with a reference point for what makes any one individual unique. Once seemingly irrelevant information now yields meaningful correlations. When businesses know everything about everyone else, it becomes easier to know a lot about you. This all puts consumers at a tremendous informational disadvantage.

Exposing the complexity of today's advertising environment puts the lie to the theory of the venture consumer. But it will not be enough, by itself, to convince the public of the informational advantages that their commercial interlocutors now possess; a reappraisal of consumer capabilities must be translated into legal reforms. An initial barrier to such reforms is judicial construction of advertisers' First Amendment rights.

Finding a Free Speech-Privacy Balance

In 1975, Ralph Nader's zealous promotion of a cause produced unforeseen, antiprogressive consequences. (It would not be the last time.) As head of the consumer group Public Citizen, Nader challenged a Virginia state law that stopped pharmacies from advertising the price of drugs. Nader thought consumers should be able to get a better deal by comparing prices. His line of argument was that shoppers' First Amendment freedoms were being violated by the state's limitation on the pharmacies' commercial speech. Nader won the case, receiving vindication at the hands of the Supreme Court, but he also opened up a Pandora's box.

Nader's legal strategy was to use the First Amendment to arm data-disadvantaged consumers with more information. The Supreme Court bought in, recognizing a constitutional "right to receive" advertising.[23] Ironically, the free speech doctrine that Nader helped create now provides marketers with a constitutional shield, immunizing their strategies for acquiring informational advantage. Instead of acknowledging the complexity of the modern marketplace, the Court's commercial speech doctrine describes a market for speech controlled by equally autonomous actors, all uniformly capable of transacting with each other for the best possible bargain. This rosy view of consumer capabilities makes laws meant to restrict invasive market research techniques appear unnecessary. Why enact legislation preventing some forms of online data collection—so-called Do-Not-Track laws—if consumers and advertisers face off on a level playing field?

The refusal to acknowledge marketplace complexity produces overly simplistic efforts to balance information privacy with the First Amendment. In attempting this balance, courts merely ask *what* kind of information is being collected instead of *how* that information is being used. As a result, most of the time when privacy protections and the First Amendment butt heads, privacy loses. Laws preventing the collection or distribution of data deemed "sensitive"—like credit scores and personal health records—can survive constitutional review,[24] but privacy statutes restricting the collection of everyday data may not fare as well. This is unfortunate because the marketing techniques described in this book rely on the quotidian data of ordinary life to develop rich digital portraits of individuals. In some ways, information on location, marital status, and shopping habits can tell marketers much more about you than health records and credit scores (although marketers are interested in those too). In stark contrast, the European Union has given consumers the ability to avoid commercial surveillance and even to have their collected data erased after the fact.[25] The danger is that the Court's commercial speech doctrine, which assumes the rational consumer's ability to handle whatever is thrown at them, will handcuff efforts to enact similar measures in the United States.[26]

The solution might be to borrow from First Amendment doctrine outside of commercial speech. In intellectual property cases, U.S. courts take a more nuanced view, recognizing that some speech contributions deserve greater protection than others. They ask not only what communicative material is being borrowed by the defendant, but how the defendant is using that material. In this analysis, unauthorized appropriations of intellectual property are immunized when they are deemed "transformative." This requires a close examination of how the intellectual property at issue is being employed by the defendant. For example, in determining whether the unauthorized inclusion of a person in a video game is transformative, judges zero in on what the video game maker actually does with that person. When Sega took singer Kieran Kirby's likeness but also contributed a dissimilar physique and different costumes and portrayed her as a twenty-fifth-century news reporter, a court concluded that a "transformation" had taken place and immunized Sega's appropriation under the First Amendment.[27] And yet when video game manufacturers import college athletes into their games without somehow altering their appearance or expected role, transformation has not been found and the defendants' First Amendment arguments fail.[28]

In other areas of First Amendment law, there is a recognition that some parties possess communicative advantages that others lack. A "newsworthiness" defense exempts unauthorized journalistic uses of celebrity communications. Courts justify the newsworthiness defense by articulating the need for the press to balance out the communicative power of celebrities. In this view, the First Amendment is meant to diagnose and rectify power disparities, not exacerbate them. Judges are particularly receptive to newsworthiness arguments involving unauthorized use of celebrity interviews or press conferences, reasoning that the media are serving a public purpose by distributing information that the famous person at issue would like to restrict or at least manage differently.

Protected "news" is defined broadly, including even a work of entertainment, so long as the work fulfills an "informative role."[29] Hence, when the eponymous entertainer Cher tried to use her publicity right to stop a tabloid from printing a past unpublished interview (under the headline "Cher: My Life, My Husbands, and My Many, Many Men"), the court ruled in the tabloid's favor. The judge explained that the newsworthiness defense prevented this kind of celebrity "censorship."[30]

Borrowing a page from these playbooks, courts could begin to acknowledge marketplace complexity and recalibrate the balance between information privacy and free speech. An analysis of not just what data is being collected, but how that data is being used might save legal reforms like Do-Not-Track laws from First Amendment annihilation. A willingness to countenance the informational advantages of advertisers and disadvantages of consumers could justify government restrictions otherwise deemed unconstitutional. This is not to say that there are no problems with the tranformativeness and newsworthiness defenses or that they map perfectly on to the different calculus of how to reconcile information privacy with free speech.[31] For my purposes, however, these areas of First Amendment doctrine reveal the potential for a more searching judicial investigation of communicative asymmetries. The complexity of the marketplace demands increased attention to what advertisers are doing with consumer information instead of just categorizing that information as sensitive or ordinary. Even if they are not imported wholesale into commercial speech doctrine, the concepts of transformativeness and newsworthiness reveal the need for additional, more flexible metrics to be added to the Court's constitutional evaluation of information privacy law.

Private Paternalism

For some, an even worse danger than marketers exploiting cognitively challenged consumers is paternalist government intervention in the advertiser-consumer relationship. As we have seen, this paternalist objection frames much of the current thinking about the proper relationship among advertisers, consumers, and government. A new consumer movement will need to respond by supplanting the narrative of meddling government officials with its own frame of paternalist advertisers who think they know what is best for consumers.

Advertiser Knows Best

The most common definition of *paternalism* emphasizes the inherently coercive nature of paternalist acts, their substitution of one party's choice for another.[32] After generating a string of legislative successes, the consumer movement of the 1960s and early 1970s hit a brick wall. Despite repeated tries, legislation creating a federal consumer protection agency (CPA) failed to pass Congress. Historians credit a concerted strategy by business leaders to paint the CPA as elitist interference with consumer decision making. Future Speaker of the House Tip O'Neill described the anti-CPA lobbying campaign as the most extensive that he had seen in his twenty-five years in Washington.[33] Yale Law School professor Ralph Winter articulated the business community's desired frame well. He contended that a CPA would make out-of-touch do-gooders and civil servants "the self-appointed vigilante of the economic system."[34]

The same fear of government coercion continues to stymie more recent regulatory efforts. One argument successfully marshaled against proposed Do-Not-Track rules was that consumers should be able to decide on their own whether to allow online tracking, not have the state make that choice for them in advance.[35] FTC commissioner Thomas Rosch contended that Do-Not-Track "would install 'Big Brother' . . ." into the benign world of consumer information collection.[36] Similarly, in its commercial speech decisions, the Supreme Court castigates elected officials and agency heads for deciding that some citizens cannot figure out which commercial choices are best for them. The Court balked at proposed FDA limits on the advertising of untested compounded drugs, saying the limits were motivated by "a fear that people would make bad decisions if given truthful information."[37] As First Amendment scholar C. Edwin Baker noted, advertising regulations typically affect only a small, clearly defined group of commercial speakers. Nevertheless, Supreme Court justices maintain that these sorts of laws are aimed at "keeping people ignorant" or "prevent men and women from hearing facts that might not be good for them," falsely implying an all-encompassing government prohibition on particular expression no matter the speaker.[38]

Ironically, fear of government coercion is even evident in the narratives of consumer advocates. "Libertarian paternalist" scholars like Cass Sunstein hold consumer choice paramount even while acknowledging the frequent failure of individuals to act in their own self-interest. Sunstein calls for a new legislative default such that consumers be required to "actively choose" to have their data collected before online harvesting of personal information could take place.[39] The Obama administration made a similar suggestion in its "Consumer Privacy Bill of Rights," proposing that consumers be required to opt in to the collection of data that is particularly sensitive or "out of context."[40] The evidence shows, however, that such policies will not work: motivated advertisers can override privacy-friendly defaults. Limiting consumer privacy reform to policies framed around individual consumer choice stems from an aversion to having government decide what is best for its citizens. Because of this fear of a national nanny, the few policy proposals addressing adcreep tend to focus on consumers instead of advertisers as levers for change.

Consumer activists need to show that all sorts of actors, not just legislatures and government agencies, can behave paternalistically. Anyone from parents to significant others to employers to the federal government can claim to know what is best for someone else. Most important, the charge of paternalism can also apply to advertisers.

Admittedly, the government is a special kind of actor. Its size and ability to invoke the machinery of the state supply it with a coercive power that other entities might lack. But what is ignored in the current governmental paternalism frame is that the new advertising's fundamentally manipulative character makes it coercive as well. Targeted advertising represents a form of social control. The power to sort individuals into different categories implies the power to discriminate. Customization makes some offers and prices available to some consumers and not to others. Advertising's colonization of civic space forces commercial appeals into our field of vision. Neuromarketing substitutes involuntary biological responses for deliberative consumer feedback. Instead of providing consumers with more or better choices, these techniques threaten to make our choices for us.

Businesses naturally downplay the coercive downside of these marketing innovations. Consider this comment of a data scientist describing the benign nature of automated advertising, targeted at individuals and based on algorithms churning through vast quantities of data: "What happens if my algorithm is wrong? Someone sees the wrong ad. What's the harm? It's not a false positive for breast cancer."[41] Advertisers might have a better case if their conduct was transparent. Another definition of *paternalism* highlights the expressive nature of acts that suggest that the paternalist actor knows better than the person acted upon.[42] Online data collection works in part because it is so unobtrusive, vacuuming up our moods and moments without our awareness. Neuromarketing relies on subterfuge for much of its selling power. By not telling consumers what they know and how they know it, today's advertisers are, in effect, saying "I know what you need better than you do."

The frame of private paternalism shows that both advertisers and regulators can act coercively. As a result, any regulation of advertiser tactics involves a trade-off, substituting a paternalist government action for paternalist private action. This potential substitution of the government's view for the individual consumer's should not be ignored, but rather acknowledged in a pragmatic assessment of consumer and government capabilities. In a variety of contexts, skepticism over government paternalism has been overcome by faith in government expertise. For example, the FDA regulates how clinical trials are performed by drug companies and determines which pharmaceuticals can come to market. While some may complain about the inefficiencies created by this regulatory screen, there seems to be widespread agreement that government intervention in the sale of new drug formulations is necessary.[43] Because it is impossible for the average consumer to assess the efficacy and safety of these formulations, in this instance, the government *is* in a better position to evaluate what will be good for us than we are. Similarly, consumers know very little about how their personal information is being used and who is using it. Perhaps the stakes are not as high as those involved in using an untested and unsafe drug. Yet as this book has shown, modern market research poses real social consequences, from market failures to discrimination to the loss of free will. Once the paternalism of private actors becomes apparent, a new regulatory edifice on the advertising law framework can be constructed, one that responds to the particular challenges of this round of marketing innovation by assessing advertising strategies as they happen.

Putting New Cops on the Advertising Beat

As it stands now, there is little to no oversight of the entities making use of consumers' digital trails. Likewise, no one watches the corporate mad scientists conducting experiments like the Facebook social contagion study. Attempting to make these practices transparent to consumers will not solve the problem;

they are often too complex for nonexperts to understand. Instead, a government watchdog should examine the data recording and handling practices of the online presences that take center stage in the modern marketplace.

Supervision of advertisers' data collection practices would not require the creation of a brand-new federal bureaucracy. Pursuant to their legal mandate, financial regulators set up shop in banks, determining compliance with relevant lending laws. Similarly, the Federal Trade Commission (FTC) already has the authority to embed examiners inside retail giants and advertising firms. Congress provides the FTC with the ability to root out "unfair" trade practices "likely to cause substantial injury to consumers."[44] As part of this mission, the FTC can demand nonpublic information from firms and did so in the 1970s, collecting data on things like profits broken down by different business lines. Since the Reagan administration, however, the FTC has retrenched, limiting its investigatory powers largely to enforcement actions against individual businesses after unfair practices have come to light.[45]

FTC supervision of corporate data practices could be accomplished practically, without imposing a large burden on business. To find out what kinds of data are being harnessed by advertisers and to what ends, FTC supervisors could be copied on the same reports already being generated by internal and external marketing teams. These reports, provided to corporate leaders for decisions about advertising campaigns, would be transmitted to regulators as well. Steps would need to be taken to keep this information confidential, but financial regulators already take similar precautions. Almost every business engages in some advertising and consumer tracking, so there would need to be some exclusions from review. Corporations like Nike, Acxiom, and Facebook should have to open up their internal processes to the FTC, but a small local business might not. These kind of size-based cutoffs apply to other kinds of regulatory ventures. The Securities and Exchange Commission exempts public offerings of less than $5 million from its typical review.[46] Odds of Internal Revenue Service auditing decrease dramatically for businesses with corporate assets of less than $10 million.[47] FTC supervision should not be rejected simply because the agency will need to concentrate on the biggest targets.

A second proposal is to mandate the creation of corporate research boards. The basic concept—establishing independent intermediaries to review the ethical consequences of online data research—has attracted academic and governmental notice and was even flagged in consumer privacy legislation sponsored by the White House.[48] Staffed by corporate actors, not government examiners, the boards may be viewed as a more politically palatable substitute for FTC review of information collection practices. Compared to the FTC, such boards could act in a more nimble and localized fashion. Moreover, given limited government resources, the boards could serve as a regulatory backstop for businesses collecting consumer data on a relatively small scale.

In some ways, corporate research boards would work in the same fashion as the internal research boards (IRBs) that review academic research. University researchers must justify experiments on human subjects to IRBs, which check the proposed research plan against the ethical compasses of peers as well as guidelines set out under federal regulations. By contrast, private companies have no obligation to have outsiders review their experiments or to comply with federal laws designed to calculate whether the harm from such experimentation outweighs its social benefits. In the case of the Facebook social contagion study, even academic researchers themselves were given immunity from the normal rules guiding IRB review because of their alliance with a private corporation. Giving corporate research boards access to the inner workings of social media companies that test the behavior of their own users would help limit the natural tendency of businesses to conduct hidden trials crossing the line from persuasion to manipulation. Admittedly, where this line is is not always self-evident. Nevertheless, the legal status quo ensures that this line will be continually crossed in the search for profits through more effective advertising.

Corporate research boards would need to follow a certain script to make sure that they provide real review and not a rubber stamp for corporate experimentation. Documentation would be key, as the research board would have to supply an adequate record for oversight if an experiment was challenged after the fact by the FTC or in a private lawsuit. Boards would be composed of personnel within the firm. Businesses chafe at the thought of turning over their confidential business decisions or intellectual property to complete outsiders. Review by a corporate research board staffed by individuals inside the corporation's walls would help alleviate these concerns. Nevertheless, there should be at least one person on the board from outside the company to ensure a certain amount of board independence. These boards will also need guiding principles. A starting point would be the principles already articulated for government-funded research. Although changes may need to be made over time to address the particularized concerns of privately funded research, the criteria of respect for research subjects, beneficence (which requires a balancing of the benefits of data use against potential harms), and compliance with any existing laws that already prohibit particular kinds of commercial experimentation are a good start.[49]

Some object to using a model based on IRBs to perform an ethical check on corporate research. They point to examples of overzealous IRB review in academia, concerned that the addition of a similar layer of review could prevent some valuable private research and drive corporate researchers underground.[50] Corporate research boards would need to be structured so as not to be too cumbersome and to render decisions in a timely fashion. But rejecting the premise of corporate research boards out of hand because of frustration with some decisions made in the university setting seems extreme. Few would advocate a return to the days when the only check on academic experimentation was the researcher's individual ethical standards. Academic research sometimes needs a gatekeeper and the benefits of a larger perspective. The same is true of corporate research, particularly now that it can be accomplished so easily, so clandestinely, and on potentially huge sample populations.

FTC data examiners and corporate research boards represent a potential counterweight to the current data collection and experimentation free-for-all. Real-time review may still miss problematic marketing strategies. Budget constraints will limit the scope of the FTC's mission, and there is always the danger of regulatory capture by the very actors under scrutiny. Internal pressure on corporate research boards may allow some experiments to go forward that consumers would find objectionable. More generally, these regulatory bodies will be on the lookout for advertising tactics they consider overly paternalistic thanks to their specific targeting of vulnerable populations or clandestine character. Overt emotional appeals that successfully stir consumers, even in ways that may not be in their best interest, would be allowed to proceed. But the perfect should not be the enemy of the good. These intermediaries can help reverse the growing information asymmetries between modern marketers and individual consumers. In the 1970s, senators opposing the creation of the CPA contended that government regulators would assume "that all consumers are mental midgets who must look to Washington to find out how to manage their personal lives."[51] Yet advertisers' informational advantages have risen steadily since the defeat of the CPA, making arguments privileging consumer autonomy over regulatory screening less tenable than they were decades ago. For the right price, almost any business can tap into a treasure trove of consumer information. It should not be considered overly paternalistic for these businesses to disclose what that information is and what they are doing with it.

Brand Tyranny

For two days in the summer of 2014, Mat Honan, a writer for *Wired* magazine, decided to like everything he saw on Facebook. His entire online experience changed. According to Honan, "after checking in and liking a bunch of stuff over the course of an hour, there were no human beings in my feed anymore. It became about brands and messaging, rather than humans with messages."[52] One might characterize Honan's behavior as a journalist's stunt, unrepresentative of actual consumer behavior. But another interpretation is that Honan's experiment exposed the advertising algorithms that constantly operate behind the scenes and control what we see. Marketers describe their customized appeals as democracy in action. One-to-one commercial messaging, they argue, gives the individual a greater voice in the marketplace. But the algorithms that Honan brought to the surface do not have our best interests at heart. They shape our choices even as they respond to them, privileging predictability over personal evolution. Programmed to sell, these automated interfaces use or discard our human connections as it serves their purpose.

Advertisers have long struggled to overcome the appearance of insincerity. To the extent there is anxiety over fashioning the self through consumption, some of this anxiety stems from advertisers calling out to us in broad terms, not acknowledging our own unique tastes and concerns. Honan's experience notwithstanding, part of the appeal of targeted advertising is its seeming authenticity. Customized commercial missives interpellate the consumer in a different way than traditional radio or television commercials do. These ads appear more authentic because they purport to represent us, not the advertiser. With the sovereign consumer seemingly in the driver's seat, personalized marketing looks like democratic empowerment for citizens seeking fulfillment in the marketplace. Yet the clandestine nature of many of today's marketing strategies calls the supposedly empowering effects of commercial customization into question. As they craft individualized appeals, marketers communicate brand meanings through hidden primes and undisclosed social media experiments. Meanwhile, as advertising becomes more narrowly tailored, it becomes harder to disentangle democratic values from a single-minded focus on personal gain. In framing the need for legal reform, consumer activists must highlight the perils of personalization. By reinforcing existing social hierarchies, weakening social ties, and silencing dissent, individualized marketing erodes democratic values instead of strengthening them. Rather than serving as a liberator, the new advertising promotes the tyranny of the brand.

The Antidemocratic Implications
of Personalized Advertising

While not always successful, advertisers sometimes manage to secure particular legal protections by tying their craft to a resonant social goal. When advertisers can convince the public of the worth of their persuasive projects, professional privileges tend to follow. Skepticism of advertisers, however, triggers legal restrictions, from legislation reining in patent medicine claims to bans on cigarette advertising. This is an evolving process as new marketing techniques produce fresh inquiries into advertiser motivations. A recurrent theme, however, has been an attempt by advertisers to frame these new techniques as aids to democratic self-governance.

Time and again, advertisers have leveraged the rhetoric of American democracy to describe their persuasive projects. In the early twentieth century, marketers trumpeted their ability to use new national advertising platforms to raise immigrants and lower socioeconomic groups to a higher, more uniform standard of living. Without broad-based marketing schemes, the argument went, things like soap, toothpaste, and home refrigerators would never have been adopted by the larger public.[53] This message of democratic progress through mass acculturation struck a chord, leading judges in the early twentieth century to strengthen the trademark protections enjoyed by successful brand owners. Later, when some courts signaled a discomfort in the 1930s and 1940s with brand owners' monopolistic control of certain industries, advertising's defenders responded by linking trademarks to patriotism. "A trademark is not a monopoly," argued trademark scholar Rudolph Callmann, "but on the contrary, a symbol of individuality and individuality is democracy."[54] In the mid-twentieth century, instead of viewing Americans as a like-minded mass, corporate America began to note how social groups were organizing along lines of race, gender, and ethnicity for political and civil rights. Advertisers used market segmentation to showcase their participation on the front lines of the identity politics of the civil rights movement and beyond.[55] At the end of the twentieth century, the celebrity public relations industry advanced a more egalitarian understanding of fame, assuaging concerns over celebrity's antidemocratic qualities and facilitating movements for broader and more long-lasting publicity rights.[56]

Once again, advertising's techniques and attendant cultural justifications are changing. Like a military drone able to pinpoint its targets with unprecedented precision, advertisers can now drop persuasive payloads on individuals, not groups. Advertisers depict modern marketing's increasingly precise nature, the ability to understand consumers on an individual level, as ushering in a new era of democratic self-fulfillment. Just as the concept of popular sovereignty confers legitimacy on the state, belief in a sovereign consumer ratifies corporate decisions to confront consumers with personalized marketing. Brand managers maintain that they work in a new paradigm where the balance of informational power has shifted to consumers. "Brand management as we knew it is dead. The increasing power of the customer has killed it," offers one marketing guru.[57] Or take the advice of an *Adweek* columnist, contending that modern communication requires brands "to be red hot in this Darwinian world of social media and empowered consumers who now can prolifically communicate with each other and form the all-powerful 'court of public opinion.'"[58]

In similar fashion, advertising campaigns explicitly link democracy and individualized consumerism. Sneaker maker Converse (a subset of athletic wear colossus Nike) labeled a marketing initiative featuring consumer-produced films touting the Converse brand as its "Brand Democracy" campaign."[59] Doritos' "Crash the Super Bowl" contest asks participants to submit thirty-second videos to a corporate Facebook page, with Doritos airing the two videos receiving the highest number of online votes during the big game. The title "Crash the Super Bowl" suggests a populist message. Winners (via their home-grown advertisements) get to participate in an event where live attendance is typically reserved for corporations, celebrities, and the rich. The dominant frame heralds the individually empowering benefits of synergistic surveillance without acknowledging its potential for social control. IBM described plans to combine massive stores of retailer data with information from Facebook and Twitter user profiles as facilitating the commercial delivery of "more relevant, more personalized services."[60] Advertisers in all these narratives react passively to their audiences, merely tabulating votes in free and open commercial elections. Framing the technology and techniques of customized advertising in these terms makes it difficult to question advertiser motivations and, by implication, property rights in the mindshare generated by the new advertising.[61]

A new consumer movement needs to change the terms of this discussion by showcasing the antidemocratic implications of existing in our own commercial echo chambers. Movement leaders must emphasize modern marketing's role in reinforcing existing hierarchies. Salesmanship that leverages behavioral biases can generate market failures and exacerbate economic disadvantage.[62] Advertisers have long tried to prey on the cognitively vulnerable, but new technologies make this easier to accomplish than ever before. Neuromarketers not only study how to exploit the particular susceptibilities of the elderly, the young, and those with addictive personalities, but use online profiling to find those kinds of consumers and reach them at their most defenseless moments.[63]

Similarly, rather than ushering in a new age of the democratically chosen celebrity, social media platforms reward those who are already popular. With the tools of social media at everyone's disposal, we are told that anyone can be famous. Advertisers need users to believe this story of technological empowerment so they continue to provide the personal disclosures critical for commercial profiling. In reality, big corporations still have an enormous amount of say over which personalities to showcase and how to tabulate the results of online popularity contests.[64] Instead of leveling the visibility playing field, social networking platforms provide celebrities with special tracking and communications tools meant to reestablish offline fame in new surroundings. As technology writer Jacob Silverman notes, "Fame is self-reinforcing and algorithmically desirable."[65]

The rhetoric of brand democracy also rings hollow when the manufactured nature of brand popularity is exposed. The supposed virality of online ad campaigns and select celebrity social media posts often reflects the work of public relations specialists, not an organic outpouring of consumer interest. Advertisers can launch memes through fake e-mail accounts or carefully planted statements posted under an assumed name. Brand managers carefully seed video-sharing sites and blogs to manipulate online rankings and gain visibility for their products. They also use buzz marketing to target designated influencers, who can propel the commercial message outward without directly implicating the advertiser.[66] "Brand democracy" does not look so democratic when you look under the hood.

Like any totalitarian state, commercial actors have an interest in silencing dissent. Advertisers frame the ability to cull unique actors out from the undifferentiated consuming herd as democracy in action, but opportunities for consumers to deliberately express themselves to commercial entities are diminishing. Neuromarketing ignores conscious discourse in favor of hidden diagnosis of the consumer's emotional state and the clandestine creation of brand-friendly somatic markers. Market researchers increasingly favor online spying over older techniques, like focus groups and surveys, that necessitated a dialogue between advertiser and consumer. Opportunities for commercial participation through the tools of social media require consumers to be surveilled and consent to opaque terms of service, hardly an ideal means of democratic governance. Meanwhile, journalistic voices are co-opted by retailers intent on blurring the line between editorial opinion and branded content. Venerable news sources now sell advertising space on their covers and front pages. Broadcast journalists feature paid-for product placement alongside their coverage of the day's events. Once the marketplace becomes unresponsive to dissenting voices, it is no longer fulfilling its democratic promise.[67]

Finally, personalized advertising weakens social ties, celebrating the cult of the individual while diminishing opportunities for collective action. Sometimes democracy endorses markets and the pursuit of individual goals, but it also sometimes supports more collective values, like distributive fairness. Mat Honan's experience reveals the willingness of advertisers and social media platforms to cast aside interpersonal bonds when it serves their commercial purposes. Online visibility metrics privilege attenuated social connections over stronger ties of dependency and friendship. To be sure, there are examples of citizens, motivated by shared political ideals, using social media to band together. But social media's prevailing ethos is one of libertarian self-branding in an ever-expanding commercial sphere. This kind of individualism is antidemocratic, at least when it operates to the exclusion of other, more communitarian visions of self-realization. The brand tyranny frame suggests that technology does not always act as a liberator. It counsels that surveillance legitimated through contractual boilerplate is not democracy in action. And it cautions against expanding property rights to further advertisers' disciplinary projects.

Reining in Intellectual Property

Intellectual property law is a key component of the advertising law ecosystem. Marketers infuse brands and celebrity spokespersons with emotional meanings. They then use trademark protections and publicity rights law to try to prevent others from challenging those meanings. With luck, a frame stressing the antidemocratic implications of modern marketing techniques will prompt a reconsideration of legal rules that propertize audience share while restricting consumer freedom. If the meanings engineered by advertisers and celebrities become more susceptible to interrogation by others, then some of the deleterious social consequences of the new advertising can be ameliorated.

Trademark law is designed to further marketplace efficiency by preventing commercial rivals from making misleading use of the advertiser's mark. But as discussed in Chapter 4, trademark law's remit now encompasses nonconfusing commercial messaging and even communications that are completely immaterial to consumer purchasing decisions. Both trademark infringement and trademark dilution law have grown to protect brand symbolism at the same time that neuromarketers have made that symbolism easier to engineer. Eye tracking, fMRI scans, and EEG readings uncover emotional secrets that can be embedded into advertisements. Advertisers' neural know-how is not at the stage where a company can make a brand mean whatever it wants; consumers still reinterpret some proffered brand meanings. And sometimes organized resistance to corporate branding efforts can attract significant public attention, as when the activist group the Yes Men created a faux marketing campaign using the Shell name and logo to protest arctic drilling. In general, however, advertiser-friendly trademark rulings make it harder for resistance to occur by stifling communications that challenge a mark's emotional message.

As techniques like neuromarketing and commercial surveillance create emotional capital with a minimum of conscious consumer input, legal actors should question the role of dilution law in protecting that emotional capital. Because it requires no proof of consumer confusion, dilution law lets brand owners stop activities that pose no risk to consumers. At the least, recent judicially crafted presumptions of dilution should be abandoned. For example, the presumption that any sexually related use of a famous mark is actionable needs to be junked. Dilution already privileges powerful brands, typically the ones that have sunk the most into advertising. Consider the case of a trade show exhibitor that hired two models to distribute condoms while perched on a Viagra-branded missile.[68] Pfizer, the maker of Viagra, successfully sued for dilution of its famous mark. But what exactly is the harm to Pfizer's reputation from the exhibitor's stunt? The Viagra brand is already synonymous with sex, so it is hard to see what sort of unsavory associations might leech into heads of onlookers who saw the missile. At the least, Pfizer should be forced to provide evidence that the exhibitor's display probably diluted the signaling power of its mark. In general, courts should require proof of dilution and not presume the dilutive impact of a particular mark use.

Another solution would be to impose a materiality requirement in trademark law, blocking only those unauthorized uses of a mark that truly matter to consumers. False advertising law already has such a materiality requirement. In assessing whether a business violated false advertising law by misleading consumers, courts investigate whether the misleading statement was actually likely to influence purchase.[69] For example, when a seller of halogen ovens was accused of wrongly contending that its product was designed by and guaranteed by the company Sharper Image, a court found for the defendant. The court relied on a survey showing that the advertised association with Sharper Image was immaterial to oven purchasers; they cared about the warranty but not about where it came from.[70]

Simply by asking whether the challenged mark use would truly matter to consumers, courts could reduce the ability of brand owners to emotionally influence their targets. Trademark law currently has no such materiality requirement. In fact, thanks to expanding doctrine, trademark suits are more likely than ever before to target brand uses that do not matter to consumers. Brand owners sue to prevent nonofficial sources from selling sweatshirts invoking state universities. Television show writers and movie producers find themselves targeted by trademark owners for innocuous brand mentions. Construction equipment manufacturer Caterpillar claimed trademark infringement when a filmmaker included a fictional scene showing the company's tractors removing trees from an environmentally sensitive area.[71] Louis Vuitton sued Warner Brothers for intentionally featuring a knock-off version of one of its luxury handbags and having a character describe it as a "Lewis Vuitton" in its comedy *The Hangover II*. Major League Baseball contended that its names and logos could not be used in a movie depicting a real-life baseball general manager.[72] Trademark owners prosecute these sort of claims because they object to the story being told, not because of a genuine fear of consumer confusion. A materiality requirement could reduce the incidence of such claims and allow other entities to compete for mindshare with their own alternative brand meanings. At the same time, material and confusing unauthorized brand uses would continue to be prohibited, still allowing for the protection of truly misled customers.[73]

Ballooning publicity rights protections need to be questioned as well. In its current state, the right of publicity protects against even oblique celebrity references and lasts, in some states, for close to a century after the celebrity's death. The backers of the right offer little justification for these expansions. Instead, they simply assume that visibility should be an important and legally protected marker of status. This description of the right comes from its foremost American scholar:

> If you see someone taking your coat from a hook in a restaurant, the natural impulse is to say "Excuse me, but you are taking something that belongs to me." In the same way, a plaintiff who asserts the right of publicity says to the defendant, "Excuse me, but you are using my identity to draw attention to your commercial advertisement. That belongs to me."[74]

Similarly, when the musician Prince died in April 2016, Minnesota lawmakers rushed to enact a retroactive posthumous publicity rights law, its chief sponsor offering the feeble reasoning that it was "really important" to stop unlicensed T-shirt vendors from profiting off the singer's fame after his demise.[75]

Visibility should not be equated with personal property like a coat unless we conclude that it makes rational sense to do so. An equally plausible view might be that visibility should not be propertized. In the past, courts chose to devalue visibility, striking down legal rules that passed the economic rewards of fame from generation to generation. Today it may again make sense to reward qualities different from visibility. Instead of reinforcing the cultural power of celebrities, the law could facilitate efforts to undermine that power and thereby discourage visibility status competitions. Rather than explicitly endorsing the status-signaling aspects of visibility, legal rules might permit outsiders to more freely structure their identities with celebrity symbols.

How would a legal regime that was not so accepting of the value of visibility look? Most important would be a willingness to limit the alienability of visibility. By making publicity rights freely tradable and inheritable, the legal system has greatly increased visibility's value. Posthumous publicity rights facilitated the creation of celebrity management companies that strategically manage diverse portfolios of famous personalities and lobby for greater legal protections. Limits on alienability, like those that existed only a relatively short time in the past, would depress the value of visibility. There are many reasons to seek fame, so reducing the alienability of publicity rights would not be a silver bullet for the problems of micro-celebrity. Even without the reward of a property right in fame, many social forces still encourage individuals to seek celebrity status. But limiting the transfer of publicity rights would be one step toward making visibility less attractive, perhaps discouraging some of the efforts to gain online attention that noncelebrities pattern their own behavior after.

Changing the right of publicity's alienable status, particularly its descendability, would be an uphill battle. Right now, it is the celebrities and their licensing agents who have the political muscle, and that muscle has created momentum, making descendible publicity rights the default rule in most states. The "property" label tends to produce particular legal assumptions, including the ability to transact away that property. Still, there have been some recent setbacks for celebrities seeking to expand publicity rights protections. Right of publicity bills pushed by Bill Cosby (before he became embroiled in a sex abuse scandal) in Massachusetts and J.D. Salinger's son in New Hampshire failed to advance. New York State remains firm in its refusal to allow postmortem rights despite numerous efforts by celebrities and their associated allies to change the law. Some call for a federal right of publicity law so advertisers need not navigate the laws of all fifty states when they roll out a new campaign.[76] Such a law could provide a vehicle for rolling back the protections for commercial visibility that have accreted in various states over the past two decades. Although most backers of such a law favor robust publicity rights protections,

Congress should consider the costs of the status quo and decline to recognize postmortem rights or, at least, make any publicity rights that exist after death of extremely limited duration.

By reducing intellectual property protections for celebrities and brand owners, lawmakers could strike an important blow against adcreep. In their current incarnations, trademark law stops nonconfusing uses of brands and the right of publicity restricts uses of a celebrity persona decades after the celebrity's death. These legal rules are not only illogical from a utilitarian standpoint; they produce deleterious social consequences. A chilling example comes from the estate of a man who sounded the alarm against the use of propaganda and surveillance to control minds. George Orwell died in 1950, yet his estate continues to vigorously assert rights in his persona as well as in trademarks and copyrights relating to his literary works. In 2015, the estate insisted that T-shirts bearing the number "1984" and mugs featuring Orwell's image and quotes from his books infringed its intellectual property rights. Quickly bowing to the estate's threatened legal action, a website removed the offending items. Orwell warned of a world controlled by authoritarian governments. His concerns might also apply to the mounting social and legal authority of celebrities and advertisers.[77]

*   *   *

When Vance Packard wrote in 1957, he shocked society with his revelations of the techniques being employed on Madison Avenue. These techniques seemed to prey on human vulnerabilities and upset a view of consumer autonomy that was widely shared. But since Packard's book, advertisers have moved on multiple fronts to normalize their presence. At a certain point, the advertisement in the school cafeteria or the neuromarketer diagnosing your psychological profile becomes part of the scenery. Normalization defangs these strategies for their targets even as it makes them more effective. In Packard's time, citizens were horrified at the idea of unseen forces surreptitiously collecting information on them, concerned that they would be turned into commercial Manchurian candidates. Modern advertising's ubiquity makes similar practices seem innocuous. Individually, the new advertising's various components are disturbing, each posing social costs that policymakers have failed to fully consider. Taken collectively, the new advertising threatens to overwhelm our faculties, to become so embedded in our daily routines that it extinguishes our will to resist.

Like the rest of us, legal actors can become numb to advertising's incursions, gradually worn down by the relentless persistence of commercial trackers pursuing their quarry. Advertising law incorporates norms of dignity, fairness, and transparency to keep the relationship between advertiser and consumer in balance, but thanks to the efforts of advertisers, these norms are changing. Commercial data collection depends not only on digital boilerplate, but on this boilerplate becoming routinized, raising a judicial eyebrow only when its terms appear particularly egregious. The antipaternalist philosophy guiding First Amendment treatment of commercial speech makes more sense if you assume that advertising is everywhere. A default of surveillance and selling in any environment, including schools, public lands, and the home, turns government regulators, not advertisers, into the intruders. Judges once balked at attempts to make themselves more visible, assuming an aura of remote contemplation. Now, caught up in an ever-present celebrity culture, judges emulate the attention-grabbing strategies of reality television stars and no longer fret over the right of publicity's antidemocratic implications. The overall pattern is of once-significant legal barriers falling away as advertising's increasingly insistent presence makes any attempt at commercial persuasion appear commonplace.

Should we accept this as a matter of legal and social evolution and allow the commercial tide to wash over us? Advertising is a necessary part of modern life. It can provide useful information, which in turn can lead to market efficiencies and innovation. Even if the bulk of advertising is devoid of factual content, commercial appeals can offer consumers aesthetic choices as well as canvases that can be reappropriated for commentary and critique. But advertising also asserts a particular point of view, one that is individualistic, materialist, and mercenary. It employs the language of democratic choice but crowds out competing narratives of civic responsibility. When advertisers gain all-hours access to our private lives and thoughts, they increase not only their powers of persuasion but also their ability to discriminate against us and appeal to our basest motives. When we start behaving like advertisers ourselves (or their celebrity partners), we compound our own informational disadvantages, disclosing data that can be leveraged against us in future commercial conversations. Life without advertising would make little sense, but neither would a dystopian society of omnipresent monitoring and commercial appeals.

History shows that resistance to the spread of advertising is not futile. Marketing innovations of the past have been beaten back or at least restrained by a combination of legal change and public will. But some expression of resistance will be needed before necessary new edifices on the advertising law framework can be built. The danger is that this critical moment will pass without consumers putting up a fight. The ads we now accept as the price of going to the movies will become the neural scans we submit to when entering the supermarket. Marketing techniques that invade once sacred territories and scrutinize once private thoughts will become part of the existing background of unrecognizable, unthreatening commercial white noise. The most powerful kind of persuasion is the kind we don't see coming.

Acknowledgments

This book is as much the product of years of scholarship and teaching in the area of advertising law as it is being a parent of two new members of the consumer society. When I became a father, commercial appeals that I once might not have noticed suddenly loomed large. Thinking about the future, I wondered how my children would experience a world of omnipresent advertising. Although I grew up in the commercial culture of the 1970s and 1980s, I felt that there was significant space in my childhood where I could focus on relationships that had nothing to do with being a consumer. I hope my kids are able to feel that way too.

The book could not have been written without the patience of my family: my children, Clara and Hank, and my wonderful wife, Christine. It also could not have been written without my colleagues at the University at Buffalo School of Law. They were exposed to all of the chapters in this book in various forms, pointed me in the right directions, suggested closing off avenues that would not be fruitful, and encouraged me to go forward with the project. Particular thanks go to Samantha Barbas, Anya Bernstein, Michael Boucai, Rebecca French, Fred Konefsky, Lynn Mather, Tony O'Rourke, Tico Taussig, and Jim Wooten for reading multiple drafts of multiple chapters of *Adcreep* and offering extremely helpful suggestions. My gratitude also goes out to friends and colleagues outside Buffalo for their ideas for making this book better, including Katya Assaf, Rob Coluantoni, Shubha Ghosh, Ravind Grewal, Sam Halabi, Peter Lee, and John Tehranian. Thanks also go to students in my advertising and law and technology seminars who were exposed to draft chapters (whether they realized it or not) and provided stimulating and valuable conversations on the content contained therein. Much appreciation goes to the research assistants who have helped me on this work over the years: Michael Caranante, Alina Hasan, Brian McSherry, and particularly Erin Goldberg.

Notes

Introduction

1. Michael J. Prince, *Don't Worry about the Government: Agency Panic in Philip K. Dick and Steven Spielberg's "Minority Reports,"* in The Dynamics of Interconnectedness in Popular Culture(s) 142, 150–52 (Ray B. Browne & Ben Urish eds., 2014); Ian Rothkerch, *Will the Future Really Look Like "Minority Report"?*, Salon, July 10, 2002, http://www.salon.com/2002/07/10/underkoffler_belker/.

2. I use the term Madison Avenue in its popular sense as a metonym for the American advertising industry. In reality, most of the advertising agencies that once clustered in this particular area of New York decamped for other locations in the late twentieth century. Deborah Leslie, *Abandoning Madison Avenue: The Relocation of Advertising Services in New York City*, 18 Urban Geography 568, 568, 577–79 (1997).

3. Helga Dittmar, Consumer Culture, Identity and Well-Being: The Search for the "Good Life" and the "Body Perfect" 2 (2008); Tim Kasser et al., *Some Costs of American Corporate Capitalism: A Psychological Exploration of Value and Goal Conflicts*, 18 Psychol. Inquiry 1, 5 (2007); Sheree Johnson, *New Research Sheds Light on Daily Ad Exposures*, SJ Insights, Sept. 29, 2014, http://sjinsights.net/2014/09/29/new-research-sheds-light-on-daily-ad-exposures/.

4. Helen Nissenbaum, Privacy in Context: Technology, Policy, and the Integrity of Social Life (2010).

5. Martin Lindstrom, Brandwashed 161 (2011).

Chapter 1

1. Ruth Deforest Lamb, American Chamber of Horrors: The Truth About Food and Drugs 296 (1936); Genevieve Forbes Herrick, *Mrs. Roosevelt Talks of Truth in Advertising*, Chi. Daily Trib., Oct. 24, 1933, at 6; *Medicine: Eyes and Dyes*, Time, Nov. 20, 1933, at 26.

2. Inger L. Stole, Advertising on Trial: Consumer Activism and Corporate Public Relations in the 1930s, at 68 (2005).

3. Gwen Kay, Dying to Be Beautiful: The Fight for Safe Cosmetics 107–08 (2005); *Lash Lure*, Cosmetics and Skin, http://www.cosmeticsandskin.com/bcb/lash-lure.php (last visited June 13, 2016).

4. Mark Bartholomew, *Advertising and the Transformation of Trademark Law*, 38 N.M. L. Rev. 1 (2008).

5. 16 C.F.R. § 255.5.

6. 21 U.S.C. § 343(a)(1); 47 C.F.R. § 73.671.

7. Spokeo, Inc. v. Robins, 136 S. Ct. 1540 (2016); Cabral v. Supple, 608 Fed. Appx. 482, 483 (9th Cir., June 23, 2015); Spencer Weber Waller et al., *Consumer Protection in the United States: An Overview*, 2011 Eur. J. Consumer L. 853 (2011).

8. The various means of regulating consumer information are duplicative. The National Advertising Division resolves the same disputes that can be prosecuted by the FTC or in a competitor's false advertising claim. On the one hand, some legal scholars worry that failure to delineate clear boundaries among these different legal regimes may produce varying results, pushing the law away from the balances of advertiser and consumer rights carefully constructed by legislators and judges. Michael Grynberg, *More Than IP: Trademark among the Consumer Information Laws*, 55 Wm. & Mary L. Rev. 1429, 1469–70 (2014). On the other hand, governmental resources to police advertising are limited, and regulatory proceedings can take a great deal of time when compared to private lawsuits. Given these limitations, it may make sense to have a backstop of private enforcement for those times when the government is unwilling or unable to prosecute offending advertisers on its own. Lee Goldman, *The World's Best Article on Competitor Suits for False Advertising*, 45 Fla. L. Rev. 487, 505 (1993).

9. Lucius Beebe, The Stork Club Bar Book viii (1946), *quoted in* Ralph Blumenthal, Stork Club: America's Most Famous Nightspot and the Lost World of Café Society 3 (2000).

10. Stork Rest., Inc. v. Sahati, 166 F.2d 348, 358 (9th Cir. 1948).

11. Lee Benham, *The Effect of Advertising on the Price of Eyeglasses*, 15 J.L. & Econ. 337 (1972).

12. *Morning Star Coop. Soc'y Ltd. v. Express Newspapers Ltd.*, [1979] FSR 113, 117.

13. *See* Barton Beebe, *The Semiotic Analysis of Trademark Law*, 51 UCLA L. Rev. 621, 623–24 (2004).

14. Coca-Cola Co. v. Chero-Cola Co., 273 F. 755, 756 (D.C. Cir. 1921).

15. *Stork Rest.*, 166 F.2d at 358–59.

16. Mark P. McKenna, *A Consumer Decision-Making Theory of Trademark Law*, 98 Va. L. Rev. 67 (2012); Rebecca Tushnet, *Running the Gamut from A to B: Federal Trademark and False Advertising Law*, 159 U. Pa. L. Rev. 1305 (2011).

17. John Kenneth Galbraith, The Affluent Society 135 (2d ed. rev. 1969).

18. See, for example, Peter Menell, *Brand Totalitarianism*, 47 U.C. Davis L. Rev. 787, 792–93 (2014).

19. Procter & Gamble Co. v. Kimberly-Clark Corp., 569 F. Supp. 2d 796, 799 (E.D. Wis. 2008).

20. William M. Landes & Richard A. Posner, The Economic Structure of Intellectual Property Law 173 (2003); Lillian R. BeVier, *Competitor Suits for False Advertising under Section 43(a) of the Lanham Act: A Puzzle in the Law of Deception*, 78 Va. L. Rev. 1, 8 (1992).

21. Zahr Said, *Embedded Advertising and the Venture Consumer*, 89 N.C. L. Rev. 99, 105 (2010).

22. *See* Micah L. Berman, *Manipulative Marketing and the First Amendment*, 103 Geo. L.J. 497, 502–15 (2015); Ryan Calo, *Digital Market Manipulation*, 82 Geo. Wash. L. Rev. 995, 1001 (2014); Jon D. Hanson & Douglas A. Kysar, *Taking Behavioralism Seriously: The Problem of Market Manipulation*, 74 N.Y.U. L. Rev. 630, 747 (1999).

23. Arthur Kallet & F. J. Schlink, 100,000,000 Guinea Pigs: Dangers in Everyday Foods, Drugs, and Cosmetics 138 (1933).

24. *Id.* at 140.

25. Donald E. Frey, America's Economic Moralists: A History of Rival Ethics and Economics 91 (2009); Lawrence B. Glickman, Buying Power: A History of Consumer Activism in America 5, 23 (2009); Karen Halttunen, Confidence Men and Painted Women: A Study of Middle-Class Culture in America, 1830–1870, at 25–31 (1982); Mark Bartholomew, *Trademark Morality*, 55 Wm. & Mary. L. Rev. 85, 111–12 (2013).

26. John Swann, *The Formation and Early Work of the Drug Laboratory, USDA Bureau of Chemistry*, Apothecary's Cabinet, Fall 2005, at 1, 6.

27. Tracy Westen, *Government Regulation of Food Marketing to Children: The Federal Trade Commission and the Kid-Vid Controversy*, 39 Loy. L.A. L. Rev. 79, 83 (2006).

28. J. Howard Beales III, *Advertising to Kids and the FTC: A Regulatory Retrospective That Advises the Present*, 12 Geo. Mason L. Rev. 873, 881 (2004).

29. Editorial, *The FTC as National Nanny*, Wash. Post, Mar. 1, 1978, at A22.

30. *Id.*

31. Ronald Reagan, *Consumerists Out: Will Return*, Manhattan Mercury, Jan. 26, 1975, *quoted in* Glickman, *supra* note 25, at 292.

32. *Id.*

33. Paul Bond, *"Astaire Bill" to Protect Deceased Celebs' Images*, Backstage, Feb. 21, 2001, http://www.backstage.com/news/astaire-bill-to-protect-deceased-celebs-images/.

34. 2 Max Weber, Economy and Society: An Outline of Interpretive Sociology 932–39 (Guenther Roth & Claus Wittich eds., 1978); Charles Kurzman et al., *Celebrity Status*, 25 Sociological Theory 347, 348–49 (2007).

35. Luten v. Wilson Reinforced Concrete Co., 263 F. 983, 985 (8th Cir. 1920); Hat Corp. of Am. v. D.L. Davis Corp., 4 F. Supp. 613, 623 (D. Conn. 1933); Dayton Eng'g Labs. Co. v. Kent, 260 F. 187, 189 (E.D. Pa. 1919); State *ex rel* Carnation Milk Products Co. v. Emery, 189 N.W. 564, 570 (Wis. 1922).

36. Katya Assaf, *Brand Fetishism*, 43 Conn. L. Rev. 83, 105–06 (2010); Frank Schechter, *The Rational Basis of Trademark Protection*, 40 Harv. L. Rev. 813, 825 (1927).

37. Letter from Justice Felix Frankfurter to President Franklin D. Roosevelt (May 7, 1934), *quoted in* Larry Tye, The Father of Spin: Edward Bernays and the Birth of Public Relations 63 (1998).

38. Mark Bartholomew, *A Right Is Born: Celebrity, Property, and Postmodern Lawmaking*, 44 Conn. L. Rev. 301, 313, 343 (2011).

39. Letter from F. Scott Fitzgerald to his daughter, Frances Scott Fitzgerald (Aug. 24, 1940), *quoted in* THE CRACK-UP 299, 300 (Edmund Wilson ed., 1945).

40. Pollara v. Seymour, 206 F. Supp. 2d 333, 337 (N.D.N.Y. 2002). Advertisements are eligible for the same basic protections under copyright law as other creative works. Bleistein v. Donaldson Lithographing Co., 188 U.S. 239, 252 (1903).

41. Valentine v. Chrestensen, 316 U.S. 52, 54 (1942).

42. Ohralik v. Ohio State Bar Ass'n, 436 U.S. 447, 455–56 (1978).

Chapter 2

1. Lisa Rein, *Harry Potter Stamp Riles Post Service Panel, Traditional Stamp Collectors*, WASH. POST, Nov. 18, 2013, http://www.washingtonpost.com/politics/harry-potter-stamp-riles-postal-service-panel-traditional-stamp-collectors/2013/11/18/95d8ebb2–4d7a-11e3–ac54–aa84301ced81_story.html.

2. Lisa Rein, *USPS "Prostituting" Its Stamp Program with Commercial Images, Prominent Former Postmaster General Says*, WASH. POST, Aug. 7, 2014, http://www.washingtonpost.com/blogs/federal-eye/wp/2014/08/07/usps-prostituting-its-stamp-program-with-commercial-images-prominent-former-postmaster-general-says/.

3. MICHAEL SERAZIO, YOUR AD HERE: THE COOL SELL OF GUERRILLA MARKETING 6 (2013).

4. Deborah Roedder John, *Consumer Socialization of Children: A Retrospective Look at Twenty-Five Years of Research*, 26 J. CONS. RES. 183, 185 (1999).

5. Marion G. Crain, *Managing Identity: Buying Into the Brand at Work*, 95 IOWA L. REV. 1179 (2010); Sophie Broach, *Talking Urinal Cake Taking Aim in DUI War*, TOLEDO BLADE, July 4, 2012, http://www.toledoblade.com/Nation/2012/07/04/Talking-urinal-cake-taking-aim-in-DUI-war.html; David Folkenflik, *Gas Station TV Capitalizes on a Captive Audience*, NPR.ORG, Oct. 15, 2014, http://www.npr.org/2014/10/15/356451263/gas-station-tv-capitalizes-on-a-captive-audience.

6. Rolfe Winkler, *Google Predicts Ads in Odd Spots Like Thermostats*, WALL ST. J. BLOG, May 21, 2014, http://blogs.wsj.com/digits/2014/05/21/google-predicts-ads-in-odd-spots-like-thermostats/.

7. Steven Ford, *Disney Encourages Fans to Show Their Disney Side at New Official Disney Vine Site*, ORLANDO SENTINEL, Oct. 1, 2013, http://articles.orlandosentinel.com/2013–10–01/the-daily-disney/os-disney-launches-official-vine-site-20131001_1_disneyland-resort-walt-disney-world-resort-fans.

8. SERAZIO, *supra* note 3, at 78.

9. Editorial, *Skip the Cinema Ads*, S.F. CHRON., Mar. 2, 2005, at B8.

10. Bruce Horovitz, *Meet the Man at the Center of the Dispute over Movie Ads*, L.A. TIMES, Oct. 10, 1990, http://articles.latimes.com/1990–10–30/business/fi-3485_1_commercials-in-movie-theaters.

11. David J. Fox, *Maryland Mulls Ban on Ads at Movies*, L.A. TIMES, Mar. 5, 1991, http://articles.latimes.com/1991–03–05/entertainment/ca-108_1_movie-theaters-adding; *see* Joe Neumaier, *Invasion of the Movie Ads!*, N.Y. DAILY NEWS, July 15, 2003, http://www.nydailynews.com/archives/nydn-features/invasion-movie-ads-article-1.518731;

Pre-Movie Ads Mislead Audience, Suit Claims, Sun-Sentinel, Feb. 20, 2003, at 5A; Kristi Turnquist, *Suit Targets Ad in Movie Theaters*, Oregonian, Feb. 21, 2003, https://www.highbeam.com/doc/1G1–97932246.html.

12. Elaine Dutka, *Landmark Sponsorship Move: The Art-House Chain, Which Has Shied Away from Ads, Signs a Deal with a Carmaker to Develop Indep-Film Material to Show Before Features*, L.A. Times, Aug. 31, 2005, http://articles.latimes.com/2005/aug/31/entertainment/et-landmark31.

13. The Arbitron Cinema Advertising Study 2007: Making Brands Shine in the Dark 6 (2007); Hollie McKay, *Are Out of Control in Theater Commercials Driving Away Moviegoers?*, Fox News, Jan. 19, 2012, http://www.foxnews.com/entertainment/2012/01/19/are-out-control-in-theater-commercials-driving-away-moviegoers/.

14. Michael J. Sandel, What Money Can't Buy: The Moral Limits of Markets 190 (2012); John Byrne & John Chase, *Digital Billboards Proposed for City Property*, Chi. Trib., Oct. 27, 2012, http://articles.chicagotribune.com/2012-10-27/news/ct-met-emanuel-billboards-deal-20121027_1_digital-billboards-emanuel-plan-emanuel-spokeswoman-kathleen-strand; Marsha Shuler, *Another Louisiana Agency Selling Advertising on State Property*, New Orleans Advocate, July 11, 2015, http://www.theneworleansadvocate.com/news/sttammany/12871645-172/another louisiana-agency-selling-advertising; Matthew Spina, *Advertising Company Putting Ads in County Jail: Lawyers, Bondsmen Can Market Services*, Buffalo News, Mar. 27, 2011; *State Farm Sponsorship of Hoosier Helpers*, Ind. Dep't Transp., Oct. 13, 2011, http://www.in.gov/indot/3005.htm; Letter from Stan Wisnlewski, Dir., L.A. County Dep't of Beaches & Harbors, to the Hon. Board of Supervisors, County of L.A., June 14, 2007, http://file.lacounty.gov/bos/supdocs/32970.pdf.

15. Mark Clayton, *America's National Parks: No Longer Ad-Free Zones?*, Christian Sci. Monitor, Mar. 31, 2006, http://www.csmonitor.com/2006/0331/p04s01–ussc.html; Toluse Olorunnipa, *Hurting for Cash, U.S. National Parks Turn to Companies*, Bloomberg, June 17, 2016, http://www.bloomberg.com/politics/articles/2016–06–17/hurting-for-cash-u-s-national-park-service-turns-to-companies; Douglas Shinkle, *Parks in Peril*, National Conference of State Legislatures, Jan. 2012, http://www.ncsl.org/research/environment-and-natural-resources/parks-in-peril.aspx; *Rick Scott Approves Ads on Florida State Greenways and Trails*, Huffington Post, May 9, 2012, http://www.huffingtonpost.com/2012/05/09/rock-scott-ads-state-trails_n_1502972.html; *State Parks Explore Corporate Sponsorship*, Huffington Post, Aug. 30, 2010, http://www.huffingtonpost.com/2010/08/30/state-parks-explore-corpo_0_n_698789.html.

16. April Moore, *A Balancing Act*, 194 Am. Sch. Board J. 28, 28–30 (2007).

17. Sandel, *supra* note 14, at 199; Joseph Blocher, *School Naming Rights and the First Amendment's Perfect Storm*, 96 Geo. L.J. 1 (2007); Jennifer L. Harris & Samantha K. Graf, *Protecting Young People from Junk Food Advertising*, 102 Am. J. Pub. Health 213, 217 (2012); Jonathan Saltzman, *Taking Ads to School: Fiscal Crunch Has 2 Districts Selling Hot Display Space*, Boston Globe, June 8, 2003, at B9.

18. National Education Policy Center, Effectively Embedded; Schools and the Machinery of Modern Marketing 4 (2010); Dana Liebelson, *How Shutterfly*

and Other Social Sites Leave Your Kids Vulnerable to Hackers, Mother Jones, May 3, 2013, http://www.motherjones.com/politics/2013/05/shutterfly-teamsnap-eteamz-ssl -hackers-kids-data; Natasha Singer, *Privacy Concerns for ClassDojo and Other Tracking Apps for Schoolchildren,* N.Y. Times, Nov. 17, 2014, at B1. Although now defunct, a company called BusRadio provided music and public service announcements designed to soothe rowdy school bus riders in three hundred school districts in twenty-four states with paid advertisements. Zach Miners, *School Bus Radio Program Plays Its Last Tune,* U.S. News & World Report, Sept. 29, 2009, http://www.usnews.com/education/blogs/ on-education/2009/09/29/school-bus-radio-program-plays-its-last-tune.

19. Alex Molnar et al., *Schools Inundated in a Marketing Saturated World, in* Critical Pedagogies of Consumption: Living and Learning in the Shadow of the "Shopocalypse" 83, 91 (Jennifer A. Sandlin & Peter McLaren eds., 2010); Kenneth J. Saltman, *Putting the Public Back in Public Schooling: Public Schools Beyond the Corporate Model,* 3 DePaul J. Soc. Just. 9, 24 (2009); *BP Helping Develop California Schools' Environmental Curriculum?,* Democracy Now, Sept. 10, 2010, http://www.democracynow .org/2010/9/10/why_is_oil_giant_bp_helping.

20. Maurice Saatchi, *The Strange Death of Modern Advertising,* Fin. Times, June 22, 2006, http://www.ft.com/cms/s/0/abd93fe6-018a-11db-af16-0000779e2340.html#axzz30 HOx5fPv.

21. Samuel Johnson, The Works of Samuel Johnson, LL.D 159 (London: Luke Hansard & Sons 1810).

22. Sandel, *supra* note 14, at 353.

23. David Marquand, The Decline of the Public: The Hollowing Out of Citizenship 41 (2004).

24. *See* Campaign for a Commercial-Free Childhood, *CCFC to Scholastic: Stop the In-School SunnyD Sugar Spree,* Nov. 30, 2010, http://www.commercialfreechildhood. org/ccfc-scholastic-stop-school-sunnyd-sugar-spree; Brodie Farquhar, *Commercialism in National Forests?,* Casper Star-Tribune, Dec. 1, 2005, http://trib.com/news/state -and-regional/commercialism-in-national-forests/article_2ca4f401-1b3a-5d86-852d -a69536a41e41.html.

25. Michel Foucault, Discipline and Punish: The Birth of the Prison 184 (Alan Sheridan trans. 1979) (1975).

26. Michel Foucault, Power/Knowledge: Selected Interviews and Other Writings, 1972–1977, at 63–77 (Colin Gordon ed., 1980). *See generally* Space, Knowledge and Power: Foucault and Geography (Jeremy W. Crampton & Stuart Elden eds., 2007).

27. Ladelle McWhorter, *Normalization, in* The Cambridge Foucault Lexicon 315, 315–21 (Leonard Lawlor & John Nale eds., 2014).

28. Janet E. Halley, *Gay Rights and Identity Imitation: Issues in the Ethics of Representation, in* The Politics of Law 115, 117 (David Kairys ed., 1998); *see also* Norah Campbell, *The Signs and Semiotics of Advertising, in* The Routledge Companion to Visual Organization 130, 139–40 (Emma Bell et al. eds., 2014).

29. See, for example, Christopher A. Summers, *An Audience of One: Behaviorally Targeted Ads as Implied Social Labels,* 43 J. Cons. Res. 156 (2016).

30. Charlie Wells, *Even Retailers Buy Into the Celebrity of Haul Videos*, S.F. CHRONI-CLE, Aug. 15, 2010, at N-1; Marisa Meltzer, *Thrill of the Haul: The Secret Joy of Displaying Your Shopping Sprees on YouTube*, SLATE, Mar. 22, 2010, http://www.slate.com/articles/double_x/doublex/2010/03/thrill_of_the_haul.html.

31. See ALICE E. MARWICK, STATUS UPDATE: CELEBRITY, PUBLICITY, AND BRAND-ING IN THE SOCIAL MEDIA AGE 164–69 (2013); Nara Schoenberg, *Big Stars in Ads "Selling Out"?, Millennials Don't Mind*, CHI. TRIB., Mar. 6, 2016; Matt Novak, *Generation Like: The Kids Sell Out (But Don't Know What That Means)*, PALEOFUTURE, Feb. 18, 2014, http://paleofuture.gizmodo.com/generation-like-the-kids-sell-out-but-dont-know-what-1524517417.

32. By 2004, over one-third of all Fortune 500 companies had directly advertised to gays and lesbians. *See* KATHERINE SENDER, BUSINESS, NOT POLITICS: THE MAKING OF THE GAY MARKET 153 (2004). Similarly, in recent decades, advertisers introduced increasingly sophisticated marketing plans targeting Hispanic consumers. Lisbeth Iglesias-Rios & Mark Parascandola, *A Historical Review of R.J. Reynolds' Strategies for Marketing Tobacco to Hispanics in the United States*, 103 AM. J. PUB. HEALTH 15 (2013).

33. FELIPE KORZENNY & BETTY ANN KORZENNY, HISPANIC MARKETING: A CUL-TURAL PERSPECTIVE 287 (2005).

34. ARLENE DÁVILA, LATINOS, INC.: THE MARKETING AND MAKING OF A PEOPLE 94–99 (2001); *see* ANTHONY J. CORTESE, PROVOCATEUR: IMAGES OF WOMEN AND MI-NORITIES IN ADVERTISING 85 (1999); Jillian M. Baez, *Mexican (American) Women Talk Back: Audience Responses to Latinidad in U.S. Advertising, in* LATINA/O COMMUNICATION STUDIES TODAY 257, 260 (Angharad N. Valdivia ed., 2008).

35. PATRICK M. GEORGES ET AL., NEUROMARKETING IN ACTION: HOW TO TALK AND SELL TO THE BRAIN 198–202 (2014); KORZENNY & KORZENNY, *supra* note 33, at 235–37; SUZANNA DANUTA WALTERS, ALL THE RAGE: THE STORY OF GAY VISIBILITY IN AMERICA 279 (2001); Utpal Dholakia et al., *A Social Influence Model of Consumer Participation in Network and Small Group-Based Virtual Communities*, 21 INTERN. J. RES. MKTG. 241, 241–63 (2004)

36. Diana Taylor, *Abnormal, in* THE CAMBRIDGE FOUCAULT LEXICON 3, 3 (Leonard Lawlor & John Nale eds., 2014).

37. DÁVILA, *supra* note 34, at 98–101.

38. KORZENNY & KORZENNY, *supra* note 33, at 6.

39. Katherine Sender, *Sex Sells: Sex, Class, and Taste in Commercial Gay and Lesbian Media*, 9 GLQ 331, 335–36 (2003).

40. Jon Binnie, *Cosmopolitanism and the Sexed City, in* CITY VISIONS 171 (David Bell & Azzedine Haddour eds., 2000); PIERRE BOURDIEU, DISTINCTION: A SOCIAL CRI-TIQUE OF THE JUDGMENT OF TASTE 7 (1984); Kylo-Patrick R. Hart, *We're Here, We're Queer—and We're Better Than You: The Representational Superiority of Gay Men to Het-erosexuals on Queer Eye for the Straight Guy*, 12 J. MEN'S STUD. 241, 246–47 (2004). Even-tually the ability to individualize commercial appeals may act as a counter to some of the broader representations of social identity described here. However, advertisers will always balance personalization with the need to inculcate group norms that facilitate

consumption. Inculcating a norm of "good taste" makes good business sense whatever a more individualized analysis reveals.

41. At the same time, advertisers are also entering into partnerships with television networks to make the line between programming and commercials more opaque. For example, ABC and Target joined forces to air a set of commercials featuring characters from three ABC shows. The commercials aired during the particular shows and offered a running storyline, similar to the shows themselves. Stuart Elliott, *Commercial Breaks That Keep a Story Going*, N.Y. Times, Nov. 19, 2013, at B4. In 2016, NBC began partnering *Saturday Night Live*'s actors and writing staff with advertisers to develop "original sponsored content." Phil Rosenthal, *Fewer Traditional "SNL" Ads, But—Excuuuuse Me—Show to Sell for Sponsors*, Chi. Trib., Apr. 27, 2016, http://www.chicagotribune.com /business/columnists/ct-rosenthal-snl-ads-0428-biz-20160427-column.html.

42. Terry O'Reilly & Mike Tennant, The Age of Persuasion: How Marketing Ate Our Culture 115 (2009); Adam Ostrow, *Get a Mac Named Ad Campaign of the Decade*, Mashable.com, Dec. 14, 2009, http://mashable.com/2009/12/14/get-a-mac-ad-campaign/.

43. Martin Lindstrom, Brandwashed 248 (2011).

44. Ronald D. Michman et al., Lifestyle Marketing: Reaching the New American Consumer 41, 71 (2003); Douglas Holt, *Why Do Brands Cause Trouble? A Dialectical Theory of Consumer Culture and Branding*, 29 J. Cons. Res. 70, 87 (2002); John W. Schouten & James H. McAlexander, *Subcultures of Consumption: An Ethnography of the New Bikers*, 22 J. Cons. Res. 43, 51–55 (1995); Meghan Casserly, *Beam Raises Bethany Frankel's Skinnygirl, Makes Her a "Lady,"* Forbes, May 2, 2012, http://www .forbes.com/sites/meghancasserly/2012/05/02/beam-inc-bethenny-frankel-skinnygirl -cocktail-drink-like-a-lady/.

45. For example, the "Disney Side" online video contest mentioned earlier prohibited references to gambling, alcohol, drugs, or "the taking up of arms against any person, government, or entity"; it also required videos to be only six seconds in length and heavily weighted references to Disney theme parks and the contest itself in determining winning entries. *Disney Side Vine Contest Official Rules*, Disney, http://disney01.plcontent.com/ sidecontest-pl1470/Content/OfficialRules.pdf?cdn=1243674109 (last visited Sept. 23, 2016).

46. Korzenny & Korzenny, *supra* note 33, at 273.

47. Girls Intelligence Agency, http://www.girlsintelligenceagency.com (last visited June 15, 2016).

48. Georges et al., *supra* note 35, at 198–202 (discussing how to use marketing "bait" to turn community leaders into "contaminants" that will spread viral marketing).

49. Michel Foucault, The History of Sexuality 92 (Robert Hurley trans. 1978) (1976).

50. *See* Julie Bosman, *Chevy Tries a Write-Your-Own-Ad Approach, and the Potshots Fly*, N.Y. Times, Apr. 4, 2006, at C1.

51. James Morris, *How European Media Companies Are Dealing with Product Placement*, Advertising Age, June 13, 2011, http://adage.com/article/global-news/ european-media-companies-dealing-product-placement/228121/; Michael Sweeney, *Vloggers Must Clearly Tell Fans When They're Getting Paid by Advertisers, ASA Rules,*

GUARDIAN, Nov. 26, 2014, http://www.theguardian.com/media/2014/nov/26/vloggers
-must-tell-fans-paid-adverts-asa-rules.

52. MICHAEL WALZER, SPHERES OF JUSTICE 315 (1983).

53. MARTHA MINOW, PARTNERS, NOT RIVALS: PRIVATIZATION AND THE PUBLIC
GOOD 32 (2002). *See also* MARQUAND, *supra* note 23, at 135.

54. J. Horace McFarland, *Why Billboard Advertising as at Present Conducted Is
Doomed,* 51 CHAUTAUQUAN 19, 20 (1908).

55. Chicago v. Gunning System, 73 N.E. 1035, 1041 (Ill. 1905).

56. Bryan v. Chester, 61 A. 894, 895 (Pa. 1905).

57. City of Passaic v. Paterson Bill Posting Co., 62 A. 267, 268 (N.J. 1905).

58. Rochester v. West, 51 N.Y.S. 482, 485 (App. Div. 1898).

59. Cream City Bill Posting Co. v. Milwaukee, 147 N.W. 25, 28 (Wis. 1914); St. Louis
Gunning Advertisement Co. v. City of St. Louis, 137 S.W. 929, 945 (Mo. 1911); David Burnett, Note, *Judging the Aesthetics of Billboards,* 23 J. L. & POLITICS 171, 199 n.148 (2007).

60. *In re* Wilshire, 103 F. 620, 623 (S.D. Cal. 1900).

61. Hav-A-Tampa Cigar Co. v. Johnson, 5 So. 2d 433, 439 (Fla. 1941).

62. Perlmutter v. Greene, 182 N.E. 5, 6 (N.Y. 1932).

63. Packer Corp. v. Utah, 285 U.S. 105, 110 (1932).

64. Early billboard restrictions eventually paved the way for even more sweeping
regulation, including complete billboard bans in four states and the federal Highway
Beautification Act of 1965, which reduced the total number of billboards in the United
States by restricting signs to areas zoned "commercial" or "industrial" by local authorities. Sociologist Mariana Valverde has criticized the aesthetic regulation of advertising
as paternalistic and reflecting middle-class preferences. MARIANA VALVERDE, EVERYDAY
LAW ON THE STREET 49 (2012). There may be some truth to Valverde's charge, but one
should also note that corporate marketers are, at best, an imperfect champion of citizen
interests. For more on the history of billboard regulation, see CATHERINE GIDIS, BUY-
WAYS: BILLBOARDS, AUTOMOBILES, AND THE AMERICAN LANDSCAPE (2004).

65. Valentine v. Chrestensen, 316 U.S. 52, 54 (1942).

66. Va. State Pharmacy Bd. v. Va. Citizens Consumer Council, 425 U.S. 748, 757
(1976).

67. *Id.* at 760.

68. Cent. Hudson Gas & Elec. Corp. v. Public Serv. Comm'n of New York, 447 U.S.
557, 566 (1980). Before evaluating the speech restriction under the three-part test, the
court must first resolve a threshold question: if the commercial speech at issue is misleading or concerns unlawful activity, then there is no First Amendment issue. Metro-
media, Inc. v. City of San Diego, 453 U.S. 490, 507 (1981).

69. Ohralik v. Ohio State Bar Ass'n, 436 U.S. 447, 456 (1978).

70. Bd. of Trustees, State Univ. of N.Y. v. Fox, 492 U.S. 469, 480 (1989).

71. U.S. v. Edge Broad. Co., 509 U.S. 418 , 433–34 (1993).

72. 44 Liquormart, Inc. v. Rhode Island, 517 U.S. 484, 505 (1996) (emphasis in original).

73. Va. State Pharmacy Bd. v. Va. Citizens Consumer Council, 425 U.S. 748, 771 &
n.24 (1976).

74. The Court explained that compelled commercial disclosures merely provide additional information for consumers and, hence, should be looked on with general favor. As a result, neither strict scrutiny nor the lesser *Central Hudson* intermediate standard of review needed to apply to cases of compelled commercial speech. Rather, only a rational basis review was needed, one requiring only the paltry showing that the compelled speech was "reasonably related to the State's interest in preventing deception of consumers." Zauderer v. Office of Disciplinary Counsel, 471 U.S. 626, 633 (1985). Following *Zauderer*, courts held that governmental interests in compelled commercial speech besides preventing consumer deception—including protecting the environment, furthering public health, and protecting consumers from manipulative marketing tactics—warranted the same relaxed standard of review. *See, e.g.,* Nat'l Elec. Mfrs. Ass'n v. Sorrell, 272 F.3d 104, 115 (2d Cir. 2001); *see also* Recent Case, *D.C. Circuit Holds That FDA Rule Mandating Graphic Warning Images on Cigarette Packaging and Advertisements Violates First Amendment: R.J. Reynolds Tobacco v. FDA,* 126 HARV. L. REV. 818, 823 (2013) ("On its own terms, *Zauderer* need not be limited to these two descriptors ["misleading" and "deceptive"]—*Zauderer* also referred to 'manipulative' and 'confus[ing]' as defective qualities that would place commercial speech under its reach.").

75. *44 Liquormart, Inc.,* 517 U.S. at 526; *see also* Thompson v. W. States Med. Ctr., 535 U.S. 357, 377 (2002) (Thomas, J., concurring) ("I continue, however, to adhere to my view that cases such as this should not be analyzed under the *Central Hudson* test.").

76. Lorillard Tobacco Co. v. Reilly, 533 U.S. 525, 572 (2001) (Thomas, J., concurring in part).

77. *See 44 Liquormart, Inc.,* 517 U.S. at 517 (Scalia, J., concurring in part).

78. *See* Alex Kozinski and Stuart Banner, *Who's Afraid of Commercial Speech?,* 76 VA. L. REV. 627 (1990); Martin H. Redish, *Commercial Speech, First Amendment Intuitionism and the Twilight Zone of Viewpoint Discrimination,* 41 LOY. L.A. L. REV. 67 (2007).

79. Edenfield v. Fane, 507 U.S. 771, 770–71 (1993); *see also* Greater New Orleans Broad. Ass'n, Inc. v. United States, 527 U.S. 173, 187 (1999).

80. R.J. Reynolds Tobacco Co. v. FDA, 696 F.3d 1205, 1218 (D.C. Cir. 2012).

81. Mainstream Mktg. Servs. v. FTC, 283 F. Supp. 2d 1151, 1161 (D. Colo. 2003).

82. The first court hearing the case noted that the Do-Not-Call law did not apply to charitable solicitations, and therefore the government was exercising unjustified authority over what kind of speech consumers would be exposed to. The appeals court relied on evidence that commercial telephone solicitations were significantly more likely to rely on aggressive, repeat phone calls and apply deceptive tactics than charitable solicitations. Mainstream Marketing Servs. v. FTC, 358 F.3d 1228, 1246 (10th Cir. 2004). Scholars note the continuing potential for the First Amendment to stymie future government initiatives like the Do-Not-Call registry. Jeffrey Rosen, *Keeping Google Good: Remarks on Privacy Regulation and Free Speech,* 20 GEO. MASON L. REV. 1003, 1005–06 (2013); Peter Swire, *Social Networks, Privacy, and Freedom of Association: Data Protection vs. Data Empowerment,* 90 N.C. L. REV. 1371, 1402 (2012).

83. Edenfield v. Fane, 507 U.S. 761, 771 (1993).

84. Thompson v. W. States Med. Cent., 535 U.S. 357, 372 (2002); U.S. v. Caronia, 703

F.3d 149, 166 (2d Cir. 2012). *See also Introduction: Paternalism—Issues and Trends, in* PATERNALISM: THEORY AND PRACTICE 1, 8–9 (Christian Coons & Michael Weber eds., 2013) (contending that antipaternalist philosophy is motivated by nonutilitarian concerns).

85. R.J. Reynolds Tobacco Co. v. FDA, 696 F.3d 1205, 1208 (D.C. Cir. 2012). The FDA referred to its prior attempts to combat the massive amounts of tobacco industry advertising with its own advertising as "like bringing a butter knife to a gun fight." *Id.* at 1221.

86. *Id.* at 1217.

87. CTIA—The Wireless Ass'n v. City & Cnty. of S.F., 827 F. Supp. 2d 1054, 1063 (N.D. Cal. 2011).

88. CTIA—The Wireless Ass'n v. City & Cnty. of S.F., 494 F. Appx. 752, 754 (9th Cir. 2012). *See also* Nat'l Ass'n of Mfgs. v. SEC, 800 F.3d 518 (D.C. Cir. 2015) (holding SEC rule requiring companies using conflict minerals from the Democratic Republic of Congo to state on their websites that their products were not "DRC conflict free" was "controversial" and violated the companies' First Amendment rights).

89. Sorrell v. IMS Health Inc., 131 S. Ct. 2653, 2670 (2011) ("The fear that speech might persuade provides no lawful basis for quieting it."); *Thompson*, 535 U.S. at 374 (law prohibiting the advertising of compounded drugs was rejected because it was motivated by "a fear that people would make bad decisions if given truthful information about compounded drugs").

90. Erika L. Rosenberg, *Mindfulness and Consumerism, in* PSYCHOLOGY AND COMMERCIAL CULTURE 107, 112 (Tim Kasser & Allen D. Kanner eds., 2004); Paul Slovic et al., *The Affect Heuristic, in* HEURISTICS AND BIASES: THE PSYCHOLOGY OF INTUITIVE JUDGMENT 397, 417 (Thomas Gilovich et al. eds., 2002).

91. NATIONAL EDUCATION POLICY CENTER, SCHOOLHOUSE COMMERCIALISM LEAVES POLICYMAKERS BEHIND 1–63 (2014). Some lawmakers have banned in-school advertising for particular low-nutrition food and drinks (as well as the products themselves). But they have not objected when the same conglomerates selling those consumables simply substituted new lower-calorie versions in their stead. As a result, most schools continue to enter exclusive beverage marketing agreements with drink makers that mandate copious in-school brand promotion.

92. Matthew A. Edwards, *The FTC and New Paternalism*, 60 ADMIN. L. REV. 323, 344 (2008).

93. Denver Area Educ. Telecomm. Consortium, Inc. v. FCC, 518 U.S. 727, 802–03 (1996) (Kennedy, J., concurring in part, dissenting in part).

94. Nat'l Cable & Telecomm. Ass'n v. Brand X Internet Servs., 545 U.S. 967 (2005); DAWN NUNZIATO, VIRTUAL FREEDOM: NET NEUTRALITY AND FREE SPEECH IN THE INTERNET AGE 21–23, 126–27 (2008). In 2015, the FCC announced new rules classifying Internet service providers as common carriers. At the time of this book's publication, these rules were being challenged by broadband providers in several federal lawsuits. Moreover, a recent federal court decision concluded that the FTC has no jurisdiction over common carriers, even when the company at issue is engaged in activities unrelated to its common carrier status. FTC v. AT&T Mobility, No. 15-16585 (9th Cir. Aug. 29, 2016).

95. Charles R. Taylor & Weih Chang, *The History of Outdoor Advertising Regulation in the United States*, 15 J. MACROMARKETING 47 (1995).

96. ALFRED RUNTE, NATIONAL PARKS: THE AMERICAN EXPERIENCE 5–9 (3d ed. 1997); Holly Doremus, *Nature, Knowledge, and Profit: The Yellowstone Bioprospective Controversy and the Core Purposes of America's National Parks*, 26 ECOLOGY L.Q. 401, 437–41 (1999).

97. Burnett, *supra* note 59, at 198 & n.141.

98. JOHN DEWEY, MORAL PRINCIPLES IN EDUCATION iv–vii (1909); *see also* John Dewey, *The School as a Means of Developing a Social Consciousness and Social Ideals in Children*, J. SOC. FORCES 513 (1923).

99. NATIONAL EDUCATION POLICY CENTER, *supra* note 91, at 17.

100. JOHN BUSCHMAN, LIBRARIES, CLASSROOMS, AND THE INTERESTS OF DEMOCRACY 42 (2012).

101. UNITED STATES GOVERNMENT ACCOUNTABILITY OFFICE, COMPETITIVE FOODS ARE WIDELY AVAILABLE AND GENERATE SUBSTANTIAL REVENUES FOR SCHOOLS 7–8 (Aug. 2005), http://www.gao.gov/new.items/d05563.pdf.

102. Melissa Maynard, *This State Park Brought to You by . . .*, STATELINE.ORG, Aug. 17, 2010, http://www.recpro.org/assets/News_from_NARRP/2010-08-19_news_from_narrp .pdf.

103. Kate Sheppard, *Should Corporations Bankroll National Parks?*, MOTHER JONES, Mar. 5, 2012, http://www.motherjones.com/environment/2012/03/corporations-national -parks-coca-cola.

104. Kurt Repansheck, *National Park Service Waived Policy to Allow Budweiser's Centennial Partnership*, NATIONAL PARKS TRAVELER, Apr. 28, 2015, http://www.national parkstraveler.com/2015/04/national-park-service-waived-policy-allow-budweisers -centennial-partnership26535.

105. Carol McGraw, *School Bus Ads Bring Needed Revenue to Colorado Springs Area Districts*, COLO. SPRINGS GAZETTE, Aug. 5, 2013, http://gazette.com/school-bus-ads-bring -needed-revenue-to-colorado-springs-area-districts/article/1505252#4ZFpiKmDTKEU 02WJ.99.

106. Bd. of Trustees, State Univ. of N.Y. v. Fox, 492 U.S. 469, 475 (1989).

107. *See* Little Pencil, LLC v. Lubbock Indep. Sch. Dist., 616 Fed. Appx. 180 (5th Cir. 2015); Mech v. Sch. Bd. of Palm Beach Cty., 806 F.3d 1070, 1071 (11th Cir. 2015) (finding in favor of school board and against math tutor/pornographer, but acknowledging that this was a "difficult" case).

108. NATIONAL EDUCATION POLICY CENTER, *supra* note 91, at 6; TEXAS ASSOCIATION OF SCHOOL BOARDS, ADVERTISING IN PUBLIC SCHOOLS 2–3 (2015); Florida Association for Pupil Transportation, *FAPT Position Paper—Advertising on School Buses*, FAPTFLORDIA .ORG, Jan. 2011, at 4–5.

109. Jennifer Levitz & Stephanie Simon, *A School Prays for Help*, WALL ST. J., June 16, 2010, http://www.wsj.com/articles/SB10001424052748704875604575280422614633564.

110. Yvonne M. Terry-McElrath et al., *Commercialism in US Elementary and Sec-*

ondary School Nutrition Environments: Trends from 2007 to 2012, 168 JAMA PEDIAT-RICS 234, 234–42 (2014); Emily Bryson York, *McD's Newest Ad Platform: Report Cards*, ADVERTISING AGE, Dec. 5, 2007, http://adage.com/article/news/mcd-s-newest-ad-plat form-report-cards/122421/.

111. BLOCHER, *supra* note 17, at 42–56. Because of First Amendment concerns, a municipal bus service in Portland, Oregon, chose to allow ads touting marijuana usage even though school-age children used the buses as transport to and from school. Randy Billings, *Portland Buses to Display Marijuana Ads Despite Objections*, PORTLAND PRESS HERALD, Oct. 2, 2013, http://www.pressherald.com/2013/10/02/marijuana _legalization_backers_unveil_bus_ads_/.

112. *See* Cuffley v. Mickes, 208 F.3d 702, 705–06 n.3 (8th Cir. 2000) (holding that prohibiting the Ku Klux Klan from participating in the Adopt-A-Highway program constituted impermissible viewpoint discrimination under the First Amendment).

Chapter 3

1. Polly Sprenger, *Sun on Privacy: "Get Over It,"* WIRED, Jan. 26, 1999, http://archive. wired.com/politics/law/news/1999/01/17538.

2. theyTOLDyou, *Google CEO Eric Schmidt on Privacy*, YOUTUBE, Dec. 8, 2009, http://www.youtube.com/watch?v=A6e7wfDHzew&noredirect=1.

3. Eric Goldman, *A Coasean Analysis of Marketing*, 2006 WIS. L. REV. 1151, 1177–94 (2006); Adam Thierer, *A Framework for Benefit-Cost Analysis in Digital Privacy Debates*, 20 GEO. MASON L. REV. 1055, 1077 (2013).

4. JULIA ANGWIN, DRAGNET NATION 82 (2014); Adrienne LaFrance, *Facebook Is Expanding the Way It Tracks You and Your Data*, ATLANTIC, June 12, 2014, http://www.theatlantic.com/technology/archive/2014/06/facebook-is-expanding-the-way-it-tracks-you-and-your-data/372641/; Steve Kroft, *The Data Brokers: Selling Your Personal Information*, CBS NEWS, Mar. 9, 2014, http://www.cbsnews.com/news/the-data-brokers-selling-your-personal-information/.

5. FRANK PASQUALE, THE BLACK BOX SOCIETY: THE SECRET ALGORITHMS THAT CONTROL MONEY AND INFORMATION 46 (2015).

6. *See* Josh Lauer, *Making the Ledgers Talk: Customer Control and the Origins of Retail Data Mining, 1920–1940, in* THE RISE OF MARKETING AND MARKET RESEARCH 153, 154–55 (Harmut Berghoff et al. eds., 2012).

7. CHARLES DUHIGG, THE POWER OF HABIT 182–212 (2012); Paul J. Schwartz & Daniel M. Solove, *The PII Problem*, 86 N.Y.U. L. REV. 1814, 1851–52 (2011).

8. Anne Flaherty, *App Developers Are Tracking Kids Despite Laws to Protect Their Privacy*, PBS NEWSHOUR, Dec. 8, 2014, http://www.pbs.org/newshour/rundown/app-devel opers-tracking-kids-despite-laws-protect-privacy/.

9. VIKTOR MAYER-SCHONBERGER & KENNETH CUKIER, BIG DATA: A REVOLUTION THAT WILL TRANSFORM HOW WE LIVE, WORK, AND THINK 90 (2013); Jinyan Zang et al., *Who Knows What About Me? A Survey of Behind the Scenes Personal Data Sharing to Third Parties by Mobile Apps*, J. TECH. SCI., Oct. 30, 2015, http://jots.pub/a/2015103001/.

10. Nicola Clark, *Airlines Use Digital Technology to Get Even More Personal*, N.Y. TIMES, Mar. 17, 2014, at B4.

11. Clark Howard, *Invasive App Permissions Cross the Privacy Line*, CLARKHOWARD .COM, July 4, 2013, http://www.clark.com/invasive-app-permissions-cross-privacy-line.

12. H.F. Lin et al., *Mobilizing Timely Location-Based Advertising: A Study of Effectiveness on Persuasion*, 3 AUSTRALIAN J. BUS. & MGMT. RES. 15 (2013).

13. Jennifer C. Kerr, *Tracking Shoppers via Phones*, BUFFALO NEWS, Feb. 20, 2014, at C6; Nick Wingfield, *Another Super Bowl Ad Fest, This Time on the Cellphone*, N.Y. TIMES, Jan. 30, 2014, at A1; Kate Tummarello, *Surveillance in Aisle Three*, THE HILL, Feb. 16, 2014, http://thehill.com/blogs/hillicon-valley/technology/198480-surveillance-in-aisle-three.

14. Natasha Singer & Brian X. Chen, *Use of Mobile "Supercookies" Seen as Threat to Privacy*, N.Y. TIMES, Jan. 26, 2015, at B2.

15. MARTIN LINDSTROM, BRANDWASHED: TRICKS COMPANIES USE TO MANIPULATE OUR MINDS AND PERSUADE US TO BUY 207 (2011).

16. JOSEPH TUROW, THE DAILY YOU: HOW THE NEW ADVERTISING INDUSTRY IS DEFINING YOUR IDENTITY AND YOUR WORTH 154 (2011); Alistair Barr & Maureen Bavdek, *Groupon Data Collection Scrutinized by Congress*, REUTERS, July 21, 2011, http://www .reuters.com/article/2011/07/21/us-groupon-congress-idUSTRE76K5OT20110721.

17. Adam Serwer, *Congress Says Netflix Can Share What You Are Watching*, MOTHER JONES, Dec. 27, 2012, http://www.motherjones.com/mojo/2012/12/netflix-video-privacy -facebook-sharing. The law amended a 1988 privacy law that prevented video rental companies from sharing a customer's rental history without specific permission. The 1988 law was passed in response to a newspaper article disclosing that Supreme Court nominee Robert Bork's home viewing choices ranged from *Sixteen Candles* to James Bond films. The change in the law allowed Netflix to integrate its service with Facebook, thereby facilitating the synching of the enormous data profiles maintained by the world's largest social network with Netflix's own consumer information. Jared Newman, *Netflix Goes Social in the U.S., But Watch Out for Your Privacy*, TIME, Mar. 13, 2013, http://techland .time.com/2013/03/13/netflix-goes-social-in-the-u-s-but-watch-out-for-your-privacy/.

18. Neil M. Richards, *The Perils of Social Reading*, 101 GEO. L.J. 689, 698–99 (2013); Cindy Cohn & Parker Higgins, *Who's Tracking Your Reading Habits? An E-Book Buyer's Guide to Privacy, 2012 Edition*, ELECTRONIC FRONTIER FOUNDATION, Nov. 29, 2012, https://www.eff.org/pages/reader-privacy-chart-2012.

19. MAYER-SCHONBERGER & CUKIER, *supra* note 9, at 53–54; CENTER FOR MEDIA JUSTICE, CONSUMERS, BIG DATA, AND ONLINE TRACKING IN THE RETAIL INDUSTRY: A CASE STUDY OF WALMART (2013), http://centerformediajustice.org/wp-content/up loads/2014/06/WALMART_PRIVACY_.pdf; Alexandra Berzon & Mark Maremont, *Researchers Bet Casino Data Can Identify Gambling* Addicts, WALL ST. J., Aug. 3, 2013, http://www.wsj.com/articles/SB10001424127887324348504578607903673679448.

20. CENTER FOR MEDIA JUSTICE, *supra* note 19, at 21.

21. *Id.* at 17.

22. DUHIGG, *supra* note 7, at 182–212; H. Brian Holland, *Privacy Paradox 2.0*, 19 WIDENER L.J. 893, 899 (2010); Richards, *supra* note 18, at 698–99.

23. Evan Williams (@ev), Twitter (Dec. 6, 2009, 7:01 PM), https://twitter.com/ev/status/6414387003.

24. Corporate Disasters: What Went Wrong and Why 134, 230–32 (Miranda H. Ferrara & Michele P. LaMeau eds., 2012).

25. Some content purveyors have struck back, refusing to deliver content to consumers using these ad-blocking technologies. Mike Isaac, *Facebook Takes Steps to Defeat Ad Blockers*, N.Y. Times, Aug. 10, 2016, at B1; Ellen Hammett, *ITV Declares War on Ad-Blockers*, Connected Consumer, Oct. 18, 2013, http://connectedconsumer.mediatel.co.uk/insight/article/itv-player-declares-war-on-ad-blockers. Others respond to consumer self-defense by making new kinds of cookies that are harder to delete or by simply waiting for the consumer to return to their website, or an affiliated website, and then installing a new cookie that enables reidentification of the consumer and this person's past online history. New means of online tracking do not rely on cookies, identifying individuals from the number of fonts in their browser, or the rate at which their computer's battery loses its charge. Moreover, technologies that facilitate truly anonymous use of the Internet often suffer from inefficiencies and a lack of compatibility with the more mainstream services used by others. Angwin, *supra* note 4, at 133, 146.

26. Paul Cockerton, *Tesco Using Minority Report Style Face Tracking Technology So Ads on Screens Can Be Tailored*, Mirror, Nov. 4, 2013, www.mirror.co.uk/news/uk-news/tesco-using-minority-report-style-face-2674367.

27. Andrew Trotman, *Minority Report Moves Step Closer as Lord Sugar Launches Face Recognition Adverts*, Daily Telegraph, Jul 9, 2013, http://www.telegraph.co.uk/finance/newsbysector/mediatechnologyandtelecoms/media/10170020/Minority-Report-moves-step-closer-as-Lord-Sugar-launches-face-recognition-adverts.html; *see also* Federal Trade Commission, Facing Facts: Best Practices for Common Uses of Facial Recognition Technologies (Oct. 2012); Jonathan Bloom, *Retailers Using Controversial Marketing Tools*, ABCLocal.go.com, June 7, 2013, http://abclocal.go.com/story?section=news/assignment_7&id=9131638.

28. Stephanie Clifford, *Billboards That Look Back*, N.Y. Times, May 31, 2008, at C1; Sydney Ember, *You See That Billboard? It's Looking Back at You*, N.Y. Times, Feb. 29, 2016, at B6; Jennifer O'Mahony, *Store Mannequins "Spy on Customers" with Hidden Cameras*, Daily Telegraph, Nov. 26, 2012, http://www.telegraph.co.uk/technology/news/9702683/Store-mannequins-spy-on-customers-with-hidden-cameras.html.

29. U.S. Patent Application No. 12/958,775 (filed Dec. 2, 2010).

30. Will Greenwald, *Dis-Kinected: What the Xbox One Can Do Without a Kinect*, PC Mag., Nov. 21, 2013, http://www.pcmag.com/article2/0,2817,2427207,00.asp.

31. David Goldman, *Your Samsung TV Is Eavesdropping on Your Private Conversations*, CNN, Feb. 10, 2015, http://money.cnn.com/2015/02/09/technology/security/samsung-smart-tv-privacy/.

32. Jeremy Polacek, *Facebook's Freaky DeepFace Program Knows Your Friends Better Than You Do*, Mic.com, Mar. 19, 2014, http://www.policymic.com/articles/85719/facebook-s-freaky-deepface-program-knows-your-friends-better-than-you-do.

33. Goldman, *supra* note 3, at 1173–74.

34. M. Ryan Calo, *Digital Market Manipulation*, 82 Geo. Wash. L. Rev. 1, 30, 36 (2014).

35. Adam Harvey, *Face to Anti-Face*, N.Y. Times, Dec. 14, 2013, http://www.nytimes .com/interactive/2013/12/14/opinion/sunday/20121215_ANTIFACE_OPART.html; *see also* Elizabeth E. Joh, *Privacy Protests: Surveillance Evasion and Fourth Amendment Suspicion*, 55 Ariz. L. Rev. 997 (2013) (chronicling various forms of "privacy protests" designed to avoid consumer and government surveillance).

36. Neil M. Richards, *The Dangers of Surveillance*, 126 Harv. L. Rev. 1934, 1949 (2013); *see also* Eli Pariser, The Filter Bubble 28–34 (2011). Those in favor of digital surveillance maintain that data scientists can build serendipity into their algorithms, satisfying the human desire for the unexpected by uncovering consumers' latent interests. Goldman, *supra* note 3, at 1219. Yet truly serendipitous encounters require an element of true randomness that is divorced from hidden thoughts and past experience, and these are the sorts of encounters that are unlikely to aid advertisers' bottom line.

37. Zeynep Tufekci & Brayden King, *We Can't Trust Uber*, N.Y. Times, Dec. 7, 2014, at A27.

38. Richards, *supra* note 36, at 1957.

39. Ad Nauseum: A Survivor's Guide to American Consumer Culture 204 (2009).

40. Evie Nagy, *Everyone Is Listening*, Fast Company, June 2015, at 40, 42.

41. Valerie Tarico, *Churches Are Using Creepy Facial Recognition Technology to Track Congregants—Here's Why*, Rawstory.com, June 27, 2015, http://www.rawstory.com /2015/06/churches-are-using-creepy-facial-recognition-technology-to-track-congre gants-heres-why/.

42. Robert D. Putnam, Bowling Alone: The Collapse and Revival of American Community 19 (2000); Janna Malmud Smith, Private Matters: In Defense of the Personal Life 27–51 (1997).

43. Illinois and Texas have laws that protect against the capture of biometric information for commercial purposes. Tex. Bus. & Com. Code § 503.001 (2009); Biometric Information Privacy Act., 740 Ill. Comp. Stat. Ann. 14/1 (LexisNexis 2008). Louisiana and Arizona regulate the capture of biometric information from students. La. Stat. Ann. § 17:100.8 (2010); Ariz. Rev. Stat. § 15–109 (LexisNexis 2008). These state laws require that consent be gained from the subject (or parent of the subject) before biometric identification capture is initiated and used; however, advertisers may be able to circumvent these restrictions fairly easily. For example, under the Texas statute, a marketer does not have to disclose the purpose behind its collection of biometric information or obtain written consent. As a result, a consumer may opt in with minimal notice.

44. Samuel D. Warren & Louis D. Brandeis, *The Right to Privacy*, 4 Harv. L. Rev. 193, 195 (1890).

45. Olmstead v. United States, 277 U.S. 438, 478 (Brandeis, J., dissenting).

46. Daniel J. Solove et al., Privacy, Information, and Technology 9 (2006).

47. Pavesich v. New England Life Ins. Co., 50 S.E. 68, 80 (Ga. 1905) ("[A]s long as the advertiser uses him for these purposes, he cannot be otherwise than conscious of the

fact that he is for the time being under the control of another, that he is no longer free, and that he is in reality a slave, without hope of freedom, held to service by a merciless master; and if a man of true instincts, or even of ordinary sensibilities, no one can be more conscious of his enthrallment than he is.").

48. Roberson v. Rochester Folding Box Co., 64 N.E. 442, 447–48 (N.Y. 1902).

49. N.Y. CIV. RIGHTS LAW § 50.

50. *See, e.g.*, Foster-Milburn Co. v. Chinn, 120 S.W. 364 (Ky. 1909); Munden v. Harris, 134 S.W. 1076 (Mo. Ct. App. 1911); Edison v. Edison Polyform Co., 67 A. 392 (N.J. Ch. 1907). In actuality, the story of legal protection of privacy rights is more complicated as some courts retracted their initial support for certain versions of the privacy right. *See* Samantha Barbas, *The Death of the Public Disclosure Tort: A Historical Perspective*, 22 YALE J.L. & HUMAN. 171 (2010). In general terms, however, the last century witnessed the increasing ability of individuals to prosecute advertisers for unauthorized use of their name or likeness. *See* Mark Bartholomew, *A Right Is Born: Celebrity, Property, and Postmodern Lawmaking*, 44 CONN. L. REV. 301 (2011).

51. *See* MARY MADDEN ET AL., PUBLIC PERCEPTIONS OF PRIVACY AND SECURITY IN THE POST-SNOWDEN ERA (2014), http://www.pewinternet.org/2014/11/12/public-privacy-perceptions/; JOSEPH TUROW ET AL., AMERICANS REJECT TAILORED ADVERTISING AND THREE ACTIVITIES THAT ENABLE IT (2009), available at http://repository.upenn.edu/cgi/viewcontent.cgi?article=1138&context=asc_papers.

52. *See* Andrea M. Matwyshyn, *Privacy, the Hacker Way*, 87 S. CAL. L. REV. 1, 27 (2013); William McGeveran, *Disclosure, Endorsement, and Identity in Social Marketing*, 2009 U. ILL. L. REV. 1105, 1158–59 (2009); Eugene Volokh, *Freedom of Speech and Information Privacy: The Troubling Implications of a Right to Stop People from Speaking About You*, 52 STAN. L. REV. 1049, 1057–61 (2000); *see also In re* U.S. for Historical Cell Site Data, 724 F.3d 600, 615 (5th Cir. 2013) (finding no constitutional barrier to government acquisition of cell phone location data and urging consumers to find a "market" solution to their privacy needs).

53. Dustin D. Berger, *Balancing Consumer Privacy with Behavioral Targeting*, 27 SANTA CLARA COMPUTER & HIGH TECH. L.J. 3, 24–25 (2011).

54. MARGARET JANE RADIN, BOILERPLATE: THE FINE PRINT, VANISHING RIGHTS, AND THE RULE OF LAW 88 (2013); Mark Bartholomew, *Intellectual Property's Lessons for Information Privacy Law*, 92 NEB. L. REV. 746, 763–64 (2014); M. Ryan Calo, *The Boundaries of Privacy Harm*, 86 IND. L.J. 1131, 1149 (2011) (arguing that consumers sell their data too often and too cheaply because of "privacy myopia").

55. Cass R. Sunstein, *Deciding by Default*, 162 U. PA. L. REV. 1 (2013); *see also* Joshua A.T. Fairfield, *Do-Not-Track as Default*, 11 NW. J. TECH. L. & PROP. 575 (2013).

56. *See* RICHARD H. THALER & CASS R. SUNSTEIN, NUDGE: IMPROVING DECISIONS ABOUT HEALTH, WEALTH, AND HAPPINESS 108–15 (2008).

57. *See* Lauren E. Willis, *When Nudges Fail: Slippery Defaults*, 80 U. CHI. L. REV. 1155 (2013).

58. *Id.* at 1174–1200; Michael Corkery & Jessica Silver-Greenberg, *Overdraft Practices Continue to Gut Bank Accounts and Haunt Customers*, N.Y. TIMES, Feb. 28, 2016, at A1.

59. Chris Jay Hoofnagle & Jennifer King, What Californians Understand about Privacy Online (Sept. 3, 2008) (unpublished article), http://papers.ssrn.com/sol3/papers .cfm?abstract_id=1262130; *see also* Somni Sengupta, *Letting Down Our Guard with Web Privacy*, N.Y. TIMES, Mar. 30, 2013, at BU1 (discussing academic research revealing inability of consumers to understand online privacy policies).

60. JERRY KIRKPATRICK, IN DEFENSE OF ADVERTISING 2 (1994).

61. Sorrell v. IMS Health Inc., 564 U.S. 552, 576 (2011).

62. *Id.* at 557, 579–80. Part of the Court's issue with the Vermont law stemmed from its singling out the use of prescribing data for marketing purposes while permitting its use in other contexts like government research. This made the law a "content-based" restriction set up to fail First Amendment review. First Amendment doctrine disfavors "content-based" limits that depend on the speech's message and favors "content-neutral" restrictions on speech that are made without regard to the speech's message.

63. Dan M. Kahan et al., *"They Saw a Protest": Cognitive Illiberalism and the Speech-Conduct Distinction*, 64 STAN. L. REV. 851, 855–56 (2012).

64. U.S. v. O'Brien, 391 U.S. 367, 376 (1968).

65. *Sorrell*, 564 U.S. at 570, 578.

66. ALAN F. WESTIN, PRIVACY AND FREEDOM 7 (1967).

67. Charles Fried, *Privacy*, 77 YALE L.J. 475, 482 (1968).

68. HELEN NISSENBAUM, PRIVACY IN CONTEXT: TECHNOLOGY, POLICY, AND THE INTEGRITY OF SOCIAL LIFE 67–88 (2010); *see* U.S. Dep't of Justice v. Reporters Comm. for Freedom of the Press, 489 U.S. 749, 763 (1989) ("[B]oth the common law and the literal understandings of privacy encompass the individual's control of information concerning his or her person.").

69. DANIEL J. SOLOVE, THE DIGITAL PERSON: TECHNOLOGY AND PRIVACY IN THE INFORMATION AGE 76–77 (2004).

70. Robert Post, *Three Concepts of Privacy*, 89 GEO L.J. 2087, 2092 (2001) (internal quotations omitted).

71. LAWRENCE M. FRIEDMAN, GUARDING LIFE'S DARK SECRETS: LEGAL AND SOCIAL CONTROLS OVER REPUTATION, PROPRIETY, AND PRIVACY 214–15 (2007).

72. DAVID LYON, SURVEILLANCE STUDIES: AN OVERVIEW 65 (2007). *See generally* MICHEL FOUCAULT, DISCIPLINE AND PUNISH: THE BIRTH OF THE PRISON (Alan Sheridan trans., Vintage Books 1979).

73. In determining that the Vermont law did not directly advance the state's regulatory goals, the *Sorrell* Court viewed doctors, pharmaceutical manufacturers, and consumers as all equally capable of making informed decisions regardless of the marketers' one-sided ability to use prescribing information to generate individually tailored commercial appeals. If Vermont is concerned about the unnecessary prescription of brand-name drugs, it "can express that view through its own speech," the Court offered, turning a blind eye to the power dynamics involved in modern data collection and aggregation. Sorrell v. IMS Health Inc., 564 U.S. 552, 578 (2011).

74. *See* Lochner v. New York, 198 U.S. 45 (1905).

Chapter 4

1. James Playsted Wood, *Leaders in Marketing: Arthur C. Nielsen*, 26 J. MARKET-ING 77, 77–78 (1962); Barbara Basler, *A.C. Nielsen, Who Devised System That Rates TV Programs, Dead*, N.Y. TIMES, June 4, 1980, at A26; Mary Gillespie, *Nielsen Makes Viewers Count by Watching Them Watch TV*, CHI. SUN-TIMES, Apr. 9, 1989.

2. NICOLAS FREUDENBERG, LETHAL BUT LEGAL 13–14 (2014); A.K. PRADEEP, THE BUYING BRAIN: SECRETS FOR SELLING TO THE SUBCONSCIOUS MIND 229 (2010); Adam L. Penenberg, *NeuroFocus Uses Neuromarketing to Hack Your Brain*, FAST COMPANY, Sept. 2011, http://www.fastcompany.com/1769238/neurofocus-uses-neuromarketing-hack -your-brain.

3. DAVID HUME, AN ENQUIRY CONCERNING HUMAN UNDERSTANDING 95, 104 (L.A. Selby-Bigge ed., Clarendon Press 1955) (1743).

4. ZACK LYNCH, THE NEURO REVOLUTION: HOW BRAIN SCIENCE IS CHANGING OUR WORLD (2009).

5. The federal government has gotten involved as well. The Obama administration partnered with companies like Google and General Electric to commit $300 million per year to neuroscientific research with the ultimate goal of mapping every neuron in the human brain.

6. Ellen Byron, *Wash Away Bad Hair Days*, WALL ST. J., June 30, 2010, http://www .wsj.com/articles/SB10001424052748704911704575327141935381092; Richard Skinulis, *Minding Your Business: Neuormarketing's Search for the Brain's Buy Button*, READER'S DIGEST CAN., Nov. 2012; Roger Dooley, *Neuromarketing: For Coke, It's the Real Thing*, FORBES, Mar. 7, 2013, http://www.forbes.com/sites/rogerdooley/2013/03/07/coke-neuro marketing/#7fddcfce2ed2; Press Release, Volvo Cars Newsroom, *Car Design Proven to be on a Par with the Most Basic of Human Emotions*, Nov. 28, 2013, available at https:// www.media.volvocars.com/uk/en-gb/media/pressreleases/136009/volvo-cars-world -first-experiment reveals the emotive power of car-design.

7. Kathryn A. Braun-LaTour & Gerald Zaltman, *Memory Change: An Intimate Measure of Persuasion*, 46 J. ADVERTISING RES. 57, 58 (2006).

8. ERIK DU PLESSIS, THE BRANDED MIND: WHAT NEUROSCIENCE REALLY TELLS US ABOUT THE PUZZLE OF THE BRAIN AND THE BRAND 64–65 (2014); PATRICK M. GEORGES ET AL., NEUROMARKETING IN ACTION: HOW TO TALK AND SELL TO THE BRAIN 42 (2013); ROBERT HEATH, SEDUCING THE SUBCONSCIOUS: THE PSYCHOLOGY OF EMOTIONAL INFLUENCE IN ADVERTISING 53, 101–04 (2012); DOUGLAS VAN PRAET, UNCONSCIOUS BRANDING: HOW NEUROSCIENCE CAN EMPOWER (AND INSPIRE) MARKETING 79–88 (2014).

9. John Wanamaker, The Quotations Page, http:// www.quotationspage.com/ quotes/john_wanamaker (last visited Oct. 1, 2016).

10. LAWRENCE R. SAMUEL, FREUD ON MADISON AVENUE: MOTIVATION RESEARCH AND SUBLIMINAL ADVERTISING IN AMERICA 66–67 (2010).

11. GEORGES ET AL., *supra* note 8, at 22–25; HEATH, *supra* note 8, at 127–28.

12. FEDERAL TRADE COMMISSION, FACING FACTS: BEST PRACTICES FOR COMMON USES OF FACIAL RECOGNITION TECHNOLOGIES (2012); HEATH, *supra* note 8, at 128; Car-

los Flavian-Blanco et al., *Analyzing the Emotional Outcomes of the Online Search Behavior with Search Engines*, 27 COMPUTERS IN HUM. BEHAV. 540, 544 (2011) (correlating particular eye movements during online search process with searcher emotions).

13. GEORGES, *supra* note 8, at 23.

14. Vinod Venkatraman et al., *New Scanner Data for Brand Marketers: How Neuroscience Can Help Better Understand Differences in Brand Preferences*, 22 J. CONSUMER. PSYCH. 143, 149 (2012).

15. Hilke Plassmann, *What Can Advertisers Learn from Neuroscience?*, 26 INTL. J. ADVER. 151, 162–63 (2007).

16. Samuel M. McClure et al., *Neural Correlates of Behavioral Preference for Culturally Familiar Drinks*, 44 NEURON 379, 379 (2004).

17. PHIL BARDEN, DECODED: THE SCIENCE BEHIND WHY WE BUY 6–9 (2013).

18. VAN PRAET, *supra* note 8, at 39–48; Michael Schaefer & Michael Rotte, *Thinking on Luxury or Pragmatic Brand Products: Brain Responses to Different Categories of Culturally Based Brands*, 1165 BRAIN. RES. 98, 101–02 (2007).

19. Carsten Murawski et al., *Led into Temptation? Rewarding Brand Logos Bias the Neural Encoding of Incidental Economic Decisions*, 7 PLOS ONE 1, 5–6 (2012).

20. BARDEN, *supra* note 17, at 6–9.

21. Plassmann, *supra* note 15, at 160–62.

22. VAN PRAET, *supra* note 8, at 83.

23. Kathyrn A. Braun et al., *Make My Memory: How Advertising Can Change Memories of the Past*, 19 PSYCH. & MKTG. 1, 1 (2002); *see also* Priyali Rajagopal & Nicole Votolato Montgomery, *I Imagine, I Experience, I Like: The False Experience Effect*, 38 J. CONS. RES. 578, 579 (2011).

24. Kathryn A. Braun, *Postexperience Advertising Effects on Consumer Memory*, 24 J. CONS. RES. 319, 320–21 (1999).

25. BARDEN, *supra* note 17, at 84, 117; HEATH, *supra* note 8, at 70–73, 87–97; Jonah Lehrer, *Ads Implant False Memories*, WIRED, May 25, 2011, http://www.wired.com /2011/05/ads-implant-false-memories/.

26. S. Adam Brasel & James Gips, *Breaking Through Fast-Forwarding: Brand Information and Visual Attention*, 47 J. MKTG. 31, 31–48 (2008).

27. Richard E. Petty et al., *Central and Peripheral Routes to Advertising Effectiveness—the Moderating Role of Involvement*, 10 J. CONS. RES. 135, 135–46 (1983); Robin J. Tanner & Ahreum Maeng, *A Tiger and a President: Imperceptible Celebrity Facial Cues Influence Trust and Preference*, 39 J. CONS. RES. 769 (2012).

28. BARDEN, *supra* note 17, at 74–75; Stewart Shapiro et al., *The Effects of Incidental Ad Exposure on the Formation of Consideration Sets*, 24 J. CONS. RES. 94, 94–104 (1997).

29. Linyun W. Yang et al., *Distinctively Different: Exposure to Multiple Brands in Low-Elaboration Settings*, 40 J. CONS. RES. 973, 975 (2014).

30. Yang et al., *supra*, at 988.

31. Tanya L. Chartrand et al., *Nonconscious Goals and Consumer Choice*, 35 J. CONS. RES. 189, 196 (2008).

32. Murawski, *supra* note 19, at 4–6; Daniel Bennett, *How to Take Control of Your*

Brain and Make Better Decisions, WASH. POST, Nov. 5, 2014, https://www.washing-tonpost.com/posteverything/wp/2014/11/05/how-to-take-control-of-your-brain-and-make-better-decisions/.

33. BARDEN, *supra* note 17, at 169.

34. Shane Baxendale et al., *The Impact of Different Touchpoints on Brand Consideration*, 91 J. RETAIL 235, 236–37 (2015).

35. Adam D.I. Kramer et al., *Experimental Evidence of Massive-Scale Emotional Contagion Through Social Networks*, 111 PROC. NAT'L ACAD. SCI. 8788, 8788–90 (2014).

36. Vindu Goel, *Facebook Tinkers with Users' Emotions in News Feed Experiment, Stirring Outcry*, N.Y. TIMES, June 29, 2014, at B1; *see also* Bruce Bower, *The Hot and Cold of PRIMING: Psychologists Are Divided on Whether Unnoticed Cues Can Influence Behavior*, 181 SCI. NEWS. 26, 29 (2012); Fadhi Chehimi et al., *Augmented Reality 3D Interactive Advertisements on Smartphones*, Sixth Int'l Conference on the Mgmt. of Mobile Bus. (2007) (discussing how typical smartphone displays can be augmented for "more subliminal effect"); Mark Yi-Cheon Kim et al., *In-Store Video Advertising Effectiveness*, 50 J. ADVERTISING RES. 386, 386–402 (2010).

37. GEORGES, *supra* note 8, at 25, 110, 143, 171

38. Paul Rose, *Mediators of the Relationship between Narcissism and Compulsive Buying: The Roles of Materialism and Impulse Control*, 21 PSYCH. ADDICTIVE BEHAV. 576, 576–81 (2007); Evan Selinger & Shaun Foster, *How'd My Avatar Get into That Sneaker Ad?*, SLATE, Jan. 4, 2012, http://www.slate.com/articles/technology/future_tense/2012/01/behaviorally_targeted_ads_and_the_ethical_dilemmas_behind_building_consumers_into_ads_.html. Some of the segmentation strategies discovered through neuroscience can be implemented through online surveillance. Advertisers can identify individual propensities toward narcissism by recording how many times someone searches for her own name or posts about his activities. Google examines search activity to determine how easily individuals get irritated. Computers studying our Facebook likes make significantly more accurate assessments of our underlying personality traits than our own parents, friends, or spouses. Wu Youyou et al., *Computer-based Personality Judgments Are More Accurate Than Those Made by Humans*, 112 PROC. NAT'L. ACAD. SCI. 1036, 1036–40 (2015).

39. Drew Harwell, *Pizza Hut Wants to Read Your Mind*, WASH. POST, Dec. 1, 2014, https://www.washingtonpost.com/news/the-switch/wp/2014/12/01/pizza-hut-wants-to-read-your-mind/.

40. Jessi Hempel, *Computers That Know How You Feel Will Soon Be Everywhere*, WIRED, Apr. 22, 2015, http://www.wired.com/2015/04/computers-can-now-tell-feel-face/; Ki Mae Heussner, *Beyond Verbal Snags $1M More for Emotion-Decoding Voice Recognition Software*, GIGAOM.COM, July 23, 2013, available at https://gigaom.com/2013/07/23/beyond-verbal-snags-1m-for-emotion-decoding-voice-recognition-software/; Press Release, Beyond Verbal, *Beyond Verbal Launches Patented Technology that Decodes Human Emotions through Raw Voice*, Aug. 5, 2013, available at http://www.prnewswire.com/news-releases/beyond-verbal-launches-patented-technology-that-decodes-human-emotions-through-raw-voice-206639221.html.

41. Elizabeth Dwoskin & Evelyn M. Rusli, *The Technology That Unmasks Your Hidden Emotions*, WALL ST. J., Jan. 28, 2015, http://www.wsj.com/articles/startups-see-your-face-unmask-your-emotions-1422472398.

42. LYNCH, *supra* note 4, at 71.

43. Ivan Martinovic et al., *On the Feasibility of Side-Channel Attacks with Brain-Computer Interfaces*, *in* PROCEEDINGS OF THE 21ST USENIX SECURITY SYMPOSIUM, USENIX, 2012; Tamara Bonaci et al., *App Stores for the Brain: Privacy and Security in Brain-Computer Interfaces*, 2014 IEEE Int'l Symposium on Ethics in Science, Technology, and Engineering 1–7, 23–24.

44. Lev Grossman, *How Apple Is Invading Our Bodies*, TIME, Sept. 10, 2014, http://time.com/3318655/apple-watch-2/; *see also* Darrell Etherington, *Apple Patent Explores Mood-Based Ad Targeting*, TECHCRUNCH, Jan 23, 2014, http://techcrunch.com/2014/01/23/apple-patent-explores-mood-based-ad-targeting/.

45. MARCO IACOBONI, MIRRORING PEOPLE: THE SCIENCE OF EMPATHY AND HOW WE CONNECT WITH OTHERS 223 (2009).

46. PRADEEP, *supra* note 2, at 58.

47. HEATH, *supra* note 8, at 107.

48. HARRY BECKWITH, THE INVISIBLE TOUCH: FOUR KEYS TO MODERN MARKETING 5–6, 17–18 (2000); SAMUEL, *supra* note 10, at 7.

49. LIZBETH COHEN, A CONSUMER'S REPUBLIC: THE POLITICS OF MASS CONSUMPTION IN POSTWAR AMERICA 55 (2003); WILLIAM LEACH, LAND OF DESIRE 6 (1993); CHARLES F. MCGOVERN, SOLD AMERICAN: CONSUMPTION AND CITIZENSHIP, 1890–1945, at 7 (2006).

50. Va. State Bd. of Pharmacy v. Va. Citizens Consumer Council, Inc., 425 U.S. 748, 763 (1976).

51. MARGARET SCAMMELL, CONSUMER DEMOCRACY: THE MARKETING OF POLITICS 166 (2014).

52. *See, e.g.*, BARDEN, *supra* note 17, at 182–83.

53. IACOBONI, *supra* note 45, at 227.

54. Jon D. Hanson & Douglas A. Kysar, *Taking Behavioralism Seriously: The Problem of Market Manipulation*, 74 N.Y.U. L. REV. 630 (1999).

55. DU PLESSIS, *supra* note 8, at 141; Wendy Melillo, *Inside the Consumer Mind*, ADWEEK, Jan. 16, 2006, http://www.adweek.com/news/advertising/inside-consumer-mind-83549.

56. Nicholas A. Valentino et al., *Cues That Matter: How Political Ads Prime Racial Attitudes During Campaigns*, 96 AM. POL. SCI. REV. 75 (2002) (showing how subtle racial cues can impact behavior without awareness).

57. Bob Garfield, *Cheetos Ads That Promote "Random Acts" Are Irresponsible*, ADVERTISING AGE, May 26, 2008, http://adage.com/article/ad-review/cheetos-ads-promote-random-acts-irresponsible/127306/.

58. NAOMI KLEIN, NO LOGO: TAKING AIM AT BRAND BULLIES 7 (2000).

59. JAMES D. NORRIS, ADVERTISING AND THE TRANSFORMATION OF AMERICAN SOCIETY, 1865–1920, at 43 (1990); DANIEL POPE, THE MAKING OF MODERN ADVERTISING

232 (1983); Robert G. Bone, *Hunting Goodwill: A History of the Concept of Goodwill in Trademark Law*, 86 B.U. L. Rev. 547, 575 (2006).

60. Samuel, *supra* note 10, at 6.

61. Henry Foster Adams, Advertising and its Mental Laws 57 (2d ed. 1922).

62. Albert T. Poffenberger, Psychology in Advertising 7 (2d ed. 1932).

63. Walter Dill Scott, The Psychology of Advertising 84 (1908).

64. Dayton Eng'g Labs. Co. v. Kent, 260 F. 187, 189 (E.D. Pa. 1919).

65. Rubber & Celluloid Harness Trimming Co. v. F.W. Devoe & C.T. Reynolds Co., 233 F. 150, 155 (D.N.J. 1916).

66. Frank Schechter, The Historical Foundations Relating to the Law of Trade-Marks 166 (1925).

67. Edward S. Rogers, *The Unwary Purchaser*, 8 Mich. L. Rev. 613, 617 (1910).

68. Coca-Cola Co. v. Chero-Cola Co., 273 F. 755, 757 (D.C. Cir. 1921); Robert Bonynge, *Trademark Surveys and Techniques and Their Use in Litigation*, 48 A.B.A. J. 329, 330 (1962).

69. Florence Mfg. Co. v. J.C. Dowd & Co., 178 F. 73, 75 (2d Cir. 1910).

70. Samuel, *supra* note 10, at 93, 115–16; Thomas Albert Bliss, *Subliminal Projection: History and Analysis*, 5 Hastings Comm. & Ent. L.J. 419 (1983).

71. *Huxley Fears New Persuasion Methods Could Subvert Democratic Procedures*, N.Y. Times, May, 19, 1958, at 45.

72. Marya Mannes, *Ain't Nobody Here But Us Commercials*, Reporter, Oct. 17, 1957, at 35, 37.

73. Kenneth Lipartito, *Subliminal Seduction: The Politics of Consumer Research in Post-World War II America*, in The Rise of Marketing and Market Research 215, 217–18 (Harmut Berghoff et al. eds., 2012); FCC Public Notice, Broadcast of Information by Means of "Subliminal Perception" Techniques, 44 F.C.C. 2d 1016 (Jan. 24, 1974).

74. Frank I. Schechter, *The Rational Basis of Trademark Protection*, 40 Harv. L. Rev. 813, 825 (1927). Schechter's article is credited with introducing the dilution concept in trademark law.

75. Mishawaka Rubber & Woolen Mfg. Co. v. S.S. Kresge Co., 316 U.S. 203, 208 (1942).

76. Mark Bartholomew, *Advertising and the Transformation of Trademark Law*, 38 N.M. L. Rev. 1, 36–38 (2008).

77. Van Praet, *supra* note 8, at 215; Jean-Baptiste Legal et al., *Don't You Know That You Want to Trust Me? Subliminal Goal Priming and Persuasion*, 48 J. Experimental Soc. Psych. 358, 358–60 (2012).

78. Theodore Voorhees, Jr. et al., Neuromarketing: Legal and Policy Issues, Covington & Burling White Paper 8 (2011), available at http://www.cov.com/files/upload/White_Paper_Neuromarketing_Legal_and_Policy_Issues.pdf.

79. Some respond to neuromarketing with a shrug because Vicary's experiment turned out to be a hoax. If 1950s subliminal advertising was more hype than reality, maybe the same is true of neuromarketing in 2017. Recent studies demonstrate, however, that subliminal messages, particularly ones involving brand names, *can* influence consumer behavior. For example, when subliminally primed with the brand name of a drink, thirsty subjects selected the primed brand over similar branded beverages.

Johan C. Karremans et al., *Beyond Vicary's Fantasies: The Impact of Subliminal Priming and Brand Choice*, 42 J. EXP. SOC. PSYCH. 792 (2006). Psychologists now acknowledge evidence that "brands can automatically activate purchase goals in individuals and that these goals can influence consumers' product preferences without their awareness or conscious intent." Chartrand, *supra* note 31, at 196. In general, rather than being discredited since Vicary's time, subliminal priming has become a linchpin of research in experimental social psychology. Dan Ariely & Gregory S. Berns, *Neuromarketing: The Hope and Hype of Neuroimaging in Business*, 11 NAT. REV. NEUROSCIENCE 284, 284–91 (2010).

80. Federal Trade Commission, Commission Statement of Policy on the Scope of the Consumer Unfairness Jurisdiction (1980), *appended to* Final Order, Int'l Harvester Co., 104 F.T.C. 949, 1070 (1984), http:// www.ftc.gov/bcp/policystmt/ad-unfair.htm.

81. The FTC also has the authority to prohibit "deceptive" trade practices. Neuromarketing might be described as "deceptive," both because it tends to lead the consumer to purchase without presenting relevant information and because it can be particularly effective against vulnerable populations. In the past, the FTC has used its resources to halt marketing schemes aimed at children and the elderly, populations also targeted by neuromarketers.

82. The FTC did ask food and beverage companies to disclose whether they have conducted neuroscientific research meant to strengthen their appeals to children, but this information has not produced any particular action by the agency as of this writing.

83. Kathryn Abrams & Hila Karen, *Who's Afraid of Law and the Emotions?*, 94 MINN. L. REV. 1997, 2003–08 (2010).

84. In addition to FTC review of advertising, false advertising laws allow private entities to use the courts to try and stop particular advertising representations. These laws have been narrowly construed, however, to apply only to factual statements that are literally or impliedly false. In a world where the bulk of modern marketing is directed at infusing brands with emotional charge, this body of law can do little.

85. Complaint and Request for Investigation, submitted by the Center for Digital Democracy, Consumer Action, Consumer Watchdog, and the Praxis Project, Oct. 19, 2011, at 2, http://case-studies.digitalads.org/wp-content/uploads/2011/10/complaint.pdf.

86. VAN PRAET, *supra* note 8, at 22.

87. *HumancentiPad*, WIKIPEDIA.ORG, http://en.wikipedia.org/wiki/HumancentiPad.

88. *See* James Grimmelmann, *Social Media Experiments and the Common Rule*, 13 COLO. TECH. L.J. 219, 240–43 (2015). Perhaps not unrelated, there is more and more cross-pollination between the business community and universities when it comes to brain study. Institutions of higher learning routinely allow businesses to use their brain imaging equipment (for a hefty fee) to perform applied market research. Meanwhile, private organizations like eBay and the National Association of Securities Dealers hire university neuroscientists to scan representative members of their clientele and refine their advertising campaigns while neuromarketing firms recruit respected scientists to serve on their corporate boards.

89. For example, Pradeep contends that "at the outset of neuromarketing research it

is critical to tease out the elements of Form that are connected in the subconscious, and match those elements with the company's protected IP, trademarks, and copyrights to determine how to best protect them (and, ultimately, leverage them)." PRADEEP, *supra* note 2, at 123.

90. Moseley v. V Secret Catalogue, 537 U.S. 418 (2003).

91. Louis Vuitton Malletier, S.A. v. Hyundai Motor Am., No. 10 CIV. 1611 PKC, 2012 WL 1022247, at *13, *20 (S.D.N.Y. Mar. 22, 2012).

92. V Secret Catalogue v. Moseley, 605 F.3d 382, 389 (6th Cir. 2010). The lingerie leviathan offered little evidence that dilution was likely, submitting only a self-serving affidavit from one of its own corporate officers and a statement from a local onlooker who contended that he was "offended" by the defendants' use of the Victoria's Secret trademark. *Id.* at 385–86. Neither piece of evidence indicates that consumers are likely to form any different impression of the Victoria's Secret brand after visiting "Victor's Little Secret."

93. Tom Reichart et al., *How Sex in Advertising Varies by Product Category: An Analysis of Three Decades of Visual Sexual Imagery in Magazine Advertising*, 33 J. CURRENT ISSUES IN RES. & ADVERTISING 1, 1–19 (2012).

94. Take, for example, the case of rapper "Rolls Royce Rizzy." A federal court deemed his stage name tarnishing to the famous luxury car brand, basing its decision, in part, on song titles like "Hoe in You" and an advertisement featuring "a scantily-clad woman." Rolls-Royce Motor Cars v. Robert D. Davis, No. 15–0417, slip op. at 15–16 (D.N.J. March 11, 2016). For other examples, see Mark Bartholomew, *Trademark Morality*, 55 WM. & MARY L. REV. 85, 134–38 (2013).

95. Some of this change occurred through legislative prompting as Congress removed limiting language from the federal trademark statute. *See* GRAEME B. DINWOODIE & MARK D. JANIS, TRADEMARKS AND UNFAIR COMPETITION: LAW AND POLICY 492–93 (4th ed. 2014).

96. Playboy Enterprises, Inc. v. Chuckleberry Pub. Inc., 687 F.2d 563, 567–70 (2d Cir. 1982); Verifine Products, Inc., v. Colon Bros., Inc., 799 F. Supp. 240, 251 (D. Puerto Rico, 1992); Suncoast Tours, Inc. v. Lambert Group, Inc., No. CIV.A.98-5627, 1999 WL 1034683, at *5 n.4 (D.N.J. 1999); Resorts Int'l, Inc. v. Greate Bay Hotel & Casino, Inc., 830 F. Supp. 826, 838 (D.N.J. 1992); Oxford Indus., Inc. v. JBJ Fabrics, Inc., No. 84 CIV 2505, 1988 WL 9959, at *3 (S.D.N.Y. 1988).

97. See Mark A. Lemley & Mark McKenna, *Irrelevant Confusion*, 62 STAN L. REV. 413 (2010).

98. Bd. of Supervisors for La. State Univ. Agric. & Mech. Coll. v. Smack Apparel Co., 550 F.3d 465, 484 (5th Cir. 2008). Trademark law contains some mechanisms for protecting free expression, including defenses that immunize descriptive and nominative mark uses not meant to brand the defendant's product. The federal dilution statute holds safe the use of famous marks in parody, comparative advertising, and noncommercial expression. But judges have limited the applicability of these defenses, often conflating them with underlying questions of confusion or dilution, and thereby reinforcing the ability of trademark owners to curtail discourse that conflicts with their own brand

message. Mark Bartholomew & John Tehranian, *An Intersystemic View of Intellectual Property and Free Speech*, 81 GEO. WASH. L. REV. 1, 41–54 (2013).

99. 15 U.S.C. § 1125(c).

100. DU PLESSIS, *supra* note 8, at 231.

101. GEORGES, *supra* note 8, at 130.

102. N.Y. State Soc'y of Certified Pub. Accountants v. Eric Louis Assocs., Inc., 79 F. Supp. 2d 331, 341 (S.D.N.Y. 1999); Lee Goldman, *Proving Dilution*, 58 U. MIAMI L. REV. 569, 580 (2004); Jess Bidgood, *Chicken Chain Says Stop, But T-Shirt Maker Balks*, N.Y. TIMES, Dec. 4, 2011, at A12.

103. Joshua Greene & Jonathan Cohen, *For the Law, Neuroscience Changes Nothing and Everything*, 359 PHIL. TRANSACTIONS ROYAL SOC'Y LONDON B 1775, 1775–76 (2004); Adam J. Kolber, *Will There Be a Neurolaw Revolution?*, 89 IND. L.J. 807, 832–35 (2014); David Eagleman, *The Brain on Trial*, ATLANTIC, July–Aug. 2011, at 112, 115.

Chapter 5

1. Jenna Wortham, *Kim Kardashian, an Unlikely Mobile Video Game Hit*, N.Y. TIMES, July 30, 2014, http://bits.blogs.nytimes.com/2014/07/30/kim-kardashian-an -unlikely-mobile-video-game-hit/. Other celebrities have sought to duplicate the success of Kardashian's game, with Taylor Swift, Britney Spears, Nicki Minaj, and TV chef Gordon Ramsay all partnering with Kardashian's games publisher, Glu Mobile. Stuart Dredge, *Taylor Swift to Front Mobile Game from Kim Kardashian: Hollywood Publisher*, GUARDIAN, Feb. 4, 2016, https://www.theguardian.com/technology/2016/feb/04/ taylor-swift-mobile-game-kim-kardashian.

2. PALMYRA SCHOOLS, http://www.palmyraschools.com/ps/Food%20Services/ Menu%20Description.pdf (last visited June 9, 2016).

3. Emma Barnett, *New Site Lets Celebrity Twitter Users "Know Their Followers,"* TELEGRAPH, Oct. 28, 2011, http://www.telegraph.co.uk/technology/news/8854052/New -site-lets-celebrity-Twitter-users-know-their-followers.html; Jasmine Jaume, *How Do People Feel about Celebrity Perfumes?*, BRANDWATCH, Mar. 4, 2013, https://www.bran dwatch.com/2013/03/how-do-people-feel-about-celebrity-perfumes/.

4. Vasily Klucharev et al., *Brain Mechanisms of Persuasion: How "Expert Power" Modulates Memory and Attitudes*, 3 SOC. COGNITIVE & AFFECTIVE NEUROSCIENCE 353 (2008); Mirre Stallen et al., *Celebrities and Shoes on the Female Brain: The Neural Correlates of Product Evaluation in the Context of Fame*, 31 J. ECON. PSYCH. 802 (2010).

5. ROBERT VAN KRIEKEN, CELEBRITY SOCIETY 87–90 (2012).

6. Christie D'Zurilla, *Kim Kardashian, Old Navy Settle over Commercial Starring Lookalike*, L.A. TIMES, Aug. 29, 2012, http://articles.latimes.com/2012/aug/29/ entertainment/la-et-mg-kim-kardashian-old-navy-settle-lawsuit-melissa-molinaro.

7. Davis v. Trans World Airlines, 297 F. Supp. 1145, 1147 (C.D. Cal. 1969) ("[I]mitation alone does not give rise to a cause of action.").

8. One must be careful before proposing a causal relationship between legal innovation and social behavior. I am not suggesting that the changing law of celebrity publicity rights controls the behaviors of everyday social media users. Instead, my goal here is the

more modest one of flagging a legal change, noting a concurrent shift in communicative practices, and asking whether there may be some relationship between the two. What should be uncontroversial, even if a causal connection cannot be conclusively proven, is that cultural practices routinely influence the law and vice versa. *See* P. John Kozyris, *Comparative Law for the Twenty-First Century: New Horizons and New Technologies*, 69 TUL. L. REV. 165, 168 (1994).

9. Mark Rogowsky, *Twitter's Problem Isn't a Lack of Tweeters*, FORBES, April 12, 2014, http://www.forbes.com/sites/markrogowsky/2014/04/12/you-dont-need-to-tweet-to-use-twitter-so-why-is-everyone-bothered-few-do/.

10. Tennessee Williams, *On a Streetcar Named Success*, N.Y. TIMES, Nov. 30, 1947, at X1.

11. DANIEL HERWITZ, THE STAR AS ICON 15 (2008); P. DAVID MARSHALL, CELEBRITY AND POWER: FAME IN CONTEMPORARY CULTURE 91 (1997).

12. Joe Flint, *Celebs Muffle the Voice of Experience*, L.A. TIMES, May 7, 2012, http://articles.latimes.com/2012/may/07/business/la fi ct voiceover 20120507.

13. ELLIS CASHMORE, CELEBRITY/CULTURE 229 (2006); Julie Creswell, *Nothing Sells Like Celebrity*, N.Y. TIMES, June 22, 2008, at BU1.

14. Katherine Rosman, *Behind That Celebrity Tweet*, WALL ST. J., May 29, 2012, http://www.wsj.com/articles/SB10001424052702303674004577434474251628002.

15. Tessa Stuart, *Secrets of a Celebrity Twitter Coach*, BUZZFEED, Feb. 19, 2013, http://www.buzzfeed.com/tessastuart/secrets-of-a-celebrity-twitter-coach#.ftvBK5ELq.

16. Chadwick Matlin, *Charlie Sheen's First Paying Twitter Customer*, ATLANTIC, Mar. 11, 2011, http://www.theatlantic.com/technology/archive/2011/03/charlie-sheens-first-paying-twitter-customer/72327/.

17. Liat Komowski, *Celebrity Sponsored Tweets: What the Stars Get Paid for Advertising in 140 Characters*, HUFFINGTON POST, Nov. 11, 2013, http://www.huffingtonpost.com/2013/05/30/celebrity-sponsored-tweets_n_3360562.html.

18. Stephanie Leonard, *Top 75 Highest-Paid Athlete Endorsers of 2014*, OPENDORSE, Feb. 26, 2015, http://opendorse.com/blog/top-75-highest-paid-athlete-endorsers-2014/.

19. Emma Bazilian, *Millennial Models Like Gigi Hadid, Fueled by Social, Are Hitting the Fashion Stratosphere*, ADWEEK, March. 30, 2015, http://www.adweek.com/news/technology/millennial-models-are-hitting-fashion-stratosphere-163745; *see also* Sapna Maheshwari, *Endorsed by a Kardashian, but Is It Love or Just an Ad?*, N.Y. TIMES, Aug., 30, 2016, at A1.

20. BUMEBOX, http://www.bumebox.com/what-we-do/ (last visited June 9, 2016).

21. Lauren Johnson, *As WhoSay's Celeb Network Grows, More Marketers Look to Stars for Branded Content*, ADWEEK, Feb. 16, 2015, http://www.adweek.com/news/technology/marketers-bet-celebrities-churn-out-branded-content-162970; *Case Study: WhoSay Helps Its Advertisers Target Celebrity Fans All Across the Web*, KRUX.COM, http://www.krux.com/customer-success/case-studies/whosay-case-study/ (last visited June 9, 2016).

22. ROBERT B. CIALDINI, INFLUENCE: THE PSYCHOLOGY OF PERSUASION 116, 212–230 (2006); JAKE HALPERN, FAME JUNKIES 122–23 (2007); SALLY SATEL & SCOTT O. LILIENFELD, BRAINWASHED: THE SEDUCTIVE APPEAL OF MINDLESS NEUROSCIENCE 45 (2013).

23. Mark R. Forehand & Andrew Perkins, *Implicit Assimilation and Explicit Contrast: A Set/Reset Model of Response to Consumer Voiceovers*, 32 J. Cons. Res. 434 (2005); Robin J. Tanner & Ahreum Maeng, *A Tiger and a President: Imperceptible Celebrity Facial Cues Influence Trust and Preference*, 39 J. Cons. Res. 769 (2012).

24. Craig L. Garthwaite, *Demand Spillovers, Combative Advertising, and Celebrity Endorsements*, 6 Am. Econ. J.: Applied Econ. 76, 78 (2014); R. Bruce Money et al., *Celebrity Endorsements in Japan and the United States: Is Negative Information All That Harmful?*, 46 J. Advertising Res. 113, 113–14 (2006).

25. Theresa M. Senft, Camgirls: Celebrity and Community in the Age of Social Media 25 (2008); Theresa M. Senft, *Microcelebrity and the Branded Self, in* A Companion to New Media Dynamics 346, 346–54 (John Hartley et al. eds., 2013); Graeme Turner, Understanding Celebrity 71–73 (2d ed. 2014).

26. Alice E. Marwick & danah boyd, *To See and Be Seen: Celebrity Practice on Twitter*, 17 Convergence 139, 149 (2011).

27. *FAQ*, Instagram, https://instagram.com/about/faq/ (last visited June 9, 2016).

28. Abby Phillip, *Online "Authenticity" and How Facebook's "Real Name" Policy Hurts Native Americans*, Wash. Post, Feb. 10, 2015, http://www.washingtonpost .com/news/morning-mix/wp/2015/02/10/online-authenticity-and-how-facebooks -real-name-policy-hurts-native-americans/.

29. Instagram, *supra* note 27.

30. Jacob Silverman, Terms of Service: Social Media and the Price of Constant Connection 12 (2015); Casey Johnston, *Facebook Is Tracking What You* Don't *Do on Facebook*, ArsTechnica, Dec. 16, 2013, http://arstechnica.com/business/2013/12/ facebook-collects-conducts-research-on-status-updates-you-never-post/.

31. Leanne Bayley, *Selfie Mania! We Spend 753 Hrs Taking Pics of Ourselves*, Glamour, May 21, 2014, http://www.glamourmagazine.co.uk/news/beauty/2014/05/21/the -body-shop-selfie-study; *see also* Suvi Uski & Airi Lampinen, *Social Norms and Self-Presentation on Social Network Sites: Profile Work in Action*, 18 New Media & Society 447 (2014).

32. danah boyd, It's Complicated: The Social Lives of Networked Teens 148 (2014).

33. Matt McFarland, *What Twitter Is, As Explained by Its Evolving Tagline*, Wash. Post, Sept. 12, 2014, http://www.washingtonpost.com/blogs/innovations/wp/2014/09/12 /what-is-twitter-as-explained-by-its-evolving-tagline/.

34. For a Marxian analysis of commodity fetishism in the appearance and behavior of pop star Lana Del Rey, see Sean Redmond, Celebrity & the Media 53–58 (2014).

35. Charles Lindholm, Culture and Authenticity 59–63 (2008).

36. Laura Grindstaff & Susan Murray, *Reality Celebrity: Branded Affect and the Emotion Economy*, 27 Public Culture 109, 119–20 (2015).

37. Erving Goffman, The Presentation of Self in Everyday Life (1959).

38. Samantha Murphy Kelly, *Celebrities Are All Up in Your Facebook Statuses*, Mashable.com, Aug. 11, 2014, http://mashable.com/2014/08/11/celebrities-facebook-status

-mentions/; Heather Kelly, *Facebook Plans Private Tools for Celebrities*, CNN, Aug. 14, 2013, http://www.cnn.com/2013/08/14/tech/social-media/facebook-vip-feature/.

39. Jeremy Beiler, *Stars Gain Control of Online Images*, N.Y. TIMES, May 8, 2011, at B5.

40. JON RONSON, SO YOU'VE BEEN PUBLICLY SHAMED 263–68 (2015).

41. Michael Cieply, *A PR Firm Alters Wikipedia Pages of Its Star Clients*, N.Y. TIMES, June 23, 2015, at B3.

42. Christine Erickson, *What to Do When Your Celebrity Client Flips Out on Social Media*, MASHABLE.COM, Feb. 17, 2012, http://mashable.com/2012/02/17/celebrity-publi cist-social-media/.

43. danah boyd, *Super Publics*, APOPHENIA, Mar. 22, 2006, http://www.zephoria.org/ thoughts/archives/2006/03/22/super publics.html.

44. Veronica Rocha, *"Revenge Porn" Conviction Is a First under California Law*, L.A. TIMES, Dec. 4, 2014, http://www.latimes.com/local/crime/la-me-1204-revenge-porn -20141205-story.html.

45. Caille Millner, *Public Humiliation over Private Photos*, S.F. GATE, Feb. 10, 2013, http://www.sfgate.com/opinion/article/Public-humiliation-over-private-photos -4264155.php#photo-416158/.

46. Nina Burleigh, *Shame, Sexting, and Suicide*, ROLLING STONE, Sept. 17, 2013, http:// www.rollingstone.com/culture/news/sexting-shame-and-suicide-20130917?page=5.

47. Jon Ronson, *How One Stupid Tweet Blew Up Justine Sacco's Life*, N.Y. TIMES MAG., Feb. 12, 2015, at MM20.

48. *Former Mabank Firefighter Says Facebook Post Taken Out of Context*, KLTV.COM, June 22, 2015, http://www.kltv.com/story/29381345/former-mabank-firefighter-says-face book-post-taken-out-of-context.

49. Andrea Chang, *New Ad Platform Targets Mobile Users by Serving Social Media*, L.A. TIMES, May 22, 2013, http://articles.latimes.com/2013/may/22/business/la-fi-tn -mobile-ads-uberads-20130521; Evie Nagy, *How Brands Are Using Your Best Instagram Shots for More Authentic Marketing*, FAST COMPANY, July 9, 2014, http://www.fastcom pany.com/3032732/most-creative-people/how-brands-are-using-your-best-instagram -shots-for-more-authentic-marketing; Jeff John Roberts, *Shutterfly Hit with Privacy Suit over "Faceprints," Use of Photos*, FORTUNE, June 18, 2015, http://fortune.com/2015/06/18/ shutterfly-lawsuit-facial-recognition/.

50. Adi Robertson, *Facebook May Know You Better Than Your Friends Do—But Does It Matter?*, VERGE, Jan. 16, 2015, http://www.theverge.com/2015/1/16/7545389/facebook -like-personality-test-behaviors.

51. Steve Rosen, *Social Media Activity Might Affect Your Credit Score*, CHI. TRIB., Nov. 2, 2015, http://www.chicagotribune.com/lifestyles/sns-201511020000-tms—kidmoney ctnsr—cc20151102-20151102-story.html.

52. *See* MARY MADDEN ET AL., PUBLIC PERCEPTIONS OF PRIVACY AND SECURITY IN THE POST-SNOWDEN ERA (2014).

53. GOFFMAN, *supra* note 37, at 107.

54. DAVID KIRKPATRICK, THE FACEBOOK EFFECT: THE INSIDER STORY OF THE COM-PANY THAT IS CONNECTING THE WORLD 199 (2011).

55. *Help Center: I Have Two Accounts. Can I Merge Them?*, FACEBOOK, https://www.facebook.com/help/203498356357867 (last visited June 9, 2016).

56. SHERRY TURKLE, LIFE ON THE SCREEN: IDENTITY IN THE AGE OF THE INTERNET (1995).

57. LINDHOLM, *supra* note 35, at 54.

58. Lauren Hansen, *What Happened to Second Life?*, BBC NEWS MAG., Nov. 20, 2009, http://news.bbc.co.uk/2/hi/8367957.stm.

59. JOSEPH TUROW, THE DAILY YOU: HOW THE NEW ADVERTISING INDUSTRY IS DEFINING YOUR IDENTITY AND YOUR WORTH (2011).

60. EVGENY MOROZOV, TO SAVE EVERYTHING, CLICK HERE: THE FOLLY OF TECHNOLOGICAL SOLUTIONISM 160–80 (2014).

61. Josh Constine, *Facebook Patents Clever Way to Advertise Just to Important People*, TECHCRUNCH, Feb. 16, 2015, http://techcrunch.com/2015/02/16/facebook-influencer-marketing/; *Tailored Audiences*, TWITTER, https://business.twitter.com/solutions/tailored-audiences (last visited June 9, 2016); *FAQ*, POPULAR PAYS, http://www.popularpays.com/faq/ (last visited May 11, 2016).

62. MICHAEL SERAZIO, YOUR AD HERE: THE COOL SELL OF GUERRILLA MARKETING 93 (2013); *Word of Mouth Marketing*, MARKETINGTERMS.COM, http://www.marketingterms.com/dictionary/word_of_mouth_marketing/ (last visited June 9, 2016).

63. WORD OF MOUTH MARKETING ASSOCIATION, THE STATE OF WORD OF MOUTH MARKETING: A SURVEY OF MARKETERS (2014).

64. Katherine Rosman, *Your Instagram Picture, Worth a Thousand Ads*, N.Y. TIMES, Oct. 15, 2014, at E1.

65. SERAZIO, *supra* note 62, at 120.

66. Kristen V. Brown, *Yelp Elites: Prolific Reviewers Get Perks, VIP Treatment*, S.F. GATE, Aug. 3, 2013, http://www.sfgate.com/restaurants/article/Yelp-Elites-Prolific-reviewers-get-perks-VIP-5664932.php; Garth Hallberg, *Who Is Grady Harp?*, SLATE, Jan 22, 2008, http://www.slate.com/articles/arts/culturebox/2008/01/who_is_grady_harp.html; Aristides Pinedo-Burns & Lauren Effron, *Turning Amazon Reviews Into Celebrity Status—and Free Stuff*, ABC NEWS, Feb. 6, 2015, http://abcnews.go.com/Lifestyle/turning-amazon-reviews-celebrity-status-free-stuff/story?id=28779976.

67. *Exclusive Monetization Opportunities for Celebrities*, IZEA.COM, http://corp.izea.com/creators/celebrities/ (last visited June 9, 2016).

68. *See generally* HELEN NISSENBAUM, PRIVACY IN CONTEXT: TECHNOLOGY, POLICY, AND THE INTEGRITY OF SOCIAL LIFE (2010).

69. Sue Campbell Clark, *Work/Family Border Theory: A New Theory of Work/Family Balance*, 53 HUMAN RELATIONS 747, 751–53 (2000).

70. Michael G. Pratt & Jose Antonio Rosa, *Transforming Work-Family Conflict into Commitment in Network Marketing Organizations*, 46 ACAD. MGMT. J. 395, 396–97 (2003).

71. SERAZIO, *supra* note 62, at 94–96.

72. Aaron Sankin, *That Facebook Post You Just Liked Is an Ad—and You Didn't Even Know It*, KERNEL, Sept. 6, 2015, http://kernelmag.dailydot.com/issue-sections/features-issue-sections/14194/facebook-sponsored-social-ftc/.

73. Ellen P. Goodman, *Stealth Marketing and Editorial Integrity*, 85 TEX. L. REV. 83, 112–15 (2006).

74. Press Release, Fed. Trade Comm'n, Sony Computer Entertainment America to Provide Consumer Refunds to Settle FTC Charges over Misleading Ads for PlayStation Vita Gaming Console: FTC Also Charges Los Angeles Ad Agency with Promoting Console Through Deceptive Twitter Endorsements (Nov. 25, 2014), http://www .ftc.gov/news-events/press-releases/2014/11/sony-computer-entertainment-america -provide-consumer-refunds.

75. Toffoloni v. LFP Publ'g Grp., 572 F.3d 1201, 1205 (11th Cir. 2009).

76. Haelan Labs. v. Topps Chewing Gum, 202 F.2d 866, 867–68 (2d Cir. 1953).

77. O'Brien v. Pabst Sales Co., 124 F.2d 167, 170 (5th Cir. 1941); Pallas v. Crowley-Milner & Co., 54 N.W.2d 595, 597 (Mich. 1952).

78. There are other limits on using trademark law to prevent appropriations of celebrity personas. For example, for an aspect of a person's identity to acquire trademark rights, that aspect has to be used as a mark. A celebrity who never commercially exploited the symbols of her identity would theoretically not be eligible for trademark protection. Mark Bartholomew, *A Right Is Born. Celebrity, Property, and Postmodern Lawmaking*, 44 CONN. L. REV. 301, 314 n.48 (2011).

79. Miller v. Comm'r of Internal Revenue, 299 F.2d 706, 711 (2d Cir. 1962).

80. Memphis Development, Etc. v. Factors Etc., Inc., 616 F.2d 956, 959 (6th Cir. 1980).

81. Hodel v. Irving, 481 U.S. 704, 716 (1987).

82. Guglielmi v. Spelling Goldberg Prods., 603 P.2d 454, 455 (Cal. 1979); Antonetty v. Cuomo, 502 N.Y.S.2d 902, 906 (Sup. Ct. 1986).

83. Sinatra v. Goodyear Tire & Rubber Co., 435 F.2d 711, 713, 718 (9th Cir. 1970).

84. Booth v. Colgate-Palmolive Co., 362 F. Supp. 343, 347 (S.D.N.Y. 1973).

85. Cardtoons v. Major League Baseball Players Ass'n, 95 F.3d 959, 967 (10th Cir. 1996); *see also* Crump v. Beckley Newspapers, Inc., 320 S.E.2d 70, 85 n.6 (W. Va. 1984).

86. Tenn. ex rel. Elvis Presley Int'l Mem. Found. v. Crowell, 733 S.W.2d 89, 96–97 (Tenn. App. 1987).

87. McFarland v. Miller, 14 F.3d 912, 916–18 (3d Cir. 1994).

88. Bartholomew, *supra* note 78, at 318.

89. Steven Semeraro, *Property's End: Why Competition Policy Should Limit the Right of Publicity*, 43 CONN. L. REV. 753, 757 (2011).

90. Lee Anne Fennell, *Adjusting Alienability*, 122 HARV. L. REV. 1403, 1404–06 (2009).

91. Tenn. ex rel. Elvis Presley Int'l Mem. Found. v. Crowell, 733 S.W.2d 89, 96 (Tenn. App. 1987).

92. Midler v. Ford Motor Co., 849 F.2d 460, 463 (9th Cir. 1988).

93. Waits v. Frito-Lay, Inc., 978 F.2d 1093, 1096, 1105 (9th Cir. 1992).

94. White v. Samsung Elec. Am., Inc., 971 F.2d 1395, 1399 (9th Cir. 1992).

95. Newcombe v. Adolf Coors Co., 157 F.3d 686, 691–93 (9th Cir. 1998).

96. Bartholomew, *supra* note 78, at 356–59.

97. Melissa B. Jacoby & Diane Leenheer Zimmerman, *Foreclosing on Fame: Explor-*

ing the Uncharted Boundaries of the Right of Publicity, 77 N.Y.U. L. Rev. 1322–24 (2002); Jennifer E. Rothman, *The Inalienable Right of Publicity*, 101 Geo. L.J. 185, 219–20 (2012).

98. Ray D. Madoff, Immortality and the Law: The Rising Power of the American Dead 139 (2010); Richard Rubin, *What Is Prince's Legacy Worth? The Tax Man Needs to Know*, Wall St. J., April 28, 2016, at A1.

99. Ray D. Madoff, *Taxing Personhood: Estate Taxes and the Compelled Commodification of Identity*, 17 Va. Tax. Rev. 759, 761–62 (1998).

100. Ellen S. Bass, Comment, *A Right in Search of a Coherent Rationale-Conceptualizing Persona in a Comparative Context: The United States Right of Publicity and German Personality Rights*, 42 U.S.F. L. Rev. 799 (2008).

101. Balt. Orioles, Inc. v. Major League Baseball Players Ass'n, 805 F.2d 663, 678 (7th Cir. 1986).

102. Moreover, in a world with no right of publicity, stars could still license the use of their personas for commercial purposes. They could not guarantee a retailer the exclusive use of their name or likeness, but some businesses would still pay handsomely for the privilege of telling consumers that they were the only retailer authorized to sell goods under the name of a particular celebrity. Even without the right of publicity, false advertising and trademark law provide a means for these authorized retailers to stop competitors from using their celebrity spokespersons in a misleading manner. *See* Abdul-Jabbar v. General Motors Corp., 85 F.3d 407 (9th Cir. 1996); King v. Innovation Books, 976 F.2d 824 (2d Cir. 1992).

103. Alice Haemmerli, *Whose Who? The Case for a Kantian Right of Publicity*, 49 Duke L.J. 383, 388 & n.11 (2000); Melville B. Nimmer, *The Right of Publicity*, 19 Law & Contemp. Probs. 203, 216 (1954).

104. Alex Heigl, *"Hot Convict" Jeremy Meeks Finally Signs That Modeling Contract . . . in Jail*, People, Mar. 4, 2015, http://www.people.com/article/hottie-thug-jeremy -meeks-modeling-contract; Alex Williams, *15 Minutes of Fame? More Like 15 Seconds of Nanofame*, N.Y. Times, Feb. 8, 2015, at ST1.

105. Stacey L. Dogan & Mark A. Lemley, *What the Right of Publicity Can Learn from Trademark Law*, 58 Stan. L. Rev. 1161, 1179–84 (2006); Mark P. McKenna, *The Right of Publicity and Autonomous Self-Definition*, 67 U. Pitt. L. Rev. 225, 252–58, 263–68 (2005).

106. Mark Bartholomew & John Tehranian, *An Intersystemic View of Intellectual Property and Free Speech*, 81 Geo. Wash. L. Rev. 1, 59 n.396 (2013). Celebrities can register their names as federal trademarks. 15 U.S.C. § 1052(e)(4), (f) (2006). Some may sympathize with celebrities for the emotional toll of having their names and faces used to sell goods without their permission. A few property theorists maintain that "private property . . . is an extension of human personality, and therefore . . . essential to human dignity." Roberta Rosenthal Kwall, *Fame*, 73 Ind. L.J. 1, 39 (1997). But most right-of-publicity cases are about maximizing profit, not protecting the personal. In fact, one can argue that the right of publicity's insistence on commodifying identity diminishes personal dignity rather than enhancing it. Moreover, to the extent that the famous suffer dignitary harms when onlookers wrongly assume they have agreed to associate their

personas with a particular commercial product, trademark protection can be pressed into service to correct these misimpressions.

107. Greenberg v. Lorenz, 178 N.Y.S.2d 407, 409 (App. Term 1958); John Lentz, *Publicity—How to Plan, Produce, and Place It*, 33 AM. J. PUBLIC HEALTH 449, 449 (1943); Stanley Walker, *Playing the Deep Bassoons*, HARPERS MAG., Feb. 1932, at 373.

108. LARRY TYE, THE FATHER OF SPIN: EDWARD BERNAYS AND THE BIRTH OF PUBLIC RELATIONS 63 (1998) (quoting letter from Justice Felix Frankfurter to President Franklin D. Roosevelt (May 7, 1934)).

109. H.H. Wilson, Book Note, 64 YALE L.J. 617, 619 (1955) (reviewing ROBERT E. LANE, THE REGULATION OF BUSINESSMEN: SOCIAL CONDITIONS OF GOVERNMENT ECONOMIC CONTROL (1954)).

110. Ryther v. KARE 11, 864 F. Supp. 1510, 1515 (D. Minn. 1994); Rufo v. Simpson, 86 Cal. App. 4th 573, 617–18 (2001); Anna Heinemann, *Lucille Ball Is the Best Dead Celeb for Your Ad Campaign*, ADVERTISING AGE, July 18, 2005, http://adage.com/article/media/lucille-ball-dead-celeb-ad-campaign/46256/.

111. Richard L. Hasen, *Celebrity Justice: Supreme Court Edition*, 19 GREEN BAG 2D 157 (2016). One website maintains an interactive map of the domestic and international appearances of both current and retired Supreme Court Justices. SCOTUS MAP, http://www.scotusmap.com/scotus_events (last visited Oct. 1, 2016). In the explicitly commercial realm, fans can purchase a large selection of "Notorious RBG" T-shirts, coffee mugs, and tote bags referencing Supreme Court Justice Ruth Bader Ginsburg. Although Ginsburg does not receive a formal commission from these sales, she clearly relishes the heightened visibility afforded from such merchandising. Zeke J. Miller, *Ruth Bader Ginsburg Says She Has Quite a Large Supply of Notorious RBG T-Shirts*, TIME, Oct. 19, 2014, http://time.com/3523180/ruth-bader-ginsburg-rbg shirts/; Hunter Schwarz, *Ruth Bader Ginsburg Goes Full Notorious RBG*, WASH. POST, April 16, 2015, http://www.washington post.com/blogs/the-fix/wp/2015/04/16/ruth -bader-ginsburg-goes-full-notorious-rbg/.

112. Katya Assaf, *Buying Goods and Doing Good: Trademarks and Social Competition*, 67 ALA. L. REV. 9/9, 984 (2016).

113. JOSHUA GAMSON, CLAIMS TO FAME 28 (1994).

114. *Id.* at 32.

115. Memphis Dev. Found. v. Factor Etc., Inc., 616 F.2d 956, 959–60 (6th Cir. 1980).

116. *Id.*

117. Lugosi v. Universal Pictures, 603 P.2d 425, 430 (Cal. 1980).

118. Jessica Evans, *Introduction, in* UNDERSTANDING MEDIA: INSIDE CELEBRITY 1, 4 (Jessica Evans & David Hesmondhalgh eds., 2005).

119. TURNER, *supra* note 25, at 70.

120. According to a 2005 study, 31 percent of American teenagers believed that they would be famous someday. *Survey of Teens in the Greater Washington, D.C. Area*, HENRY J. KAISER FAM. FOUND. (Oct. 2005), https://kaiserfamilyfoundation.files.word press.com/2013/01/survey-of-teens-in-the-greater-washington-dc-area-toplines.pdf. If anything, more recent research demonstrates that this belief in the ability of anyone to

become famous has only intensified. Daryl Nelson, *Why Are Young People So Obsessed with Being Famous?*, Consumer Affairs, Jan. 21, 2013, http://www.consumeraffairs .com/news/why-are-young-people-so-obsessed-with-becoming-famous-012113.html; *Reality TV Turning Young Girls into Fame Monsters?* (NPR broadcast Oct. 19, 2011), http:// www.npr.org/2011/10/19/141508287/reality-tv-turning-young-girls-into-fame-monsters.

121. 1 J. Thomas McCarthy, The Rights of Publicity and Privacy § 3:2 (2d ed. 2016).

122. Fraley v. Facebook, 830 F. Supp. 2d 785, 804–05 (N.D. Cal. 2011).

123. Perkins v. LinkedIn Corp., 53 F. Supp. 3d 1190, 1211 (N.D. Cal. 2014).

124. Lynne M.J. Bosineau, *Giving the Right of Publicity a Much-Needed Makeover for the Social Media Revolution*, 5 Landslide 22, 23 (2012).

Chapter 6

1. #McDStories, Twitter, https://twitter.com/hashtag/mcdstories; Tiffany Hsu, *McDonald's #McDStories Twitter Marketing Effort Goes Awry*, L.A. Times, Jan. 23, 2012.

2. Mike Isaac & Mark Scott, *WhatsApp to Provide User Data to Facebook*, N.Y. Times, Aug. 26, 2016, at B1; Garett Sloane, *WhatsApp and 7 Other Startups That Hated Advertising, Like Facebook*, Adweek, Feb. 20, 2014, http://www.adweek.com/news/technology/ whatsapp-and-7-other-startups-hated-advertising-facebook-155849.

3. Daniel Kahneman, Thinking Fast and Slow 40–42, 81 (2011); Erika L. Rosenberg, *Mindfulness and Consumerism, in* Psychology and Consumer Culture: The Struggle for a Good Life in a Materialistic World 107, 115–17 (Tim Kasser & Allen D. Kramer eds., 2004); Kirk Warren Brown & Richard M. Ryan, *The Benefits of Being Present: Mindfulness and Its Role in Psychological Well-Being*, 84 J. Personality & Soc. Psychol. 822, 822–23 (2003).

4. Robert Benford & David Snow, *Framing Processes and Social Movements: An Overview and Assessment*, 26 Ann. Rev. Soc. 611 (2000); Theodore Ruger, *Social Movements Everywhere*, 155 U. Pa. L. Rev. 18, 22 (2006); *see also* Jack M. Balkin & Reva B. Siegel, *Principles, Practices, and Social Movements*, 154 U. Pa. L. Rev. 927, 946–50 (2006); Tomiko Brown-Nagin, *Elites, Social Movements, and the Law: The Case of Affirmative Action*, 105 Colum. L. Rev. 1436, 1488–90 (2006).

5. Douglas NeJaime, *Framing (In)equality for Same-Sex Couples*, 60 UCLA L. Rev. Discourse 184 (2013).

6. Amy Kapczynski, *The Access to Knowledge Mobilization and the New Politics of Intellectual Property*, 117 Yale L.J. 804, 814 (2008); Nicholas Pedriana, *From Protective to Equal Treatment: Legal Framing Processes and Transformation of the Women's Movement in the 1960s*, 111 Am. J. Soc. 1718, 1727 (2006).

7. John A. Noakes & Hank Johnston, *Frames of Protest: A Road Map to a Perspective, in* Frames of Protest: Social Movements and the Framing Perspective 1, 2 (Hank Johnston & John A. Noakes eds., 2005).

8. Rita K. Noonan, *Women Against the State: Political Opportunities and Collective Action Frames in Chile's Transition to Democracy*, 10 Soc. F. 81, 94–105 (1995).

9. Lyndi Hewitt & Holly J. McCammon, *Explaining Suffrage Mobilization: Balance,*

Neutralization, and Range in Collective Action Frames, in FRAMES OF PROTEST, *supra* note 7, at 33, 39.

10. Mayer N. Zald, *Culture, Ideology, and Strategic Framing, in* COMPARATIVE PERSPECTIVES ON SOCIAL MOVEMENTS 261, 266–67 (Doug McAdam et al. eds., 1996).

11. SIDNEY A. SHAPIRO & JOSEPH P. TOMAIN, ACHIEVING DEMOCRACY: THE FUTURE OF PROGRESSIVE REGULATION 100 (2014); *see also* MANCUR OLSON, THE LOGIC OF COLLECTIVE ACTION 46–48, 165–67 (1965).

12. Historians chart three separate sustained periods of consumer activism in the United States—one in the early 1900s, one during the Great Depression, and one coinciding with the movements for social and civil rights in the 1960s and 1970s. *See* ROBERT N. MAYER, THE CONSUMER MOVEMENT: GUARDIANS OF THE MARKETPLACE 10–33 (1989).

13. ARTHUR LEFF, SWINDLING AND SELLING 148 (1976).

14. Elizabeth Warren, *Unsafe at any Rate,* DEMOCRACY J., Summer 2007, at 9–10.

15. *Id.* at 10.

16. Barton Beebe, *Search and Persuasion in Trademark Law,* 103 MICH. L. REV. 2020, 2023 (2005) ("[T]rademark doctrine has based itself upon . . . the 'sovereign consumer' . . . a utility-maximizing agent of unbounded rational choice."); Vincent Manzerolle & Sandra Smeltzer, *Consumer Databases and the Commercial Mediation of Identity: A Medium Theory Analysis,* 8 SURVEILLANCE & SOC'Y 323, 334 (2011) (describing "the principle of consumer sovereignty" as "the ideological lynchpin of a neoliberal, free market economy").

17. LAWRENCE B. GLICKMAN, BUYING POWER: A HISTORY OF CONSUMER ACTIVISM IN AMERICA 279 (2009); MATTHEW HILTON, PROSPERITY FOR ALL: CONSUMER ACTIVISM IN AN ERA OF GLOBALIZATION 249–50 (2009).

18. George A. Chressanthis et al., *Determinants of Pharmaceutical Sales Representative Access Limits to Physicians,* 14 J. MED. MARKETING 220, 224 (2014); *Persuading the Prescribers: Pharmaceutical Industry Marketing and its Influence on Physicians and Patients,* PEWTRUSTS.ORG, Nov. 11, 2013, http://www.pewtrusts.org/en/research-and -analysis/fact-sheets/2013/11/11/persuading-the-prescribers-pharmaceutical-industry -marketing-and-its-influence-on-physicians-and-patients.

19. Sorrell v. IMS Health Inc., 131 S. Ct. 2653, 2671 (2011).

20. Lawrence O. Gostin, *Marketing Pharmaceuticals: A Constitutional Right to Self-Prescriber Identified Data?,* 307 JAMA 787, 787 (2012).

21. Farhad Manjoo, *Ad Blockers and the Nuisance at the Heart of the Modern Web,* N.Y. TIMES, Aug. 19, 2015, at B1.

22. Deepa Seetharaman, *Facebook Begins Hosting News Articles from Nine Publishers,* WALL ST. J. BLOG, May 13, 2015, http://blogs.wsj.com/digits/2015/05/13/facebook-begins-hosting-news-articles-from-nine-publishers/; *see also* Lev Grossman, *Our Attention Is Just a Pawn in the Great Game of Silicon Valley,* TIME, Oct. 19, 2015, at 27–28.

23. Va. State Pharmacy Bd. v. Va. Citizens Consumer Council, 425 U.S. 748, 757 (1976).

24. Trans Union Corp. v. FTC, 245 F.3d 809, 818–19 (D.C. Cir. 2001); Ass'n of Am. Physicians & Surgeons, Inc. v. U.S. Dep't of Health & Human Servs., 224 F. Supp. 2d 1115, 1125 (S.D. Tex. 2002).

25. Case C-131/12, Google Spain SL v. Agencia Española de Protección de Datos (May 13, 2014), http://curia.europa.eu/juris/document/document.jsf?text=&docid=15 2065&pageIndex=0&doclang=EN&mode=lst&dir=&occ=first&part=1&cid=549703; David Jolly, *The European Union Takes Steps Toward Protecting Data*, N.Y. Times, March 13, 2014, at B2.

26. Although some maintain that proposals like Do-Not-Track do not implicate "speech" at all, various authorities, including the Supreme Court, maintain that setting privacy limits on data sharing represents a government effort to censor expression. Sorrell v. IMS Health Inc., 131 S. Ct. 2653, 2667 (2011); *see also* Jane Bambauer, *Is Data Speech?*, 66 Stan. L. Rev. 57 (2014); Jeffrey Rosen, *The Right to Be Forgotten*, 64 Stan. L. Rev. Online 88, 88 (2012).

27. Kirby v. Sega of Am., Inc., 50 Cal. Rprt. 3d 607, 616 (Ct. App. 2006).

28. Davis v. Elec. Arts, Inc., 775 F.3d 1172, 1177–78 (9th Cir. 2015); *In re* NCAA Student-Athlete Name & Likeness Licensing Litig., 724 F.3d 1268, 1276–79 (9th Cir. 2013); Hart v. Elec. Arts, Inc., 717 F.3d 141, 166–69 (3d Cir. 2013).

29. Davis v. Elec. Arts, Inc., No. 10–0332RS, 2012 WL 3860819, at *7 (N.D. Cal., Mar. 29, 2012); Gionfriddio v. Major League Baseball, 114 Cal. Rptr. 2d 307, 314 (Ct. App. 2001).

30. Cher v. Forum Int'l, Ltd., 692 F.2d 634, 637–38 (9th Cir. 1982); *see also* Falwell v. Penthouse Int'l, Ltd., 521 F. Supp. 1204, 1210 (W.D. Va. 1981); Mark Bartholomew, *Intellectual Property's Lessons for Information Privacy*, 92 Neb. L. Rev. 746, 794 (2014).

31. Some criticize these defenses as too malleable, giving judges too much discretion to restrict valuable expression. See Authors Guild v. Google, Inc., 804 F.3d 202, 215 (2d Cir. 2015) (cautioning, in copyright law, against "oversimplified reliance on whether the copying involves transformation"); Kienitz v. Sconnie Nation, LLC, 766 F.3d 756, 757 (7th Cir. 2014); Rebecca Tushnet, *Content, Purpose, or Both?*, 90 Wash. L. Rev. 869, 883–86 (2015). Yet the breadth of these defenses can also be viewed as a strength, allowing judges to adjust their assessments of autonomy and fairness concerns as their understanding of existing technology deepens. Others might point to the First Amendment's constitutional pedigree and informational privacy's lack thereof as reason for allowing the former to trump the latter. But this is a misplaced view. After all, the privacy cases that restrained the invasive activities of early twentieth-century advertisers surely prevented certain kinds of speech from being made. Courts of the time believed that the trade-off—limiting commercial speech in return for protecting individuals from the unauthorized use of their images—made sense. Admittedly, the First Amendment has undergone a significant strengthening since the early twentieth century, including late twentieth-century recognition of a value in commercial speech. But I doubt that most people, then or now, would look at the pioneering decisions preventing marketers from emblazoning someone's face on thousands of packages or advertisements without permission as a low point in this country's history of free expression.

32. Gerald Dworkin, *Paternalism*, Stanford Encyclopedia of Philosophy, June 4, 2014, http://plato.stanford.edu/archives/sum2014/entries/paternalism/.

33. Lawrence Glickman, *Consumer Protection Redux: The Lessons of History*, Base-

line Scenario, Sept. 7, 2009, http://www.baselinescenario.com/2009/09/07/consumer-protection-reduxh.

34. Ralph K. Winter, Jr., The Consumer Advocate Versus the Consumer 1 (1972), *quoted in* Glickman, Buying Power, *supra* note 17, at 291.

35. Howard Baldwin, *New FTC "Do Not Track" Recommendations: Clueless?*, PC World, Mar. 26, 2012, http://www.pcadvisor.co.uk/opinion/security/new-ftc-do-not-track-recommendations-clueless-3347070/.

36. Morgan Little, *FTC Pushes for "Do Not Track," Draws Comparison to "Big Brother,"* L.A. Times, Mar. 27, 2012, http://articles.latimes.com/2012/mar/27/news/la-pn-ftc-pushes-for-do-not-track-draws-comparison-to-big-brother-20120327.

37. Thompson v. W. States Med. Ctr., 535 U.S. 357, 374 (2002).

38. Lorillard Tobacco Co. v. Reilly, 533 U.S. 525, 575 (2001) (Thomas, J., concurring); 44 Liquormart, Inc. v. Rhode Island, 517 U.S. 484, 517 (1996) (Scalia, J., concurring in part and concurring in the judgment); C. Edwin Baker, *The First Amendment and Commercial Speech*, 84 Ind. L.J. 981, 984 (2009).

39. Cass R. Sunstein, *Deciding by Default*, 162 U. Pa. L. Rev. 1, 54–55 (2013).

40. *See Administrative Discussion Draft, Consumer Privacy Bill of Rights Act*, White-house.gov (2015), https://www.whitehouse.gov/sites/default/files/omb/legislative/letters/cpbr-act-of-2015–discussion-draft.pdf.

41. Steve Lohr, *If Algorithms Know All, How Much Should Humans Help?*, N.Y. Times, Apr. 6, 2015, at A3.

42. Nicolas Cornell, *A Third Theory of Paternalism*, 113 Mich. L. Rev. 1295, 1316 (2015).

43. In a 2014 survey, 58 percent of respondents viewed the FDA favorably as compared to 32 percent for the federal government as a whole. Alexander Gaffney, *Public View of FDA Continues to Improve in New Poll*, Reg. Affs. Prof. Soc'y, Oct. 2, 2014, http://www.raps.org/Regulatory-Focus/News/2014/10/02/20463/Public-View-of-FDA-Continues-to-Improve-in-New-Poll/.

44. 15 U.S.C. § 45(n).

45. Rory Van Loo, *Helping Buyers Beware: The Need for Supervision of Big Retail*, 163 U. Pa. L. Rev. 1311, 1379 (2015). The FTC does issue recommendations for best practices involving new advertising technologies that implicate privacy, including facial recognition technologies and data collection via mobile devices. But the bulk of these recommendations are merely advisory, leaving businesses free to assess whether the benefits of invasive data collection practices outweigh their potential costs. Even those who highlight the FTC's role in shaping privacy boundaries for business admit that the amount of financial and human resources the agency actually commits to protecting consumer privacy is minimal. Daniel J. Solove & Woodrow Hartzog, *The FTC and the New Common Law of Privacy*, 114 Colum. L. Rev. 583, 600–02 (2014).

46. 15 U.S.C. § 77c(b).

47. Anthony Nitti, *What Are Your Odds of Being Audited by the IRS?*, Forbes, Mar. 25, 2013, http://www.forbes.com/sites/anthonynitti/2013/03/25/what-are-your-odds-of-being-audited-by-the-irs/.

48. Ryan Calo, *Consumer Subject Review Boards: A Thought Experiment*, 66 Stan.

L. Rev. Online 97, 102 (2013); *Administrative Discussion Draft: Consumer Privacy Bill of Rights Act, supra* note 40, at 18.

49. Jules Polonetsky et al., *Beyond the Common Rule: Ethical Structures for Data Research in Non-Academic Settings,* 13 Colo Tech. L.J. 333, 356–62 (2015).

50. Zachary M. Schrag, Ethical Imperialism: Institutional Review Boards and the Social Sciences, 1965–2009 (2010); danah boyd, *Untangling Research and Practice: What Facebook's "Emotional Contagion" Study Teaches Us,* 10 Res. Ethics 1, 4 (2015).

51. 143 Cong. Rec. 19160 (daily ed. June 13, 1974) (statement of Senators Ervin, Nunn, and Brock in minority report on S. 707), *quoted in* Glickman, Buying Power, *supra* note 17, at 292.

52. Mat Honan, *I Liked Everything I Saw on Facebook for Two Days. Here's What It Did to Me,* Wired, Aug. 11, 2014, http://www.wired.com/2014/08/i-liked-everything-i-saw-on-facebook-for-two-days-heres-what-it-did-to-me/.

53. Daniel Pope, The Making of Modern Advertising 257–58 (1983); Frank Presbrey, The History and Development of Advertising 608–18 (1929).

54. Rudolph Callmann, *Unfair Competition without Competition?,* 95 U. Pa. L. Rev. 443, 464 n.105 (1947).

55. Lizbeth Cohen, A Consumers' Republic: The Politics of Mass Consumption in Postwar America 309–10 (2003); David M. Skover & Kellye Y. Testy, *LesBiGay Identity as Commodity,* 90 Cal. L. Rev. 223, 242–43 (2002).

56. Mark Bartholomew, *A Right Is Born: Celebrity, Property, and Postmodern Lawmaking,* 44 Conn. L. Rev. 301, 346–53 (2011).

57. Nick Johnson, The Future Of Marketing: Strategies from 15 Leading Brands on How Authenticity, Relevance, and Transparency Will Help You Survive the Age of the Customer 32 (2015).

58. Dean Crutchfield, *A Brand by Any Other Name...,* Adweek, Jan. 25, 2010, http://www.adweek.com/news/advertising-branding/brand-any-other-name-101392.

59. Tracy L. Tuten, Advertising 2.0: Social Media Marketing in a Web 2.0 World 5 (2008).

60. Klint Finley, *Facebook and IBM Team Up to Supercharge Personalized Ads,* Wired, May 6, 2015, http://www.wired.com/2015/05/facebook-ibm-team-supercharge-personalized-ads/.

61. Academics offer their own arguments for brand democracy, correcting what they see as an elitism that blinded earlier scholars to consumer recoding of commercial culture's proffered meanings. Daniel Miller, A Theory of Shopping (1998); Roberta Sassatelli, *Virtue, Responsibility and Consumer Choice, in* Consumer Cultures, Global Perspectives: Historical Trajectories, Transnational Exchanges 219, 237 (John Brewer & Frank Trentman eds., 2006). According to the influential work of media scholar John Fiske, "Popular culture [of which advertising is a part] is made by the people, not imposed on them; it stems from within, from below, not above." John Fiske, Understanding Popular Culture 25 (1989). More recently, replacing the term consumer with one meant to highlight consumer agency in the age of social media, a group of sociologists write: "Prosumers produce the meaning that surrounds brands

such as McDonald's, BMW, and Nike." George Ritzer et al., *The Coming Age of the Prosumer*, 56 Am. Behav. Sci. 379, 383 (2012). These works offer valuable insights but, at least when assessed in the current era, perhaps fail to recognize the structural, technological, and legal forces that erode consumer agency.

62. Jim Hawkins, *Using Advertisements to Diagnose Behavioral Market Failure*, 51 Wake Forest L. Rev. 57 (2016).

63. A. K. Pradeep, The Buying Brain: Secrets for Selling to the Subconscious Mind 81 (2010); Amanda S. Bruce et al., *Branding and a Child's Brain: An fMRI Study of Neural Responses to Logos*, 9 SCAN 118, 118–22 (2012); Karen C. Sokol, *Tort as a Disrupter of Cultural Manipulation: Neuromarketing and the Dawn of the E-Cigarette*, 66 S.C. L. Rev. 191, 209 (2014); Peter E. Weiss & Adam Gazzaley, *External Distraction Impairs Categorization Performance in Older Adults*, 29 Psychol. & Aging 666, 666–671 (2014).

64. Helen Havlak, *The Celebrities and Brands That Lost the Most in the Facebook Purge*, Verge, Mar. 27, 2015, http://www.theverge.com/2015/3/27/8299437/facebook-like -purge-biggest-losers; Hannah Jane Parkinson, *Instagram Purge Costs Celebrities Millions of Followers*, Guardian, Dec. 19, 2014, http://www.theguardian.com/technology/2014/ dec/19/instagram-purge-costs-celebrities-millions-of-followers.

65. Jacob Silverman, Terms of Service: Social Media and the Price of Constant Connection 206 (2015).

66. Michael Serazio, Your Ad Here: The Cool Sell of Guerrilla Marketing 95 (2013).

67. Peter S. Menell, *2014: Brand Totalitarianism*, 47 U.C. Davis L. Rev. 787, 802– 05 (2014); Michael Sebastian, *Time Inc. Starts Selling Ads on Magazine Covers, Breaking Industry Taboo*, Advertising Age, May 22, 2014, http://adage.com/article/media/ time-starts-selling-ads-magazine-covers/293361/.

68. Pfizer, Inc. v. Sachs, 652 F. Supp. 2d 512, 525 (S.D.N.Y. 2009).

69. N. Am. Med. Corp. v. Axiom Worldwide, Inc., 522 F.3d 1211, 1226 (11th Cir. 2008).

70. Hearthware, Inc. v. E. Mishan & Sons, Inc., No. 11 C 5233, 2012 WL 3309634, at *11 (N.D. Ill. Aug. 10, 2012).

71. Caterpillar, Inc. v. Walt Disney Co., 287 F. Supp. 2d 913, 917 (C.D. Ill. 2003).

72. Louis Vuitton Malletier S.A. v. Warner Bros. Entm't Inc., 868 F. Supp. 2d 172 (S.D.N.Y. 2012); Michael Cieply, *Despite Big Names, Prestige Film Falls Through*, N.Y. Times, July 2, 2009, at B1.

73. *See generally* Rebecca Tushnet, *Running the Gamut from A to B: Federal Trademark and False Advertising Law*, 159 U. Pa. L. Rev. 1305 (2011); Mark A. Lemley & Mark McKenna, *Irrelevant Confusion*, 62 Stan. L. Rev. 413 (2010). Certain judicially crafted defenses to trademark infringement arguably immunize some of these "immaterial" mark appropriations. These defenses, however, often cannot be resolved early in the litigation, leaving defendants making expressive use of trademarks to choose between gambling on an expensive litigation or simply bowing to the desires of the mark owner. Leah Chan Grinvald, *Shaming Trademark Bullies*, 2011 Wis. L. Rev. 625, 653–56; William McGeveran, *Rethinking Trademark Law Fair Use*, 94 Iowa L. Rev. 49, 102–14 (2008).

74. 1 J. Thomas Mccarthy, The Rights of Publicity and Privacy § 2:2 at 83–84 (2d ed. 2009).

75. Associated Press, *Prince Death Sparks Minnesota Bill to Clarify Artist Rights*, Chi. Trib., May 10, 2016, http://www.chicagotribune.com/entertainment/music/ct-prince -minnesota-bill-artist-rights-20160510–story.html.

76. Tamlin Bason, *Should Congress or Supreme Court Help Curb Ongoing Right of Publicity Free-for-All?*, 88 Pat. Trademark & Copyright J. (BNA) 1558, Oct. 16, 2014; Alex J. Berger, *Righting the Wrong of Publicity: A Novel Proposal for a Uniform Federal Right of Publicity Statute*, 66 Hastings L.J. 845, 848 (2015).

77. Alison Flood, *George Orwell's Estate Denies "Big Brother Values" after Challenge to 1984 Merchandise*, Guardian, Oct. 28, 2015, http://www.theguardian.com/books/2015/ oct/28/george-orwell-estate-disputes-allegations-orwellian-cafepress; *Orwell Estate Sends Copyright Takedown over the Number "1984,"* TorrentFreak, Oct. 27, 2015, https://tor rentfreak.com/orwell-estate-sends-copyright-takedown-over-the-number-1984–151027/.

Index

Girls Intelligence Agency, 44
Goffman, Erving, 135
Goldman, Eric, 75, 204n36
Goodman, Ellen, 143
Guerrilla marketing: in civic spaces, 29,
    32–34; in commercial spaces, 29–32;
    controlling discourse through, 43–45;
    definition of, 29; desensitizing effects
    from, 29–30, 35, 37; hiding the adver-
    tiser's role, 30–31, 41–44; projection of
    desired norms, 36–40

Haul videos, 37
The Hidden Persuaders (Packard), 18, 107,
    184
Honan, Mat, 175, 179

Iacoboni, Marco, 104
Identity formation: advertising's role
    in, 36–41, 44–45; influence of social
    media, 135, 139; interpellation, 36–41,
    44, 175; limits on advertising's influ-
    ence, 45–46
Instagram, 67, 74, 132–133, 137, 139, 144,
    154; celebrity use, 127–130; Popular
    Pays app, 141
Institutional review boards (IRBs),
    117–119, 173–174
Intellectual property, 3–4, 12, 23, 212n89;
    protection for celebrities, 23, 145, 150–
    151, 158, 184; suggested reforms, 167,
    173, 180, 184. *See also* Dilution law,
    Right of publicity, Trademark law

Journalists: destabilizing effects of digital
    technology on, 139–140; relationship
    with advertisers, 5–7, 79–80, 164, 175,
    179; relationship with celebrities, 126,
    136, 167

Kardashian, Kim, 127–129, 132, 144;
    Hollywood app, 123–124, 214n1; law-
    suit against Old Navy, 124–125, 148

Key, Wilson Bryan, 108
Kid-vid controversy, 20. *See also*
    Television advertising
Klein, Naomi, 108
KnowYourFollowers, 123, 130
Kutcher, Ashton, 127–128, 136

Lash Lure, 9–10
Libertarian paternalism, 169–170
Lindholm, Charles, 134, 138–139
Location-based advertising, 66–68

Madoff, Ray, 149
Madonna, 154
Marquand, David, 35
McCarthy, J. Thomas, 182
Memory, advertising's influence on,
    98–99, 108
Micro-celebrity, 7, 133, 135, 150, 156; defi-
    nition of, 131; potential relationship to
    right of publicity, 183
Micro-expressions, 2, 96, 102–103
Microsoft, 67, 74, 94
Midler, Bette, 148
Miller, Glenn, 146
Minority Report, 1, 73
Morozov, Evgeny, 140
Movies, advertising in. *See* Cinematic
    advertising

Nader, Ralph, 166
National Advertising Division, 12, 190n8
National Park Service (NPS), 33, 60;
    response to commercialization of
    Niagara Falls, 59
Neoliberalism, 86. *See also* Privatization
NeuroFocus, 92, 94, 107
Neuromarketing: avoidance of IRB
    review, 118–119; business investment
    in, 94, 106, 212n88; Cheetos study,
    92, 107; Coke study, 96–97, 105–106;
    comparison to other psychological
    techniques in advertising, 93–95, 108,